BLAKE AND TORREY GENEALOGY

*The Ancestry and Allied
Families of*

Nathan Blake 3rd
and
Susan (Torrey) Blake

*Early Residents of
East Corinth, Vermont*

*Almira Torrey Blake
Fenno-Gendrot*

HERITAGE BOOKS
2010

HERITAGE BOOKS

AN IMPRINT OF HERITAGE BOOKS, INC.

Books, CDs, and more—Worldwide

For our listing of thousands of titles see our website
at
www.HeritageBooks.com

A Facsimile Reprint
Published 2010 by
HERITAGE BOOKS, INC.
Publishing Division
100 Railroad Ave. #104
Westminster, Maryland 21157

Originally published by the author
at the
Stanhope Press
Boston, Massachusetts
1916

International Standard Book Numbers
Paperbound: 978-0-7884-1612-5
Clothbound: 978-0-7884-8489-6

PREFACE

THIS gathering of Family Genealogical Records, and bits of personal history of my Ancestors, was commenced many years since, with frequent searches in old Burial Grounds and old Town Records. In the year 1907 my friend Mr. Felix A. Gendrot became interested to aid me in my research — bringing great enthusiasm, trained knowledge and untiring patience in following obscure clews; delving in Libraries and Vital Statistics, thereby obtaining exact facts from the local records in many Towns and States — to him I give sincere thanks. May other families be inspired to pay a like tribute, thereby showing our gratitude for Noble Ancestors.

ALMIRA TORREY BLAKE
FENNO — GENDROT

BOSTON, *June* 7, 1915

CONTENTS

PART I

PART II

LIST OF ILLUSTRATIONS

"And after all to go back to the study of ancestry, what is there petty or ill advised, in the study of one's family line? It is natural to desire to learn who and what the men and women were whose blood flows through our veins, many of whose traits we more or less consciously illustrate, and to whom we owe what we have and are, in a far higher degree than we often appreciate.

There is inspiration in discovering that one is descended from this man or that woman, once loved and honored among the sturdy pioneers, who settled our country, perhaps even famous in church or state here, or on the other side of the Atlantic. It is helpful to manhood, to culture, to piety to know one's self akin to those who suffered oppression and made noble sacrifices for the sake of conscience; helped to found our great Western civilization, or rallied to the defense of the infant nation when its life hung in the balance."

The Congregationalist, August 4, 1898.

PART I

ANCESTRAL LINE OF BLAKES AND BRANCH
FAMILIES IN ENGLAND AND AMERICA

BLAKE COAT-OF-ARMS

BLAKE-TORREY GENEALOGY

BLAKES IN ENGLAND.

1. de BLAKELAND Robert, who was assessed in the Wiltshire Roll of Subsidies granted in 1286 to Edward I. His son who dropped the particle " de " from his name and the terminal " land " was:

2. BLAKE Robert, who had his residence in Calne, County of Wiltshire, England. By his wife Anne, daughter of William Cole, he had:

3. BLAKE Henry, who married a daughter of Edward Durant and had a son:

4. BLAKE William, who married Elizabeth, daughter of Thomas Power. Their son:

5. BLAKE Henry, of Calne, married Margaret, daughter of Mr. Billett, and had:

6. BLAKE Robert, of Calne and Quemberford. He married Alice, daughter of John Wallop, Esq. They were buried under, and have a memorial window in Calne church. Their son:

7. BLAKE William resided in White Parish, Wiltshire, and died in 1471, and had:

8. BLAKE William, who resided at Old Hall in the parish of Andover. He married Mary, daughter of Humphrey Coles. He made his will in 1547, which was proved on the 20th of June 1547. His son:

9. BLAKE Humphrey, removed in the early part of the 16th century into Somersetshire, seated himself in Over Stowey, and became Lord of the Manor of Plainfield. The manor house is still standing; a portion of it evidently as originally built, pleasantly situated on the eastern side of the Quantock Hills. In the great hall of the Manor house in Plainfield are the sculptured arms of this Blake family as borne by its ancestors — a shield bearing three sheaves, two above and one below a chevron. He died in 1558. By his wife Agnes, he had seven children.

(The second son Robert was grandfather of the renowned Admiral Robert Blake.)   His eldest son:

10. BLAKE John, born in 1521, succeeded to the Manor of Plainfield.   His wife was Jane and they had seven children. He was buried at Over Stowey church 10 Dec. 1576.

11. BLAKE William, the eldest son of John, by the will of his father was bequeathed lands in Over Stowey, Bishops Lydiard and elsewhere.   No subsequent trace of him is found upon the parish registers and he is the man who is supposed to have settled in Pitminster. — The Manor Rolls of Taunton, Somerset-shire, show that a *William Blake* in 1586 bought lands in Pit-minster.   Of his birthplace and parentage nothing is known, but it is a natural inference that he is the William whose name appears on the register of that parish in 1588 and in subsequent years.   He may, too, be the one who was buried in the same parish June 13, 1642.   There is no record of his wife's name, but there was a widow Anne Blake buried there 14 Aug. 1644. The parish register of Pitminster which begin in the year 1544 is in a good state of preservation and, from it the following items are obtained:

"Anno Domino, 1588.   Grace Blake, daughter of William Blake, was baptized the 9th day of February.

1592.   Anne Blake, daughter of William Blake was baptized the third day of December.

1594.   William Black[12] son of William Blake was baptized the Xth day of July.

1597.   John Black son of William Blacke was baptized the XIXth day of June.

1600.   Ane Blaak daughter of William Blaak was baptized the sixteen day of October.

1603.   Richard Blaak son of William Blaak was baptized the seventeenth day of Aprill."

Later on appear the following entries which must prove interesting to all descendants in America.

"**1617.   William Blake** ((12) in England and (1) in America) was married to Agnes Band widow the XXIIIth day of September.

1618.   John Blake,[2] sonne of William Blake, and Ane Blake, daughter of William Blake was baptized the XXXth of August.

1620.   William Blake sonne of William Blake was bapt. 6th of September.

1624. James Blake sonne of William Blake was baptized 27th April."

With this record from Pitminster before us there cannot be a shadow of doubt that we have here the family of William of Dorchester. We know that he had a wife Agnes and children John, Anne, William and James, and to make the case still stronger, the age of the father at death, and also of three of the children, Anne, William and James, corresponds with the date of the baptism at Pitminster. No record has been found of the baptism of Edward, another son of William and Agnes.

"YE OLD BLAKE HOUSE"
Dorchester, Mass. (built 1648)

BLAKES IN AMERICA

FIRST GENERATION.

WILLIAM BLAKE AND AGNES BAND.

BLAKE William ((1) in America and (12) in England), son of William, was baptized in Pitminster, England, 10 July 1594. He married 23 Sept. 1617, widow Agnes Band, whose maiden name has not been ascertained. In the same parish are to be found recorded the baptism of four of their children, John, Anne, William and James. Of the baptism of their son Edward there is no record there, nor has any evidence been found of the place of the father's residence between the year 1624 (when his son James was baptized) and 1636 when he was found in America. On the 14 and 16th of May 1636, he was with Mr. Pynchon and at which time they with their associates drew up and signed the articles of Association at Agawan (now Springfield), but his name is not found upon the records subsequent to the first business transacted there. There are good reasons for concluding that he was in Dorchester earlier than indicated by the records there, but the first mention of his name is under date of 2 Jan. 1637/8 when it is ordered that certain persons, including Mr. Blake, should have " confirmed to them the ground joyneing to their hoame lotts to the other pale alowing 3 goad for a highway," which certainly is evidence that he was already in possession of land for a dwelling, but unfortunately the date of his first grant of a house lot does not appear. He was made freeman in 1638, and in 1645 we find him one of the Selectmen. His great-grandson records in his " Annals of Dorchester," under date 1663, " This year Died Mr William Blake who had been Clerk of ye Writs for ye County of Suffolk and Recorder for ye Town near 8 years. He was also Clerk of ye Training band. He died ye 25 of ye 8th mo. 1663 in ye 69th year of his age." In his will dated 3rd of September 1661, he mentions wife and "five children " without naming them, and the inventory taken 6 Nov.

1663, amounted £224. 12. 00.   His wife Agnes removed to
Boston, probably to live with her son John or her only daughter
Anne Leager, and joined the church there 6.(1) 1669/70.   She
died in Dorchester 22 July 1678.   From researches made by me
I locate his home lot on Stoughton St. on " Jones Hill " opposite
the burying ground, which was such an eyesore to him, that he
left 20 shillings to the town " to be bestowed for the repairing of
the burying place soe ye swine and other vermine may not anoy
the graves of the saints."   The present Everett Ave. dividing
the lower part, the lot running to the top of the hill, in all containing about 9 acres.   (See illustration.)

CHILDREN:

> John, bapt. Pitminster, Eng., 30 Aug. 1618, m. (1) abt. 1640, ? **Breck,**
> d. abt. 1645; m. (2) 16 Aug. 1654, Mary (Souther) Shaw; d. at
> Boston, 25 Jan. 1688/9.
>
> ANN, bapt. Pitminster, Eng., 30 Aug. 1618, m. before 1651 (1) Jacob
> Legar of Boston, d. 24 Feb. 1662; m. (2) ———— Hollowell; d. at
> Boston, 12 July 1681, ae. 63 yrs.   Her tombstone is now in possession
> of the Bostonian Society, having been taken from the Granary
> Burying Ground.
>
> WILLIAM, bapt. Pitminster, Eng., 6 Sept. 1620, m. Ann ? abt. 1649, d.
> at Milton, 3 Sept. 1703, ae. 83 yrs.
>
> JAMES, bapt. Pitminster, Eng., 27 April 1624, m. (1) 1651, Elizabeth
> Clap of Dorchester; m. (2) 1695, Elizabeth Hunt of Rehoboth; d. at
> Dorchester, 28 June 1700, ae. 76 yrs.
>
> EDWARD, b. in England, abt. 1625, m. Patience Pope (1653 ?), d. at
> Milton, 3 Sept. 1692.

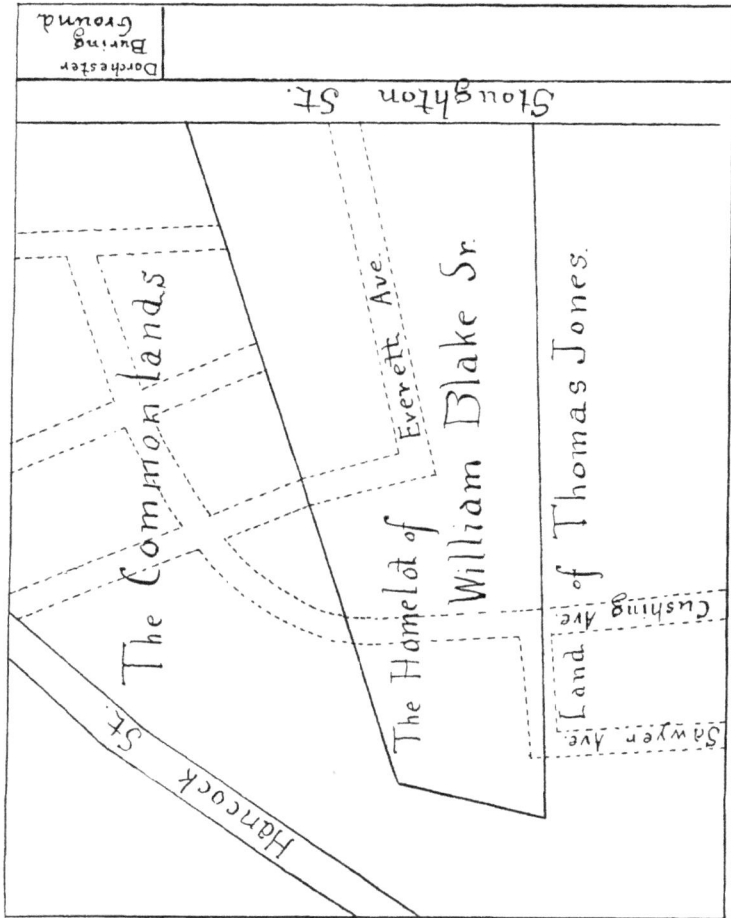

HOME LOT OF WILLIAM BLAKE, SR., JONES' HILL, DORCHESTER

SECOND GENERATION.

JOHN BLAKE AND BRECK FAMILY.

BRECK FAMILY.

BRECK Edward,[1] who came to Dorchester with the company of the Rev. Richard Mather in 1635, is usually called yeoman, though of ancient lineage and possessing kinsmen mentioned in the heralds visitation (e.g., Chester), as "gentleman." He was the son of Robert and the grandson of Hugh or Thomas; probably the former, who died at Rainforth (now Rainford) part of the parish of Prescot, Lancashire in 1591. Edward who was born in or near the year 1600 was probably left by his father in good circumstances for he was a land holder and " man of distinction " before he left Rainforth for New England. He began at once to take an important part in public life of the Dorchester settlement and served the town in various capacities including repeated terms as selectman. The loss of his first wife, as well as of a son and a daughter is referred to in a letter written to him about the year 1646. He married for his second wife, Isabell, who was the widow of John Rigby. (She married for her third husband Anthony Fisher of Dorchester on the 14th of Nov. 1663.) He lived on what is now called Adams Street very near where the Hon. John Howe since lived and built the mill on Smelt Brook Creek now known as the " tidemill or Tilestons Mill." He died Nov. 2, 1662, leaving an estate the value of which ran into hundreds of pounds sterling. In his will of 30 Oct. 1662, he mentions wife Isabell and all his living children and the deceased daughter referred to. " My will is, that all my dau. Blak's Children shall have each 40 s. out of my Estate."

CHILDREN:

By first wife:

(———— a daughter name not found), b. in England, prob. abt. 1618, d. in England prob. abt. 1628.

ROBERT, b. in England, prob. 1620, m. (1) 1642, Margery ————, d. abt. 1652; m. (2) Sarah Hawkins; d. in Boston after 1662.

7

———— (a daughter, name not known), b. in England abt. 1622, came
to America with her parents, where she m. *"Blake" abt. 1640* and d.
abt. 1645 *leaving several children.*

A son, b. in England prob. abt. 1625. No doubt left in England by
his father to attend school, d. abt. 1645.

Elinor, b. in Dorchester, prob. abt. 1636, m. Benjamin Crane of Medfield, 12 Sept. 1656, prob. d. before 1662.

By second wife:

Mary, b. in Dorchester, bapt. 6 Aug. 1648, m. (1) Samuel Paul, 9 Jan.
1667; m. (2) John Tolman, 15 June 1692; d. 25 Aug. 1720.

John, b., ——— 1651, m. ———, d. 17 Feb. 1691, a. 40 yrs.

Elizabeth, b. abt. 1652, m. John Minot, 11 March 1670, d. 6 April 1690.

Susanna, b. abt. 1654, m. John Harris, 20 March 1674/5, d. ———.

BLAKE JOHN[2] (of Boston), (*William*[1]), son of William and
Agnes (Band) Blake, baptized at Pitminster, England, 30 Aug.
1618. We think he married the daughter of Edward Breck of
Dorchester about 1640, for his first wife; she died about 1645,
leaving children. He married at the age of 36 in Boston, 16 Aug.
1654, Widow Mary Shaw, daughter of Nathaniel and Alice
Souther and widow of Joseph Shaw of Weymouth. He is re-
corded a new member recruited of the Honorable Artillery
Company in the year 1642–3 and was made freeman in 1644.
On the 27th 2nd Mo. 1657, he went bonds in Boston for his brother
Edward, and the same year was appointed Constable. In Feb.
1662/3 he purchased a portion of his sister Anna Leager's estate
on what is now Washington Street, and on the site of the present
Adams House, to which he subsequently added another lot
(what is now Keith's Theater) and without doubt resided there.
(See illustration, page 13.) (Shown by the dotted lines.) His
nephew John Blake of Dorchester who inherited the property
sold it in 1694 to Edward Durant, who a few years afterwards
conveyed it to James Blinn, at which time there was a tavern
there known as the "Sign of the Lamb." He was "clerke of ye
Market" at Boston 1669/70. On the 18: 12: 1671, he was dismissed from the church in Dorchester "to Joyne to ye 3rd
Church in Boston."

He was appointed Surveyor for Boston in 1671–2. A
merchant of Boston, evidently a man of considerable influence
and of high social standing in the town. Was one of the
executors of the will of Governor John Winthrop in 1676. He

died in Boston 25 Jan. 1688/9, leaving a will, but no inventory of his estate has been found. He gave his wife £200 and the use and improvements of all his estate " if she continued a widow," and made generous bequests to his brothers William, James and Edward and their children, his " Cosin " Bethia Shaw and her children, Hannah Walker, Kinswoman Hannah Wiswell and " Cosin " John (son of his brother James) to whom he gave all his houses and lands in Boston. A bequest was also made to John Winthrop, son of Waite Winthrop, Esq., the latter being named as one of the overseers of the will. The widow died in Boston 7 Jan. 1693/4.

Presumable children of the daughter of Edward Breck:

John (?), b. abt. 1640, m. **Bridget** ———, ? abt. 1660, lived in Sandwich, d. at Wrentham 25 May 1700.

CALEB (?), b. abt. 1642. He is recorded as having been killed in the "King Phillips War," 1676. Home town given as Sandwich.

A CHILD (?), b. abt. 1644.

By second wife:

HANNAH, b. 16 Jan. 1657 at Boston, d. at Boston 30 Aug. 1659.

THIRD GENERATION.

BLAKE John[3] (of Wrentham), (*John,*[2] *William*[1]), was the son, we think, of John Blake of Boston and the daughter of Edward Breck of Dorchester, and was born in Dorchester about 1640. He married Bridget, her maiden name and place of marriage not known. The first positive record we have of him is in the will of John Wampus, an Indian, and made in England and dated 5 Sept. 1679, in which John Blake and Edward Pratt are bequeathed land in Assanamascock of the Nipmug country in New England. They both are named as executors of his will. John Blake is called of " Plymouth in New England, husbandman." (See " Genealogical Gleanings in England," by Henry F. Waters.) He is next recorded in the deed of transfer of this land dated 25 Aug. 1686 and he is then called " late of Sandwich; and now of Wrentham." (See Suffolk deeds, liber 16, Folio 89.) In the town records of Wrentham we find that he was chosen on the first list of selectmen 1686, and in 1688 found amongst 36 taxpayers is Ensign Blake, who was the wealthiest, which leads us to believe that he was a military man. In 1689 the records refer to a Mr. Blake, and in the tax list of the year 1691, he having the sum of £ 9. 11 s. against his name. John Blake died in Wrentham 25 May 1700 and he is buried in the Wrentham Center Cemetery (see illustration) " Brigit Blake Wid. of Jo— died 30 May 170– " (Wrentham Vital Records). This is no doubt John Blake's widow. (Perley Derby of Salem, gives Bridget Blake's death as 30 May 1706.)

CHILDREN:

ANDREW, b. abt. 1662, m. Sarah Stephens, 14 Aug. 1696, d. at Norfolk, Mass., 22 June 1755, a. 94 yrs.

JOHN, b. 166[?], m. Joanna Whiting, 6 Feb. 1689, d. ———. Made a will before taking voyage in 1729. His widow d. 10 Oct. 1739, a. 75 yrs.

ISAAC, b. ———, d. at Wrentham, 8 March 1689.

Robert, b. abt. 1676, m. **Sarah Guild**, 7 Jan. 1702/3, d. at Wrentham, 4 Oct. 1735, a. 60 yrs.

10

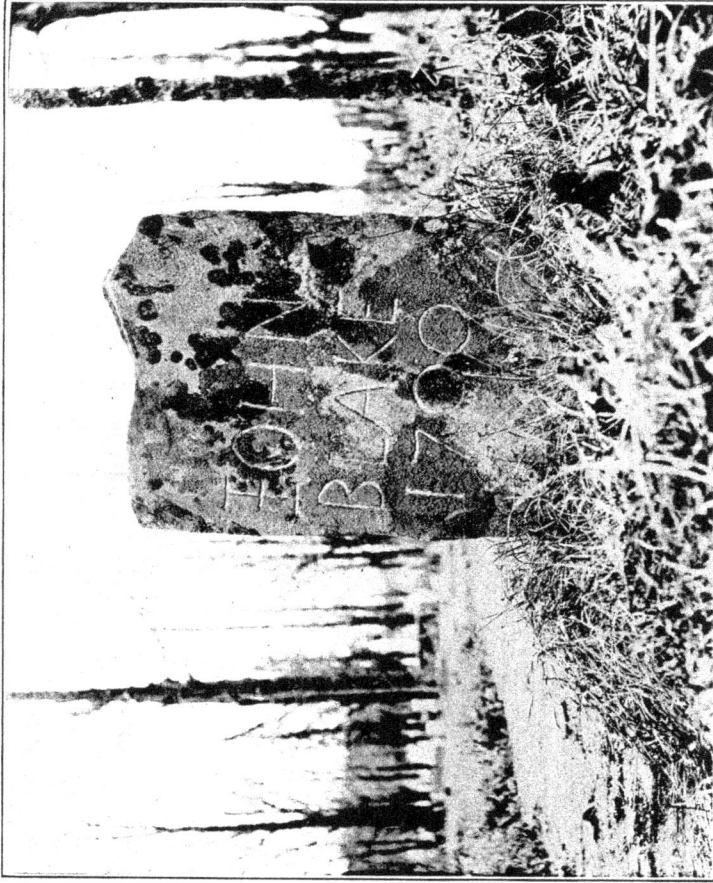

HEADSTONE OF JOHN BLAKE
Wrentham Centre Cemetery

ARGUMENTS.

In the genealogy of the Blake family in New England we have been successful in finding positive records, connecting the various Blakes of our line up to Robert of Wrentham and the priority of John Blake in Wrentham is found, but no positive connection by record can be made between them. To connect John Blake of Wrentham with some of the Blakes of New England has been my natural desire, and after much research it seems to me that a connection with the Dorchester Blakes might be made, as I have found records that would give supposition to that effect, but positive connection is again lacking. It is my theory that the eldest son John of William Blake Sr. of Dorchester, was previously married before he married Mary Shaw and had a son John, who may have been John Blake of Wrentham and that John of Wrentham was the father of Robert of Wrentham.

This is considerable to assume in view of the fact that William Blake Sr. in his will stated therein that his son John, " had no charge," while a greater argument against such a theory is found in the will of said John Blake of Boston, in which he gives his wife considerable money and all of his house and land to a nephew John, son to his brother James, but mentions no children. For all that I feel arguments can be made otherwise. In considering the subject there are three points to determine. *First*, was John Blake, son of William and Agnes, married previous to his marriage with Mary (Souther) Shaw? *Second*, was the above John Blake of Dorchester and Boston, father to John Blake of Plymouth, Sandwich and Wrentham? *Third*, was the above John Blake of Wrentham father to Robert Blake of that town, and was Robert any relation to John (of a younger generation than the one above), Andrew and Isaac, all found in Wrentham at his period ? In considering the first point, my belief that John Blake, son of William Sr. of Dorchester, was previously married is founded on the facts that his marrying for the first time at the age of 36 years seems rather late in life for those days. Furthermore, in the will of Edward Breck of Dorchester made in the year 1662, in which he says: " My will is that all my dau. *Blak's children* shall have each 40 s. out of my estate." This would lead one to believe that it could only be one of William Blake's sons, they being the only Blakes in Dorchester at that time; that

argument is strengthened when we know that William Blake
Sr. and Edward Breck were passengers on the same ship, for
Ebenezer Clap Jr., in his History of Dorchester, says " that they
came to America in the same ship with Rev. Richard Mather in
1635." Now John the son of William Blake Sr. was born in 1618,
while the birth of Edward Breck's daughter is placed at 1622,
so John Blake in 1635 would have been 17 years of age, while the
Breck girl would be about 13 or 14 years old. It does not seem
fanciful to assume that during the long voyage across that a
young man of the susceptible age of 17 would strike up a friendship that would ripen into marriage a few years later. In the
Breck Genealogy they place the birth of this daughter at about
1622 and her marriage to Blake at about the year 1640 and her
death in 1645, so she must have had from two to four children.
In an old letter found and written to Edward Breck from his old
pastor in England, Rev. James Wood, and the date of the writing
is placed in the year 1646, that is to say, after the death of Edward Breck's first wife, as well as a son in England and the death
of this daughter " Blak," and which I now quote " but me thinks
my thoughts return this Apollogie for my old frend, he is in
sorrowe for his dear wife, for his sweet daughter, both were I
here, God, hath of late taken unto himselfe. So Hopefull a
sonne here, so gracious & sweet a wife & daughter there, cannot
but lye closse to a tender father & loveing husbands hart " —
A reason that might be advanced to account for no records being
found of her marriage and death, as well as the birth of her
children, is, that a fire occurred in Dorchester in 1649, destroying
many old records. These facts combine to confirm my conclu-
sions. *Second*, was John Blake of Dorchester and Boston, father
to John Blake of Plymouth, Sandwich and Wrentham? We
find in the Plymouth Colony Records under date of 7 March
1659–60 the following. " In answare to the request of Mr. John
Blake of Boston: in the behalfe of himselfe & sister Mistris
Hannah Johnson, that according to a former grant of the Court
unto Mr. Nathaneal Souther, their father, deceased that hee
the said Blake might have libertie to looke out a pacell of lana
to accomodate them according to aforesaid grant, the Court gave
him libertie to seeke out and in case hee can find any land yett
undesposed of within our jurisdiction that may bee suitable unto
him and answerable to his expectation hee is to signify it to the

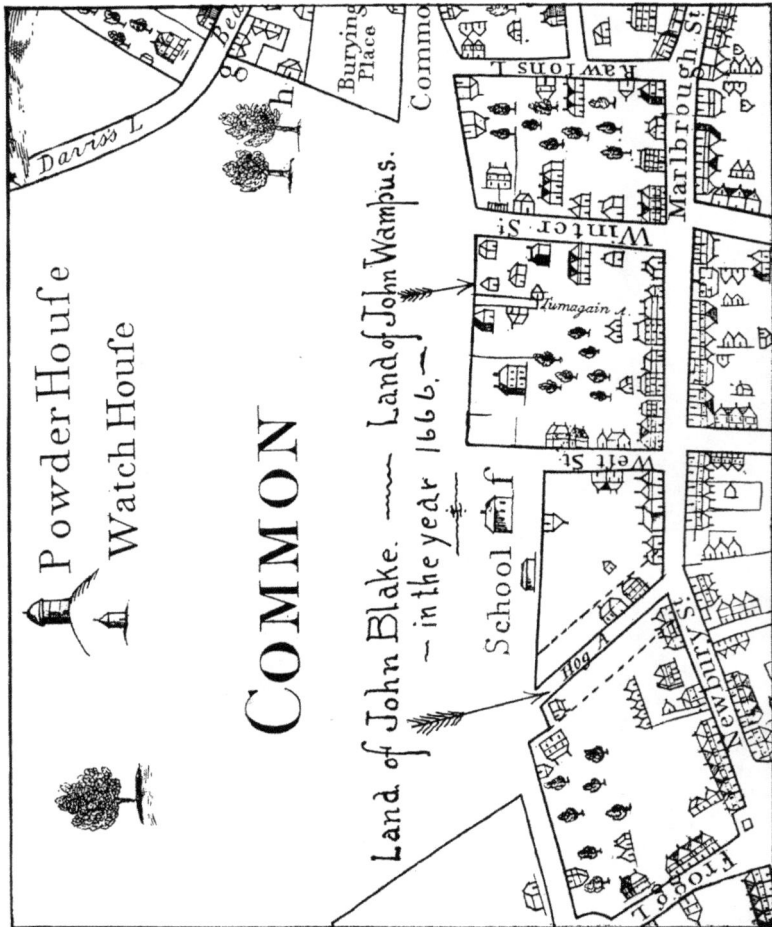

SECTION OF OLD BOSTON MAP, SHOWING LAND OF JOHN BLAKE

Court and shall have a competencye thereof confeirmed unto them."* Again in an invoice of the estate of Richard Taylor of Yarmouth taken the 13th of the 10th month in the year 1673, we find the following item: " due from Mr. John Blake of Boston 16 s." From these records it will be seen that John Blake of Boston had business negotiations in Plymouth Colony. Now John Blake of Wrentham was also of Plymouth and Sandwich, for in a will (made in England and dated 5 Sept. 1679) of John White alias Wampus, an Indian, and in which John Blake and Edward Pratt are bequeathed land in Assanamascock of the Nipmug country in New England. They both are named as executors of the will. John Blake is called of Plymouth in New England. (See Genealogical Gleanings in England by Henry F. Waters.) While in a deed dated Boston, 25 Aug. 1686, as an executor to the estate of said John Wampus, John Blake is called now of Wrentham formerly of Sandwich. (See Suffolk deeds, lib. 16, Folio 89.) These facts it would seem to me, would tie in a way, these two men together. That there was a Blake family in Sandwich, there is no doubt for we find in the records of soldiers of King Phillips War that a Caleb Blake was slain and home town given as Sandwich. Now another strange coincidence is the fact that in the year 1666 " Robert Wayard of Hartford, Conn., conveyed by deed a tract of land situated in Boston to John Wampus, an Indian of Boston, bounded on the common etc. with a dwelling house thereon." This tract is now partly covered by St. Paul's Church. My theory is that John Blake of Boston living in 1666 on what is now the Adams House, and John Wampus living at what is now St. Paul's Church were practically neighbors (see illustration), and that a son of John Blake could have become friendly to this John Wampus, thus easily explaining this mark of confidence in making him one of the executors of his will in 1679. Studying carefully these several interlacing bits of history, we can surely find corroborative evidence to assume that John Blake of Boston is father to John Blake of Sandwich in Plymouth Colony and who died in Wrentham in 1700.

Third: Was John Blake of Sandwich and Wrentham father to Robert Blake of Wrentham, and was Robert any relation to the

---

* If this land was secured, it is natural to think that John Blake of Boston might have given it to a son.

other Blakes found in Wrentham in his time? John Blake of Sandwich and Wrentham died in the latter place in 1700 and his wife Bridget died there in 1706. We find in the Wrentham Town Records of the year 1688 that among thirty-six tax payers, that Ensign Blake was the wealthiest. Now Robert Blake married in 1703 and soon after we find him located on a large farm in Wrentham, which fact would denote wealth; furthermore, he too in 1709 was called Ensign in the Queen's service, and at his death was known as Captain, as will be seen by the inscription on his gravestone. I point out these facts as showing a similar position in the community, that might be handed down from father to son. Another substantial evidence of relationship is the fact that their gravestones are found very near together in the Wrentham Cemetery. As to the relationship between the other Blakes of Wrentham of that period to either older John or Robert, we find in the births of the children of the younger John Blake (who married Joanna Whiting in 1689) that he had a daughter named Bridget, thereby plainly indicating by his own name and that of his daughter's a relationship with John and Bridget Blake; again we find that the oldest son of John and Joanna Blake whose name was James, was a witness to the will of Robert Blake in 1735, while Andrew Blake who married Sarah Stephens in 1696 named his oldest son Isaac, in that way connecting him with John and Bridget Blake who had a son Isaac, we think, and who died in Wrentham in 1689. It is my opinion that John Blake Sr. had extensive land holdings and that he divided it between his three sons. John and Andrew having their land on Stop River in that part of Wrentham now called Norfolk, as shown by deeds, and no doubt lived in that vicinity. Andrew certainly did for he is buried in the Norfolk cemetery. While Robert being the youngest remained on the home farm with his father and mother and at their death inherited it.

This chain of separate records seemingly links itself together in corroborative support of my theory, that we have here the true line of descent: this is my belief from all data given and I trust that future research will confirm my contentions.

CONTENTS

FOURTH GENERATION.

ROBERT BLAKE AND SARAH GUILD.

GUILD FAMILY.

GUILD John,[1] weaver, supposed to have been born in England about 1616, came to America in the year 1636 with his brother Samuel and sister Ann. He married 24 June 1645, Elizabeth Crooke of Roxbury who transferred her relation from the church of that place to the church in Dedham 4 July 1649. She died 31 Aug. 1669. He was admitted to the church at Dedham, Mass., 17 July 1640 and bought in this year twelve acres of upland on which he built a house which was occupied by himself and descendants for more than two hundred years. He was made a freeman 10 May 1643 and as one of the original grantees had assigned to him and his heirs forever, three roods and twelve rods more or less to which he added by grants and purchase considerable other real estate in Dedham, Wrentham, Medfield and Natick. He was thoroughly honest in all his dealings and in his habits. He never held any office, and the town records show his attendance at meeting but once in several years, that on an occasion of considerable excitement in relation to making alterations and additions to the meeting house. He died 4 Oct. 1682, leaving a will dated 3 Oct. 1682 and proved 3 Nov. 1682, in which he names children Samuel, **John,** Elizabeth. " I give and bequeath unto my son John Guild all my land lying in Wrentham as well upland as midow as also my lott near Meadfield in the dividend called ' Meadfield Dividend,' to him and his heirs forever; also I give unto my son John my looms and four sleays, which are suitable for present use as also one wheel w'th ye blades, and a book called ' Sound Believer.' " It was certified in court 3 Nov. 1682, "that he was to the understanding of the witness of disposing mind." The following inventory of his estate was made 4 Nov. 1682 and amounted to £153. 11 s.

CHILDREN:

All born in Dedham, Mass.:

JOHN, 1st, b. 22 Aug. 1646, died young.

SAMUEL, b. 7 Nov. 1647, m. Mary Woodcock, d. ———, alive in 1682.

John, 2nd, b. 29 Nov. 1649, m. **Sarah Fisher** (prob. in Dedham ?), 22 May 1677, d. in Wrentham, 24 Jan. 1722–3, a. 72 y.

ELIEZER, b. 30 Nov. 1653, d. 30 June 1655.

EBENEZER, b. 21 Dec. 1657, d. 21 April 1661.

ELIZABETH, b. 18 Jan. 1660, ?, mentioned in father's will of 1682.

BENJAMIN, b. 25 May 1664, not mentioned in his father's will of 1682.

FISHER FAMILY.

FISHER Anthony, lived in the latter part of Queen Elizabeth's reign in the parish of Syleham, County Suffolk, England, on the south bank of the Waveney River which separates Suffolk from Norfolk on a freehold estate called " Wignotte." His wife was Mary, daughter of William and Anne Fiske of St. James, South Elmsham, County Suffolk, an old Puritan family of that country which had suffered during the religious persecution of Queen Mary's reign. The Parish Records of Syleham contain several references to Anthony Fisher and his descendants, which are annexed in the language of the Records, namely:

Anno Domini 1585, Joshua Fysher, et Maria Fysher, Gemini, baptisadi fuer 24th die Februarii ano superdicto.

Anno Domini 1591 *Antonius Fysher*, bapt. erat 23 Aprilis anno sup. dicto.

Anno Domini 1599 Cornelius Fysher, the sonne of Anthonye Fisher was bap. the six day of Augusti.

Anno Domini 1621 Joshua Fysher, the sonne of Joshua Fysher was baptized on the II days of Aprille.

Anno Dom. 1633 Amos Fysher and Ann Lord were married September 24.

Joshua Fysher and Ann Luson were married 7 February, Anno Dom 1638.

Anthony Fysher was buried the eleventh day of April 1640. This last entry evidently is Anthony Fisher Senior.

FISHER Anthony,[1] son of Anthony of Syleham, County Suffolk, England, was baptized 23 April 1591, came to New England with his first wife Mary and children probably from Yarmouth in the ship " Rose," arriving in Boston 26 June 1637 and settled in Dedham. He subscribed to the Dedham Covenant, 18 July 1637. On the 1 January 1638 he was one of the committee "Chosen to Contrive the Fabricke of a Meetinghouse." On 28 July 1638 he was assigned his house lot of twelve acres, more or less. His wife Mary joined the Dedham church 27 March 1642, "but he was not comfortably received into ye church on account of his proud and haught sprit untill 14 March 1645." He was made freeman May 1645, was chosen Selectman of Dedham ("to act in town affairs") in 1646 and 1647. County Commissioner, 3 Sept. 1660 and a Deputy to the General Court 2 May 1649, was Wood-reeve in 1653-54-55-57-58-61 and 62. From a Minute in the handwriting of Eleazer Lusher bearing date 9 March 1652, we would infer that he, Anthony, gave the bulk of his property to his sons and they bound themselves to support their mother if she were left dependent. We find in the Dedham Records that his property was assessed on 2 Feb. 1656/7 at £117. 3 s. We have been unable to learn the date of the death of his wife Mary, but he married again the 14th of Nov. 1663, Isabell, widow of Edward Breck of Dorchester, being at the time of this marriage about 72. He was chosen commissioner 8 March 1666 and selectman of Dorchester Dec. 1664-65-66. "He died at Dorchester in the 80th year of his age 18 April 1671." "His widow Died the 22 June 1673." The inventory of his estate showing only personal property in Dedham and Dorchester was presented by Ensign Daniel Fisher 20 July 1671, and an agreement for the distribution was made as follows, and dated 26 July 1672: "We whose names are hereto written being ye sons and ye daughter of our late deceased father Anthony Fisher, sometimes called of Dorchester decease," etc. and signed by Daniel, Nathaniel and Cornelius Fisher, Daniel Morse and **Joanna Fisher.**

CHILDREN:

Anthony, b. ———, m. **Joanna Faxon** at Dedham, 7 Sept. 1647, d. 13 Feb. 1670.

DANIEL, b. in England abt. 1619, m. Abigail Morrett, 16 Nov. 1641, d. 8 Oct. 1683.

NATHANIEL, b. in England abt. 1620, m. Esther Hunting at Dedham, 26 Dec. 1649, d. at Dedham, 23 May 1676.

Cornelius, b. in England, m. (1) at Dedham, 22 Feb. 1653, Leah Heaton, d. 12 Nov. 1664; m. (2) at Dedham, 24 July 1665, **Sarah Everett,** d. 28 Feb. 1675; d. at Wrentham, 2 Jan. 1699.

LYDIA, b. in England abt. 1621, m. Daniel Morse of Sherborn before 1639, d. at Sherborn, 29 Jan. 1691, ae. 70 y.

A John Fisher d. at Dedham 5 Sept. 1637 and by another record John d. at the same place 15 July 1638.

FAXON FAMILY.

FAXON Thomas,[1] was born in England about 1601, came to America before 1647 with his wife Joane and three children. The earliest record of him is found at Dedham, Mass., in the marriage of his daughter Joanna to Anthony Fisher Jr., 7 Sept. 1647. His wife Joane appears upon the records in a single instance, in giving her assent to a deed of an eighth part of Block Island conveyed by Thomas Faxon to John Williams, etc.; the date of her acknowledgment of the deed is 4 June,1663. Her name seems to account for that of her daughter Joanna. The record of her death is not found, but is between 1663 and 1670 for Thomas Faxon was married 5 Sept. 1670 to Mrs. Sarah Savil, widow. He was generally termed Mr. Thomas Faxon. He was a freeman 1656 and a representative or deputy from Braintree in 1669 and one of the selectmen there in 1670–72. In his will he mentions his wife Sarah and widow **Mrs. Fisher** (his daughter). He died 23 Nov. 1680 at Braintree.

CHILDREN:

Joanna, b. in England, m. 7 Sept. 1647, **Anthony Fisher Jr.,** d. 16 Oct. 1694.

THOMAS, b. in England abt. 1628 or 29, m. 11 April 1653, Deborah Thayer, d. 25 May 1662.

RICHARD, b. in England, m. Elizabeth, d. 20 Dec. 1674.

FISHER Anthony[2] (*Anthony*[1]) was the eldest son of Anthony and Mary Fisher of Dorchester. Married in Dedham 7 Sept. 1647 Joanna only daughter of Thomas and Joane Faxon of Braintree. He came with his parents to New England and settled in Dedham 1637, was a member of the Ancient and Honorable Artillery Company in 1644; made a freeman 6 May 1646. Joined the Dedham church 20 July 1645. He was chosen surveyor at Dedham 1654–1664. In 1652 he settled the estate of Henry Brookes. Anthony Fisher Jr. was among the first to go to Wollomonopoag (Wrentham) in 1661 and to claim part of the

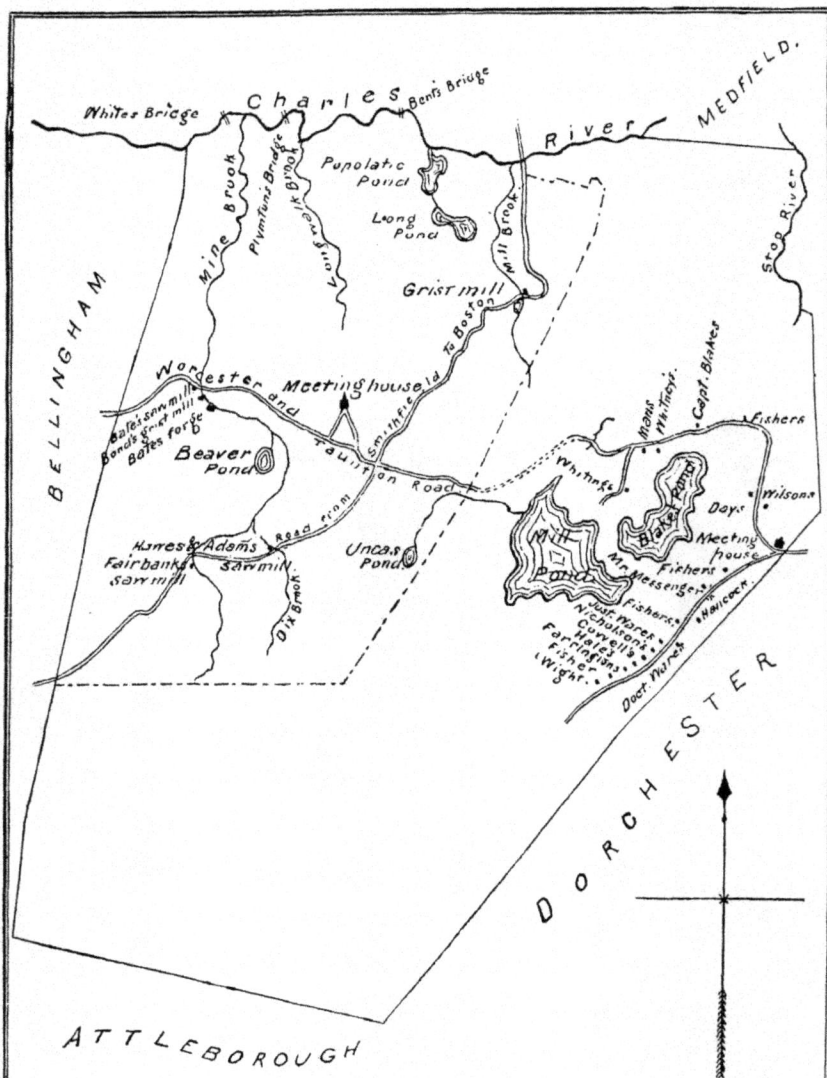

MAP OF WRENTHAM, SHOWING HOME SITE OF BLAKE, DAY
AND FISHER FAMILIES

600 acres for the encouragement of that plantation.   In March 1663 " in behalf of them that have improvements there (Wrentham) that they might take their lots with the rest of the proprietors." . . . These persons were the first persons to break up and improve lands at Wollomonopoag.   Anthony located his " improvements " (so called) upon the easterly and south easterly side of Whitings Pond or Great Pond (previously known as Mill Pond), but their houses were some distance from the Pond, probably on what is now Franklin Street and South Street.   (See illustration.)   On 8 Nov. 1669 he was one of those who went and treated with Philip Sagamore and bought the land at Wrentham.   Anthony's name is in the records as paying the town and county rate in 1648, in which year his house was valued at £10. 8 s.   Soon thereafter he rented land of Gov. Stoughton and on 6 Jan. 1652 he paid his annual rent in 5 bushels of Indian corn 0–15–0.   He was assessed for £95. 10 s., 20 Feb. 1656–57.   The following does not tell exactly where he lived in Dorchester but gives much information.   " To the much Honord Gouvenor, the Deputie Gouvenor and the Assitants and Deputies assembled in General Court at Boston 7 of 3 mo 1662. — The petition of Anthony Fisher and Nathaniell Stearnes Humbly sheweth: That wheras we your petitioners being inhabitants in Mr. Stoughton's Farme within the Bounds of Dorchester but yet distant about Seaven or eight miles or more from Dorchester meeting house and being neere ajacient to the Towne of Dedham by reason of which our scituation we are uncapeable to attend publike ordenances at Dorchester ordinarly: and we for our owne and our Familyes conveniencie doe constantly attend at Dedham, where each of our selves and our wives are enjoyed in Church Fellowship in that church."   He probably lived on the land bought of Mr. Stoughton situated near the Neponset River, but within the bounds of Dorchester.   He died 13 Feb. 1670, his widow Joanna died 16 Oct. 1694.   The inventory of his estate made 7 April 1670 includes: " House and land thereof belonging in Dedham £40.   Land purchased of Mr. Stoughton £50 etc etc."

CHILDREN:

MEHITABLE, b. 27 June 1648, prob. d. young.
EXPERIENCE, bapt. 11, 1650, prob. d. young.

JOSIAH, b. 1 May 1654, m. (1) 27 Jan. 1679, Meletiah Bullen, d. 23 Apr.
    1693; m. (2) 1 Sept. 1693, Joanna Morse; m. (3) Abigail Greenwood?,
    m. (4) Mehitabel Veazie; d. prob. 12 April 1736.
ABIAH, bapt. 3 Aug. 1656, m. Benjamin Colburn of Dedham, 5 March
    1685, d. 18 Nov. 1688.
Sarah, b. 29 Oct. 1658, m. John Guild 22 May 1677, d. ————.
DEBORAH, bapt. 24 Feb. 1661, m. James Fales, 20 Oct. 1679, settled at
    Walpole.
JUDITH, bapt. 5 July 1663, m. John Bullen, 3 Jan. 1684, d. ————.
ELEAZER, b. 18 Sept. 1669, m. Mary Avery, 13 Oct. 1698, d. ————.

GUILD John² (*John¹*), son of John and Elizabeth (Crooke)
Guild, born in Dedham, Mass., 29 Nov. 1649, married 22 May
1677, Sarah, daughter of Anthony and Joanna (Faxon) Fisher
of Dedham. She was born 29 Oct. 1658. He moved from
Dedham to Wrentham, Mass., in 1681 and is in the first list of
selectmen chosen in 1686, united with the church there 13 April
1692 and was elected a deacon 7 Dec. 1707. " As the Puritan
standard of fitness for church membership and espacially for the
office of deacon was very rigid; there can be no hesitation in
ascribing to him all those qualities of mind and heart which
constitute a trustworthy citizen and exmplary Christian." He
was a witness to the purchase of land from the Indians at Lancaster in 1701 and died at Wrentham 24 January 1722/3 in his
72 year, and is buried in the Wrentham Center Cemetery.

CHILDREN:
    b. in Dedham:
BETHIAH, b. 4 Oct. 1678, m. Samuel Sears, Jan. 7, 1703, d. ————.
SARAH, 1st, b. 30 Oct. 1680, d. 7 Dec. 1682.
    In Wrentham, Mass.:
Sarah, 2nd, b. 3 June 1683, m. (1) **Robert Blake**, 7 Jan. 1703, d. 4 Oct.
    1735; m. (2) Nathaniel Perry, 30 March 1738; d. in Wrentham, 30
    July 1757, a. 75 y.
ELIZABETH, b. 7 July 1685, m. William Puffer, 25 May 1710, d. ————.
JOANNA, b. 4 Nov. 1687, m. Samuel Kingsbury, 12 May 1715, d. ————.
JOHN, b. 7 Nov. 1690, m. (1) 21 June 1711, Mercy Foster, d. 3 May
    1730; m. (2) Phebe Mann; d. in Wrentham, 28 Jan. 1762, a. 72 y.
JOSIAH, b. 14 July 1694, m. Deborah ————, d. ————.
JUDITH, b. 19 Sept. 1697, m. Nathaniel Briggs, 16 June 1720, d. ————.
EBENEZER, b. 9 Sept. 1700, d. 13 Sept. 1701.

BLAKE Robert⁴ (*John,³ John,² William¹*), was born about
1675 and was undoubtedly the son of John and Bridget Blake.

CAPT. ROBERT BLAKE HOUSE
Wrentham, Mass.

He married 7 Jan. 1703 at Wrentham, Mass., Sarah, daughter of
John and Sarah (Fisher) Guild. She was born at Wrentham
3 June 1683. His farm (doubtless inherited from his father) was
situated on the side of Blake's Pond (now Archers) in Wrentham
and he built his home on the crown of the hill, parts of which are
incorporated into the house now occupying the site. (See illustration.) No other place can be as fitting as this to tell of the very
desirable location and beautiful outlook over the pretty sheet of
water which was the home of several of the Blake family. The
remaining trunk of an old oak which was left in clearing the forest
and stood for generations as a landmark by the roadside is still
carefully supported and guarded as a precious heritage from an
earlier settler. The grandson Phillip in his memoirs tells that when
he was a boy the old people called it " The Old Oak." Robert
Blake was owner of much property in Wrentham, an active and
useful citizen; an officer and Captain of the Troops. A family
of ten children was born to him, and as is often the case we learn
much of the real character of a person by their last will; this not
only reveals the fine nature of the man but gives interesting sidelights and clews to colonial customs. He died at Wrentham and
we read on the brown slate headstone (in the old part of the cemetery at Wrentham Center). (See illustration, page 24.) This
headstone stands close by a new roadway, recently projected.
The mound or grave has surely vanished, and as I stood by the
spot I invoked Shakespeare's Malediction upon the vandalism of
modern improvements. Just to one side and in what was doubtless the same lot, stands a headstone to his wife, who remarried
after his death, which reads " Sarah Perry, formerly wife of
Captain Robert Blake, died July 30, 1757 in her 75th year."

Extracts of the Will of Robert Blake. " In the Name of God
Amen. The first Day of Oct in the 9th year of Reign of Souereign
Lord George the Second, etc. King. I, Robert Blake of Wrentham in County of Suffolk in New England, yeomen, etc. I give
and bequeath to Sarah my Dearly beloved Wife, The One half
part of my Dwelling House and Barn, also one half part of my
land within the Township aforsaid — To eldest Son Robert
having given him considerable already, etc I give him my
Leading Staff. To son Josiah having given him a Trade etc
I give him £23 and one Cow Common Right. — I give to my Son
Nathan one Cow Comon right throughout the Comon undivided

land within the Township of Wrentham aforesaid. I also Give him eighty Pounds in money, which is to be accounted the whole and full of his Portion out of my Estate after my descease. To Son Ezra one Cow Comon right, one half part of my land, in Wrentham provided he pay his Brother and Sisters, Legacies mentioned etc. To Son Obidiah Forty Pounds. Desinging he shall have a Trade and one Cow Comon right. To son Elijah I give the one half part of all my lands in Wrentham, one half part of Dwelling house and Barn; that half part I left to my wife, provided he stay with his mother and also provided he pay legacies mentioned to his brothers and sisters, also one Cow Comon right. — To daughter Betty Hall £5 having given her considerable upon her marriage. To Daughter Sarah Fisher £5 having given her considerable upon her marriage. To Daughter Hipzabath £32. 10 shillings. To Daughter Ester £32. 10 shillings. — etc etc." Probated at Boston 28 Oct. 1735. In the inventory of his estate, his home lot by estimation comprised 100 acres, with very near 100 acres more in different places. The total amount of the estate was £1269. 5. 6.

CHILDREN:

BETTY, b. 21 July 1703, m. Benjamin Hall, 15 Nov. 1727, d. ———.

SARAH, b. 18 Aug. 1705, m. (1) 1 Nov. 1727, Thomas Fisher, d. 5 Aug. 1760; m. (2) 8 Dec. 1760, James Newe; d. 1804, ae. 99 yrs.

ROBERT, b. 22 Dec. 1707, m. Keziah Bacon, 14 Jan. 1741/2, d. 22 Dec. 1800, ae. 93 yrs.

JOSIAH, Ensign, b. 4 March 1709/10, m. Martha Cowell, 3 March 1736/7, d. at Wrentham, 25 Feb. 1795, ae. 85 yrs.

Nathan, b. 13 March 1711/12, m. (1) abt. 1741, **Elizabeth Graves,** d. 19 July 1804; m. (2) 2 Jan. 1806, Mrs. Mary Brinton; d. at Keene, 4 Aug. 1811, ae. 99 yrs.

EZRA, Deacon, b. 4 May 1714, m. Esther Ware, 8 Feb. 1737/8, d. 8 March 1775, ae. 61 yrs.

HEPHZIBAH, b. 8 Oct. 1716, m. Benjamin Shephard, 14 Dec. 1737, d. 26 Aug. 1804, ae. 88 yrs.

OBEDIAH, Dr., b. 9 June 1719, m. (1) 27 Nov. 1749, Zipporah Harris, d. 25 Feb. 1785; m. (2) Lydia, d. at Keene, 14 June 1810, ae. 91 yrs.

ESTHER, b. 23 July 1721, m. Dr. David Jones, 11 Nov. 1741, d. at Abington, Mass., 28 Sept. 1758, ae. 37 yrs.

ELIJAH, b. 13 Oct. 1723, m. Sarah Pray, 4 March 1746/7, d. ———. Removed to Keene, N. H., but death is not found there.

HEADSTONE OF CAPTAIN ROBERT BLAKE
Wrentham Centre Cemetery

CONTENTS

FIFTH GENERATION.

NATHAN BLAKE AND ELIZABETH GRAVES.

GRAVES FAMILY.

GRAVES Thomas,[1] was born in England before 1585 and came to New England with his wife Sarah and five children before 1645. His children were all born in England and were all of mature age when they came to this country; the youngest of his sons being about 16 years old. The first official record of him in this country is found at Hartford, Conn., 1645. He was not an original proprietor there; "an old man and was excused from military training." He is put down as having three pieces of real estate; one described as being the one "where on his house standeth." The sons took up homes nearby, the family remained together as far as it is known until the removal to Hatfield, Mass. I know nothing of the daughter Elizabeth; the son Samuel never married and probably did not live to accompany the rest. While Nathaniel for the sake of remaining near his wife's relations did not remove with the rest of the family to Hatfield, which removal was in Sept. 1661, reaching there in Oct. 1661.

Thomas Graves was now an aged but honored member of the community, past his 76th birthday and was not given a separate assignment or grant of land, but was counted in with his eldest son Isaac, while the lands of his son John were contiguous. He and his wife were inmates of the family of Isaac during the remainder of their lives, his death occurring Nov. 1662, one year after removal to Hatfield, his son Isaac being administrator upon his estate in Massachusetts; while his son Nathaniel performed the same service on his estate in Connecticut. His wife Sarah survived him four years and died on 17 Dec. 1666. Isaac administered upon her estate.

ISAAC, b. in England, m. Mary Church, killed by the Indians, 19 Sept. 1677.

John, b. in England, m. (1) **Mary Smith,** d. 16 Dec. 1668; m. (2) 20 July 1671, Wid. Mary Wyatt; killed by the Indians, 19 Sept. 1677.

SAMUEL, b. in England.   Did not marry.   Died prob. before removal of
family to Hatfield.

ELIZABETH, b. in England, m. ——, d. ——.

NATHANIEL, b. in England abt. 1629, m. Martha Betts, 16 Jan. 1655,
d. at Wethersfield, Conn., 28 Sept. 1682, age about 53 yrs.

SMITH FAMILY.

SMITH Lieut. **Samuel,**[1] came from England in the ship
" Elizabeth," from Ipswich in 1634 and by the custom-house
records his age is given as 32 with wife Elizabeth 32, and children,
Samuel 9, Elizabeth 7, Mary 4, and Philip 1.   He was admitted
freeman 3 Sept. 1634.   Was first perhaps at Watertown where
most of the passengers of that ship planted, but in a few years
went to Wethersfield, Conn.   He was representative there from
1641–53, and in 1659 removed to Hadley, Mass., where he was
in very high repute holding important office in both church and
state.   Was representative often from there from 1661 to 1673.
Lieutenant in command of the military from 1663 to 1678.
Was made a magistrate for the town.   He died Dec. 1680 age
about 78 years.   Of the four children he brought, three were
named in his will, though he gave the eldest son only 5 s., no
doubt for sufficient reason, yet not expressed.   Chileal and John
his sons are mentioned.   The inventory of his estate was taken
17 Jan. 1681.   His widow died 16 March 1686 age 84 years.

SAMUEL, b. in England abt. 1625, m. Elizabeth Smith, d.——, removed to Virginia.

Elizabeth, b. in England abt. 1627, m. (1) 1646, Nathaniel Foot, d.
abt. 1654; m. (2) William Gull, d. 1701; d. after 1701.

Mary, b. in England abt. 1630, m. John Graves before 1653, d. at Hatfield, 16 Dec. 1668.

PHILIP, b. in England abt. 1633, m. Rebecca Foot, 1657, d. 10 Jan. 1685.

CHILEAL, b. on this side abt. 1 March 1635, m. Hannah Hitchcock,
2 Oct. 1661, d. 7 March 1731, "almost 96."

JOHN, m. Mary Partridge, 12 Nov. 1663, slain by Indians, 30 May
1676.

GRAVES John[2] (*Thomas*[1]), son of Thomas and Sarah Graves,
was born in England and came to this country with his father.
He married (1) Mary daughter of Lieut. Samuel and Elizabeth
Smith; she died probably 16 Dec. 1668.   Married (2) 20 July

1671 Mary daughter of John Bronson and widow of John Wyatt of Haddam, Conn. He made his home in Wethersfield, Conn., the lands granted to him in 1652 were described as those " whereon his house standeth." Was made freeman 18 May 1654. He was a man of probity and education and was employed in 1655 and again in 1659 to run the boundary line between Weathersfield and Mattabessett (now Middleton). He owned land in Hartford and Wethersfield, which he retained when he removed to Hatfield in 1661, and became a member of the Hadley church 19 Feb. 1668/9. He was killed by the Indians in the raid of Ashpelon in their attack upon Hatfield 19 Sept. 1677, at the same time his brother Sergeant Isaac Graves was killed. His widow married 3rd, Lieut. William Allis 25 June 1678 and 4th, Capt. Samuel Gaylord.

> JOHN, b. at Wethersfield abt. 1653, m. Sarah White, 12 Feb. 1678, settled in Hatfield, d. 2 Dec. 1730.
>
> MARY, b. at Wethersfield abt. 1654, m. (1) 15 Jan. 1671, Samuel Bell of Springfield, and from this line is descent of the parents of Hon. Grover Cleveland, President of U. S.; m. (2) April 1679, Benjamin Stebbins; d. ———.
>
> ISAAC, b. at Wethersfield abt. 1655, m. (1) 5 Apr. 1679, Sarah Wyatt, d. 9 Jan. 1690; m. (2) 1691, Abigail, d. 13 July 1697; m. (3) Deliverence, widow of Samuel Graves; d. abt. 1740.
>
> Samuel, b. at Wethersfield abt. 1657, m. **Sarah,** d. at Sunderland, 11 March 1731.
>
> SARAH, b. at Wethersfield abt. 1659, m. Edward Stebbins, Apr. 1679, d. 1700.
>
> ELIZABETH, b. at Hatfield, 9 Dec. 1662, m. Thomas Jones, d. ———.
>
> DANIEL, b. at Hatfield, 7 Dec. 1664, m. Hannah Warriner, settled in Springfield, d. 18 May 1724.
>
> EBENEZER, b. at Hatfield 20 Nov. 1666, m. ———, was a soldier in 1688 and settled at Springfield, d.
>
> BETHIAH, b. at Hatfield, 17 June 1668, d. 21 Jan. 1669.
>
> NATHANIEL, b. at Hatfield, 10 June 1671, m. Rebecca Allis, 30 April 1702, d. abt. 1757, prob. at Whately.

GRAVES Samuel[3] (*John,*[2] *Thomas*[1]), son of John and Mary (Smith) Graves, was born at Wethersfield, Conn., 1657. He married Sarah before 1688; what her maiden name was or when she was born is not known by me. He removed to Hatfield with his parents in the year 1661. In the campaigns against the Indians he was engaged under Capt. Poole stationed at Hadley

24 Aug. 1676. We find him taking the oath of allegiance at Hatfield on the 8 Feb. 1678. After some years residence in Hatfield he removed and was one of the pioneers of the second settlement of Swampfield (now Sunderland), having removed there prior to 1718 for his name appears as one occupying a lot on that date. He was a Selectman in 1722 and again in 1724. He died the 11 March 1731, and his widow died 15 Oct. 1734.

> SARAH, b. 1 Jan. 1688, m. Daniel Smith, 7 April 1709, d. ————.
>
> JONATHAN, b. 27 Oct. 1689, m. (1) 2 June 1715, Mrs. Elizabeth Combs; m. (2) Hannah ————; d. 21 May 1773.
>
> **Abraham,** b. 12 Dec. 1691, m. **Thankfull Bardwell,** 23 May 1717, d. at Swanzey, N. H., 28 Oct. 1777.
>
> DAVID, b. 9 Dec. 1693, m. Abigail Bardwell, 26 June 1720, d. at Whately, 25 Aug. 1781.
>
> NOAH, b. 19 Dec. 1695, m. (1) Rebecca Wright, d. 8 Feb. 1744; m. (2) 8 Apr. 1754, Widow Rachel Newton; d. at Sunderland, 17 Mar. 1773, ae. 78 y.
>
> MEHITABLE, b. 19 Dec. 1695, m. John (Bardwell?) before 1727, d. ————.
>
> SAMUEL, b. 30 Jan. 1698, m. Grace Hitchcock, 9 Apr. 1728, d. at South Deerfield, 6 May 1774.

GULL FAMILY.

GULL William,[1] was of Wethersfield in 1649, married after 1654, Elizabeth, daughter of Lieutenant Samuel and Elizabeth Smith and Widow of Nathaniel Foot. She was born in England about 1627. He removed from Wethersfield, Conn., to Hatfield, Mass., 1663. Was made freeman 1673. Took the oath of allegiance at Hatfield 8 Feb. 1678 and may have lived in that part of the town that was called the " North Farms." His will is dated 12 April 1701 and proved 18 Dec. 1701, and in it he mentions his wife Elizabeth and Ann, wife of Jonathan Root, daughter **Mary,** wife of **Robert Bardwell;** Mercy, wife of Jeremiah Alvord, and a child of his deceased daughter Ester who had been wife of Joseph Gillet.

> **Mary,** b. ————, m. **Robert Bardwell,** 29 Nov. 1676, d. 12 Nov. 1726.
>
> ANNA, b. ————, m. Jonathan Root, 1680. He was of Northampton, Mass., d. after 1701.

ESTHER, b. in Hatfield or Hadley, 21 Nov. 1665, m. Joseph Gillett, 3 Nov. 1687, d. before 1701.

MERCY, b. in Hatfield or Hadley, 27 June 1668, m. Jeremiah Alvord between 1696 and 1701, d. after 1710.

BARDWELL FAMILY.

BARDWELL Robert,[1] came from London where he was an apprentice to a hatter in 1667. He married Mary, daughter of William and Elizabeth (Smith) Gull, 29 Nov. 1676. He was in Boston 1670. He learned here a new branch of the business, the making of wool hats. Was a soldier in the famous " Swamp fight " when the power of the " Narrangasetts " was broken 19 Dec. 1675. And on 7 April 1676 he was a Sergeant under Capt. Turner and stationed with 44 men under him at Hatfield, and he held the same office in the " Falls fight " 19 May 1676. After the war he settled at Hatfield and set up a hatters shop. He is found among others taking the oath of allegiance at Hatfield on 8 Feb. 1678. One of his descendants, Elijah Bardwell, to whom we are indebted for many items, says he lived at " North Farms." He died 9 Jan. 1726 and his widow died 12 Nov. 1726.

CHILDREN:

EBENEZER, b. 19 Oct. 1679, m. Mary Field, 25 April 1706, d. 13 July 1732.

MARY, b. 15 Oct. 1681, m. ————, d. ————.

JOHN 1st, b. 16 Sept. 1683, d. 1685.

SAMUEL, b. 26 Sept. 1685, m. Martha Allen, d. prob. at Deerfield, 18 Mar. 1771.

JOHN 2nd, b. 28 Aug. 1687, m. Mehitable Graves before 1727, d. 25 May 1728.

ELIZABETH, b. 30 July 1689, m. ————, d. ————.

THOMAS, b. 8 Dec. 1691, m. Sarah Belding, 16 June 1722, d. prob. at Deerfield, 8 Feb. 1781.

HESTER, b. 8 Aug. 1693, m. Joseph Belding, 23 Oct. 1717, d. before 1727.

SARAH, b. ————, m. Jonathan Barrett of Hartford, 19 May 1713, d. ————.

Thankful, b. ————, m. Abraham Graves, 23 May 1717, d. at Swansea, N. H., 12 Mar. 1775.

ABIGAIL, b. abt. 1699, m. David Graves, 6 June 1720, d. prob. at Whately, 31 Oct. 1786, ae. 87 yrs.

GRAVES Abraham[4] (*Samuel*,[3] *John*,[2] *Thomas*[1]), was the son of
Samuel and Sarah Graves; he was born in Hatfield, 12th Dec.
1691. He married Thankful, daughter of Robert and Mary
(Gull) Bardwell of Hatfield, 23 May 1717. He settled in Deerfield and removed to Swanzey, N. H., where his name is found
on a list of early settlers there 6 Dec. 1739, probably returned to
Deerfield during the period of Indian raids from Canada. We
find on a plan of house lots dated 1747 that his was number 49
and located to the east of the meeting house. His name and that
of his son-in-law Nathan Blake are found among others to
subscribe to the church covenant 21 Aug. 1753. The churches
of Swanzey and Keene met at the school house in Swanzey and
mutually and unanimously agreed to be one religious society.
His name is found again in Swanzey Factory Village in 1759,
where he was chosen on a committee to lay out the land extending
from Keene line southwesterly so as to include the entire privilege.
He died 28 Oct. 1777, and his wife Thankful died 12 March 1775.

CHILDREN:

THANKFUL, b. 10 Feb. 1718, d. young.

Elizabeth b. 19 July 1721, m. **Nathan Blake** of Keene, N. H., 1741, d.
at Keene, N. H., 19 July 1804, ae. 83 exactly.

ASAHEL, b. abt. 1722, m. ———. Was killed in Taylor fight at Hins-
dale, 14 July 1748.

ABRAHAM, b. 1723, m. ———, d. 16 Nov. 1745.

JOSHUA, b. 1724, m. Lydia Woodcock of Swansea, N. H., 12 Oct. 1758,
d. after 1774.

LYDIA, b. 1726, m. Charles Howe of Marlboro, Mass., 8 April 1746,
d. ———.

MARY, b. 1728, m. Elijah Scott of Sunderland, 25 May 1756, removed
to Swansea, N. H. in 1788, d. ———.

SARAH, b. 1729, m. Samuel Hills, 25 June 1758, d. ———.

MEHITABLE, b. 1731, m. William Wright of Northfield, 27 Aug. 1758,
d. ———.

ELIJAH, b. abt. 1732, m. Submit Dickinson, 13 May 1752, d. after 1763.

ABNER, b. abt. 1734, m. Dorcas Belding before 1765, d. at Stratton, Vt.,
2 Feb. 1787.

LUCY, b. abt. 1737, m. David Belding 2nd, 7 Feb. 1770, d. ———.

BLAKE Nathan[5] (*Robert*,[4] *John*,[3] *John*,[2] *William*[1]), fifth child
of Robert and Sarah (Guild) Blake was born in Wrentham,
13 March 1711/2. He married Elizabeth, daughter of Abraham
and Thankfull (Bardwell) Graves in 1741. She was born 19 July

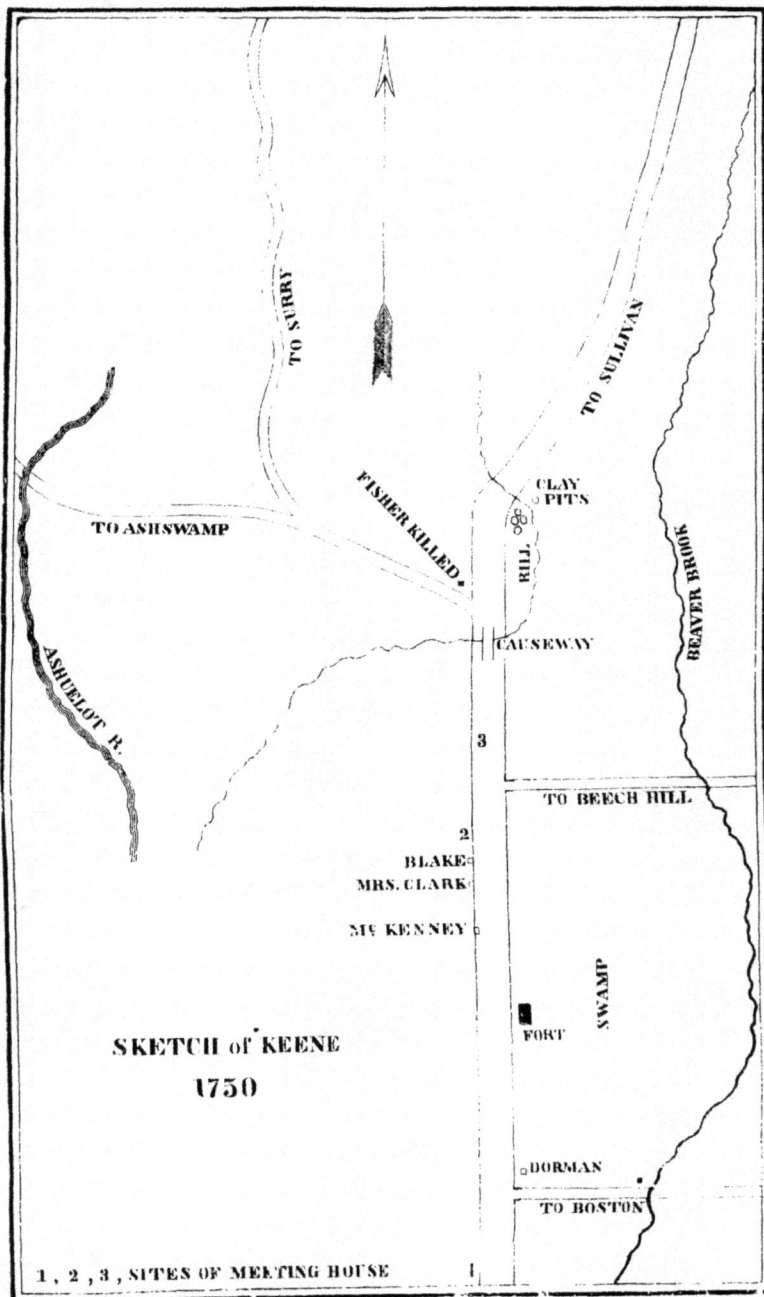

TO SURRY

TO SULLIVAN

FISHER KILLED.

CLAY PITS

TO ASHSWAMP

HILL

BEAVER BROOK

ASHUELOT R.

CAUSEWAY

3

TO BEECH HILL

2

BLAKE

MRS. CLARK

McKENNEY

SWAMP

FORT

SKETCH of KEENE

1750

DORMAN

TO BOSTON

1, 2, 3, SITES OF MEETING HOUSE

1

1721. Records show, that he was a husbandman, inheriting much land and also a goodly sum of money from his father. To give a clear idea of the movements of this period in the colonies we will state that the government had initiated Colonial Grants in New Hampshire, which proved an attractive magnet to those with money and a greater one to the brave spirits who thirsted for adventure. Thus we find that Nathan Blake at the age of 24 possessed of much land and property in Wrentham, surrounded by a good degree of civilization, good homes, and established colonial government, upon the death of his father, abandoned all these comforts and with his brother Obidiah and others took up grants in Upper Asheulot, now Keene, N. H., where he built the first house ever built in Keene in the year 1736 (see illustration) braving the terrors of frontier life, knowing full well the fierce Indian raids of a previous decade in the neighboring valley of the Connecticut. The annals of Keene give graphic account of this stirring period; even I, as a child, was often told thrilling stories by my father as he related the exploits of his grandfather.

The following quotations from annals of Keene tell the story in succinct form. " Nathan Blake and party from Wrentham laid out house-lots, roads, voted to build a Meeting House and took up pioneer work in every direction. The Blake house at the south end of the street was headquarters for meetings, a general rallying point. He with two others essayed to spend the winter of 1736–7 in their new quarters, but the terrible cold and lack of provisions soon proved too much for their endurance and in February their provisions were exhausted and hearing nothing from Heaton, whom they had sent to Northfield for meal, he and Smeed left the oxen they had brought from Wrentham, with free access to the hay gathered during the summer, and on snowshoes proceeded either to Deerfield or Wrentham. Anxious for the oxen they returned early in the spring, finding them much emaciated, feeding upon twigs and dead grass. The oxen recognized their owners and exhibited so much pleasure it drew tears from their eyes. In 1738 the town voted to build a Fort and in this, as in all town activities, among the foremost is always found the name of Nathan Blake.

" The settlers acquired the habit of repairing for safety through the night to the Forts, but even with the knowledge that Indians were lurking in the vicinity, the men must go to their barns to feed and care for their cattle. Early on 23 April 1746, Mr. Blake had gone to his barn; upon hearing the cry of Indians he determined that his cattle should not be burnt if the barn was fired; he threw open the door, letting them loose, and attempted to leave by a back door and find safety by crossing the river. He had gone but a few steps when he was hailed by Indians who had been concealed in a shop between him and the street. Seeing their guns pointed at him and knowing he was in their power, he gave himself up. They shook hands with him, he told them he had not breakfasted, to which they smilingly replied, ' it must be a poor Englishman who cannot go to Canada without his breakfast.' Passing a cord around his arms above the elbows fastening them close to his body, they gave him to the care of one of their party who conducted him to the woods. The number of Indians was about 100. After travelling about two miles, they came to a small stony brook. The Indian stooped to drink, and as Blake's hands were not confined, he thought he could easily take up a stone and beat out his brains. He silently prayed for direction, and his next thought was, that he should always regret that he had killed an Indian in that situation, and he refrained. No particulars of his journey to Canada have been obtained, except that he passed by Charlestown. At Montreal he with another prisoner of the name of Warren, were compelled to run the gauntlet. Warren received a blow in the face, knocked down the Indian who gave it, upon which he was assaulted by several who beat him unmercifully, making him a cripple for life. Blake exhibited more patience and forti- tude, received no considerable injury. He was then conducted to Quebec and thence to an Indian village several miles north of that place, called Conissadawga. He was a strong athletic man and possessed many qualities which procured him the respect of the savages. He could run with great speed, and in all the trials to which he was put, and they were many and severe, he beat every antagonist. Not long after his arrival at the village, the tribe lost a chief by sickness. As soon as his decease was made known, the women repaired to his wigwam and with tears, sobs and clamorous lamentations mourned his death. The funeral ceremonies performed, the men sought Blake, dressed him in the Indian costume, and invested him with all the authority and privileges of the deceased, as one of the chiefs of the tribe, and as husband of the widow. In the family to which he now stood in the relation of father, there were, as he has often remarked, several daughters of uncommon beauty. Yet, notwithstanding this good fortune, he still had difficulties to encounter. The tribe was divided into two parties, his friends and his enemies. The former consisted of the great mass of the tribe, who respected him for qualities, to which they had not equal pretensions; the latter of those who were envious of his success, and had been worsted in their contests with him. These, to humble his pride, sent far into the northern wilderness and procured a celebrated Indian runner to run against him. At the time assigned, the whole tribe assembled to witness the race; and a Frenchman, from Quebec, happened to be present. Perceiving the excitement among them, he advised Blake to permit himself to be beaten, intimating that fatal consequences might ensue if he did not. The race was run, and Blake, as advised by the Frenchman, permitted his antagonist to reach the goal a moment before he did. He persisted, however, after his return from captivity, in declaring that he might have beaten him if he had tried. The event of the race restored harmony to the tribe, and Blake was permitted to live in peace. But remembering the family he had left, he felt anxious to return to his home. After much intercession, the tribe proposed that if he would build a house like those of the English, he should be permitted to go to Quebec. Presuming that, when there, he could more easily obtain his liberty, he gladly acceded to the proposition; and with such tools as the Indians possessed, he prepared the necessary timber, splitting the boards from the tree, and soon completed his task. He then went to Quebec and gave himself up to the French. He had been there but a short time, when his Indian wife came in a canoe to reclaim him. He refused to return, but she soliciting and even demanding it, he declared to her that if he should be compelled to set out with her he would overturn the canoe and drown her, upon which she concluded to return without him. In the fall, the French commandant gave Blake his election to pass the winter as a laborer with a farmer, in the vicinity of Quebec, or be confined in the common gaol. He chose the latter, and had no reason to regret his choice, as he had a comfortable room and sufficient rations assigned him. He remained in confine-

CHARTER, TOWN OF KEENE.
APRIL 11, 1753.

BACK OF CHARTER.
LIST OF GRANTEES OF KEENE.

ment until spring, when his liberation was procured in the manner which will now be related.

" As a connecting link in the chain of events mention must be made of Lieutenant Pierre Raimbout, a young Frenchman who commanded a small squad of Indians in an attempted raid near Ashuelot at Winchester in the autumn of 1747. He was fired upon by a party of Colonial Scouts, who supposing him to be mortally wounded, took from him his arms, and fearing the report of the musket would attract the remainder of the party they hastened on to Northfield.

" The Indians returning and finding their commander wounded, but alive, removed him to the bank of the river, where they left him, and being alarmed for their own safety precipitately fled to Canada, informing his father that his son had been killed by the English.

" Raimbout remained as he was left, until the next morning — when feeling his strength revive he succeeded in rising and after much difficulty reached a road leading to Northfield, where upon arrival he surrendered himself. He was conveyed to the home of Dr. Doolittle who was a surgeon, physician and clergyman of the place, where he was carefully attended and his wounds completely cured.

" Raimbout being anxious to return to Canada and to his father's home, and having much influence, he succeeded in his application to the Governor of Massachusetts in effecting an exchange of prisoners; promising that not only Samuel Allen of Deerfield should be returned to his home, but that one other prisoner should be included, it was arranged that if the Governor of Canada ratified this compact the second prisoner should be Nathan Blake. A party consisting of John Hawks, Matthew Clesson and John Taylor, escorting Raimbout left Deerfield in Feb. 1748. Mrs. Blake fearing that the French Governor might refuse to ratify the engagement of the Lieutenant furnished Hawkes with funds to redeem her husband. At Montreal, Raimbout was delivered to the French Commander — the party then proceeded to Quebec, stopping on the way at the home of Raimbout senior, whose joy was great at seeing before him the son he supposed dead. Arriving at Quebec, he made application for the release of Blake, according to the engagement of Raimbout. The Governor refused, alleging that the Lieutenant had no authority to make such an engagement. Hawks persisted in urging his claim as a matter of right. He also appealed to his feelings, as a man, representing to him the forlorn situation of Mrs. Blake, and the expectations she had been permitted to indulge, and prayed that he might not be sent back the messenger of disappointment. The Governor still refusing, he declared that he could not return to her without her husband, and requested to know what sum was required as his ransom, adding that he would endeavor to pay it. The Governor, pausing a moment, replied, 'take him and keep your money.' Expressing his gratitude, Hawks hastened to the prison, and gave to Blake the glad tidings of his release. On their way to New England the party again stopped at the house of old Raimbout. The neighbors were invited; a sumptuous feast was prepared; 'wine,' to use the language of Blake 'was as plenty as water.' The evening and the night were spent in dancing, the happy father and mother opening the ball, and displaying all the liveliness of youth.

"Quebec, it should be remembered, had then been settled nearly a century and a half, and was far in advance of all the English colonies in refinement of manners. To the rough and sedate Englishmen, who had seldom been out of the woods, the whole scene was novel and excited emotions, to which they had not been accustomed. It was about the middle of April when the three envoys with their two exchange captives left Montreal on their return. Raimbout with a guard of soldiers was sent with them as far as the ridge of the Green Mountains between Otter Creek and Black River. When leaving them the French soldiers advised them to hasten on, avoiding the regular trail. On 27 April they followed down Black river, reaching the Fort at Great Falls the next day — and on the following day Fort Dummer, and on 30 April were in Deerfield, where there was great rejoicing." It is probable that Mr. Blake at once joined his family in Wrentham, Mass., but in 1750 he is again recorded among the active citizens of Keene, as one of Capt. Hobbs company to fight the Indians, also engaged in building (upon the site of his log-cabin burned by the Indians) a fine strong home of heavy hard-wood timber, the partitions of yellow pine, 2 or 3 inches thick, set on end, a sort of block house, for protection from the Indians. This house was on Main Street, corner of Winchester Street. In 1751 his name appears on a petition to Gov. Wentworth for Incorporating the Town of Keene. (See illustration, pages 35–36.) In 1754 he was on the list of selectmen and in 1764 Town-Meetings are recorded as being held at the house of Nathan Blake.   1771 he was petit juror for the several courts, and 1773 on the Alarm List.   In 1775 his name is among those who signed resolutions to the Continental Congress, pledging their lives and fortune to oppose the hostile proceedings of the British Fleets and Armies, against the United American Colonies.   In this year 1775 also recorded " Grist Mill and Saw Mill sold to Nathan Blake," and for many years known as " Blake's Mills," and conducted by him and his sons.   Nathan Blake was ever interested in church work, working to found the church, to raise money for support of the minister and to build a parsonage.   With his family he lived on his farm during the later years of his life.   His wife Elizabeth died 19 July 1804 aged 83 and is buried alongside of her husband in the Washington St. Cemetery, Keene.   In 1805, at the age of 94, he married Mrs. Mary Brinton " a fascinating widow of 64."   " Mr. Nathan Blake died Aug. 4th 1811 in the hundredth year of his age " (see illustration), and as I stood at his grave and read this record, knowing that his long ˙life had been filled with stirring episodes, had been consecrated to duty, patriotism and loyalty to friends and country, I bowed my head in reverence to the memory of a great-grandfather, saying: " He has proved his truth by his endeavor."

CHILDREN:

ESTHER, b. 29 Dec. 1742, m. Isaac Billings before 1772, d. 1806, a. 64.

ELIZABETH, b. 11 Dec. 1744, m. Benjamin Balch, 23 Nov. 1768, d. 10 May 1793.

ASAHEL, b. 24 June 1749, m. (1) 22 Oct. 1722, Sarah Blake, d. 1 Sept. 1775; m. (2) before 1777, Ithamar, d. ———.

Nathan, b. 1 May 1752, m. **Bathsheba Day,** 1 May 1777, d. in Chelsea, Vt., 10 Jan. 1813, ae. 61 yrs.

ABEL, b. 14 Feb. 1759, m. (1) before 1789, Salle Richerson or Eveleth, d. 16 July 1803; m. (2) 1805, Mrs. Jemima Hart; d. in Keene, N. H., 27 Aug. 1839, ae. 80 yrs.

ABNER, b. 23 Nov. 1760, d. in Keene, 7 July 1766, a. 5 y. 7 m. 14 d.

HEADSTONES OF MR. NATHAN AND ELIZABETH BLAKE
Washington Street Cemetery, Keene, N. H.

CONTENTS

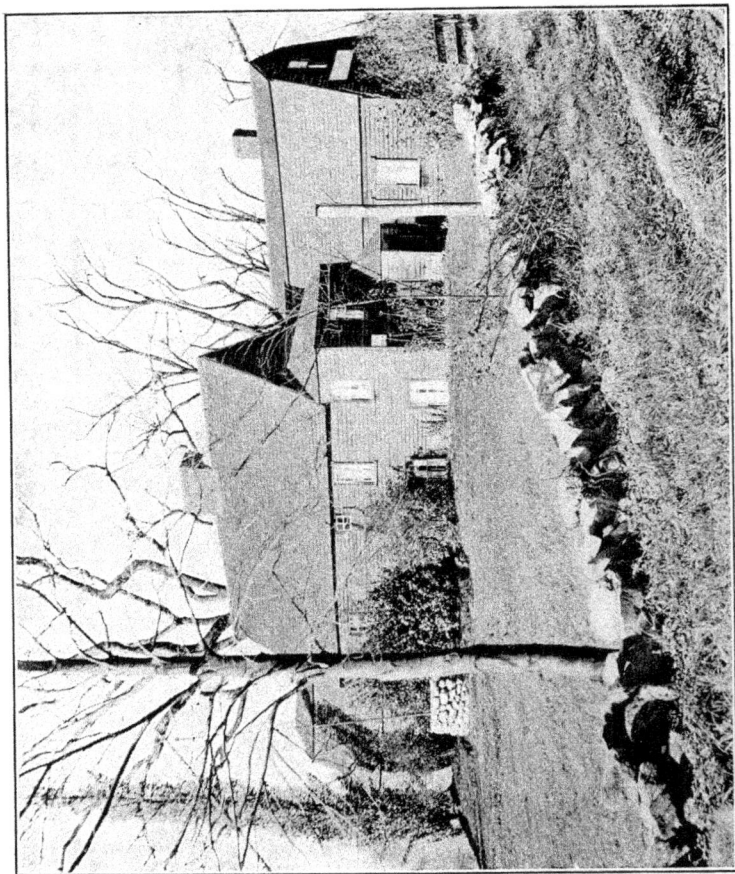

OLD FAIRBANKS HOUSE
Dedham, Mass. built 1636)

SIXTH GENERATION.

NATHAN BLAKE AND BATHSHEBA DAY.

FAIRBANKS FAMILY.

FAIRBANKS Jonathan[1] came from Sowerby in the West Riding of Yorkshire, England to Boston, Mass., in year 1633; he married Grace Lee, probably in England, and in 1636 settled in Dedham, where he built the noted "Old Fairbanks House," which is still standing as an ancient landmark; the oldest dwelling-house in New England, that for the same period of time has been continuously owned and occupied by the builder and his lineal descendants. This house is now historically famous and is an object of great interest to many visitors to the old town of Dedham. It is warped and worn by the sunshine and the storms of its nearly 300 years. (See illustration.) On the 10 of 7 mo. 1636, he with others signed the petition to "Dedham Covenant." He joined the church there 14 d. 6 m. 1646. By his will executed 4 June 1668 (the year of his death, 5 Dec. 1668), he bequeathed his whole movable estate to his wife Grace. To his second son George, To dau. Mary wife of Christopher Smith To Jonas, Jonathan and Sarah eldest daughter of his sonne John and to **Ralph Day** my sonne-in-law (husband of Susan) and to each of the four children of the said Ralph. Finally bequeaths to John eldest son all his house and land. His wife died 28 Dec. 1673.

CHILDREN:

JOHN, b. ——, m. Sarah Fisher, 1641, d. 13 Nov. 1684.

GEORGE, b. ——, m. Mary ——, before 1647, d. at Medfield, 10 Jan. 1682–3.

MARY, b. 18 April 1622, m. (1) 2 or 12 Apr. 1644, Michael Metcalf, d. 24 Dec. 1654; m. (2) before 19 (9) 1655, Christopher Smith, d. 7 (9) 1676; d. 4 June 1684.

JONAS, b. ——, m. Lydia Prescott, 28 May 1658, killed by Indians, 10 Feb. 1676.

JONATHAN, b. ——, m. Deborah Shepard before 1654, d. between 1690 and 1705.

Susan, b. ——, m. **Ralph Day,** 12 Oct. 1647, d. at Dedham, 8 July 1659.

DAY FAMILY.

DAY Ralph,[1] born probably in England. He married at Dedham for his 1st wife, Susan, daughter of Jonathan and Grace (Lee) Fairbanks, 12 Oct. 1647; she died at Dedham, 8 July, 1659. He then married 2nd 15 Nov. 1659, Abigail Ruggles. He was a Dedham townsman 11 Jan. 1644 and was made a freeman May 1645. "Beat the drum for meetings." In his will of 12 Sept. 1677 and probated 1 Feb. 1677/8, he mentions wife Abigail and children **John,** Ralph, Mary Payn and Abigail. "To son John all my Masons tools. To son Ralph my drum, one of my swords to son-in-law John Ruggles." The inventory of his estate was filed 1 Feb. 1677/8 and includes mason's tools. He died at Dedham, 28 Oct. 1677.

CHILDREN:

First wife:
ELIZABETH, bapt. 3 July 1648, d. 1648.
MARY, b. 9 Nov. 1649, m. John Payn, 7 Feb. 1677, d. 25 Oct. 1694.
SUSAN, b. 1652, d. ————, not mentioned in father's will of 1677.
John, b. 15 April 1654, m. **Abigail Pond,** 22 May 1678, d. at Wrentham, 11 Sept. 1727.
RALPH, bapt. 11 Feb. 1656, m. Sarah Fuller, 10 Aug. 1681, d. ————.

Second wife:
ABIGAIL 1st, b. 22 Apr. 1661, d. April 1661.
ABIGAIL 2nd, b.————, m.————, mentioned in her father's will of 1677, d.————.

POND FAMILY.

POND Robert[1] was from County Suffolk, England. Settled in Dorchester, Mass., about 1632, though not found in the list of Dr. Harris; was there to partake, 1636, in division of Cow Common. He died 1637. The inventory of his estate was taken 27 Dec. 1637. A chest of carpenter's tools and pump tools are mentioned. Mary and William Pond petitioned the Court for administration of the estate, and it was ordered 10 May 1648. His widow married in 1649 or 1650, Edward Shepard of Cambridge, who conveyed 24 Feb. 1650/1 to John Blackman, son-in-law to the late Robert Pond, one half the house and lands which Widow Pond had owned. In the memoirs by Rev. Mr. Mitchell written in 1658, we find this extract. " Mary now wife of Edward Shepard was dismissed hither from Church at Dorchester and is in full communion with us. Her daughter Mary Pond, baptized at Dorchester was eleven years old at her mothers joyning with us (1643)." Mrs. Mary Pond lived at Cambridge, she being widow of Robert Pond, who died in 1637; it is also probable that she brought other children with her to Cambridge and that Daniel Pond who married Abigail Shepard (daughter of Edward Shepard) was her son.

CHILDREN:

> ROBERT, b. in England, m. Mary Ball abt. 1656, d. before middle life.
> WILLIAM, b. in England, m. Mary Dyer abt. 1640, d. 4 April 1690.
> Daniel, b. ———, m. (1) before 1652, **Abigail Shepard,** d. 5 July 1661; m. (2) 18 Sept. 1661, Ann Edwards; d. at Dedham, 4 Feb. 1697/8.
> MARY, bapt. at Dorchester, 1632, m. John Blackman, d. ———.

SHEPARD FAMILY.

SHEPARD Edward[1] bought land in Cambridge 1639, and we gather from memoirs by Rev. Mr. Mitchell written in 1658 that " Edward Shepard was a member of his church in full communion in 1643. So also was his wife Violet, deceased. Their children were in minority when he joyned, Abigail (now living at Dedham) was 12 years, Deborah (also at Dedham) 10, and Sarah (dwelling at Braintree) 7." His wife Violet died 9 Jan. 1648–9, and he married for his second wife, Mrs. Mary Pond, who was the widow of Robert Pond. His name appears in the town and county records in various relations. He is mentioned in the records of the steward of Harvard College, 1654 of two importations of wheat " from aboard Edward Shepheard's vessel." In his will dated 1 Oct. 1674, he calls himself of Cambridge and a mariner, mentions wife Mary, son John, daughters Elizabeth and Deborah. To the children of **Daniel Pond** which he had by my daughter **Abigail,** and to daughter Sarah. He gave a deed to W. Fessenden, 18 Feb. 1679, and his will was proved 20 Aug. 1680. So he must have died between these two dates.

CHILDREN:

> JOHN, b. abt. 1627, m. (1) 1 Oct. 1649, Rebecca Greenhill, d. 26 Dec. 1690; m. (2) 3 Aug. 1691, Susan, widow of William Goodman; m. (3)

Martha, widow of Arthur Henburg; removed to Hartford, d. 12 June 1707.

ELIZABETH, b. abt. 1629, m. and had children, was living in 1674.

Abigail, b. abt. 1631, m. **Daniel Pond** before 1652, d. prob. at Dedham, 7 July 1661.

DEBORAH, b. abt. 1633, m. Jonathan Fairbanks Jr., before 1654, d. 7 Sept. 1705.

SARAH, b. abt. 1636, m. Samuel Thompson, 27 April 1656, d. at Braintree, 15 Jan. 1679, ae. 43 y.

POND Daniel[2] (*Robert*[1]), son of Robert and Mary Pond. He married 1st Abigail, daughter of Edward and Violet Shepard of Cambridge, before 1652. She died at Dedham, 5 July 1661 and he married 2nd Ann Edwards, 18 Sept. 1661. He is called a husbandman and appeared in the town of Dedham, Mass., about the year 1652, having purchased land on the 30 March that year. He was received into full communion in the Dedham church 8 : 11 : 1653. He was one of the Selectmen of the town in 1660. In 1661 the southern portion of Dedham was set off into a separate township called Wrentham and he immediately became an owner of real estate there, obtaining a grant of Lot No. 15 as early as 22 March 1662/3. He probably never lived in Wrentham. He was a Lieutenant of the militia and took the freeman's oath in 1690. He died 4 Feb. 1697/8 at Dedham. His will was made 2 : 12 : 1697/8 and proved 3 March 1697/8. In it he mentions wife Anne, sons John, Ephraim, Robert, and daughter **Abilgail Day.** " To children of daughter Rachel Stone, etc To daughter Hannah Devotion etc., To sons William, Caleb and Jabez, etc and To daughter Sarah Pond etc etc." His widow Anne died 6 June 1732, age 92 years.

CHILDREN:

First wife:

Abigail, b. at Dedham, 5 Nov. 1652, m. **John Day,** 22 May 1678 at Dedham, d. after 1721.

DANIEL ? (a son, the name not given, of Daniel was bapt. 22 of Jan. 1653 at Dedham), d. 4 March 1661/2.

JOHN, b. ———, m. (1) Hannah, d. 2 June 1691; m. (2) Rachel Stow; m. (3) Judith, d. 26 April 1708; settled in North Franklin and living in 1734.

EPHRAIM, bapt. 6 July 1656, m. Deborah Hawes, 6. Jan. 1685/6, d. at Wrentham, 22 Dec. 1704.

RACHEL, bapt. 5 Sept. 1658, m. ———— Stone, July 1681, d. before 1698.
HANNAH, b. 27 Sept. 1660, m. (John ?) Devotion, d. ————.

Second wife:

DANIEL, b. 17 April 1663, m. Tabitha, d. before 1698.
ROBERT, b. 5 Aug. 1667, m. (1) Joanna (Lawrence ?); m. (2) 16 Jan. 1728/9, Abigail Fisher; m. (3) 17 Nov. 1747, widow Sarah Shuttleworth; d. 3 July 1750, ae. 83 y.
WILLIAM, b. 20 Nov. 1669, m. ————, d. (at Dedham, 16 Nov. 1723 ?).
CALEB, b. 13 Feb. 1672, m. Priscilla Colburn, d. 23 Feb. 1705/6.
JOSHUA, b. 3 Jan. 1674, d. 24 April 1676.
JABEZ, b. 6 March 1677, m. (1) 11 Jan. 1698/9, Mary Gay, d. at Dedham, 11 June 1731; m. (2) at Medfield, 22 Nov. 1732, Mary Plympton; d. at Dedham, 6 Nov. 1749.
SARAH, b. 10 July 1679, m. Eleazer Holbrook of Sherborn, 14 June 1698, d. ————.

DAY John[2] (*Ralph*[1]) was the eldest child of Ralph and Susan (Fairbanks) Day, and was born at Dedham, Mass., 15 April 1654. He married at Dedham, 22 May 1678, Abigail, daughter of Daniel and Abigail (Shepard) Pond. She was born at Dedham, 5 Nov. 1652. We find him in a list of Capt. Samuel Moseley's Company of Volunteers taken at Dedham the 9th day of Xber 1675, and is credited with military service under Capt. Moseley at Dunstable and is paid £02 : 14 : 09 on the 24 July 1676, and on the 24 Aug. 1676 he is again paid and called of " Dedham Town." (In the claims for Narragansett township No. 4 (now Greenwich) Mass. (under date of 4 June 1685? we find " John Day, Soldier Grantee, and the claiment to be John Day a son.") He removed to Wrentham about 1680. In his will dated 16 June 1621, he mentions Abigail his wife, and children **John,** Jonathan, Ralph; daughter Susannah and daughter Abigail, who was then married. The will was probated 24 Jan. 1727/8. He died at Wrentham, 11 Sept. **1727.**

CHILDREN:

John, b. at Dedham, 11 Oct. 1679, m. **Ruth Puffer** at Wrentham, 12 Dec. 1706, d. at Wrentham, 2 Apr. 1758, ae. 79 y.
RALPH, Lieut., b. at Wrentham, 9 Dec. 1681, m. Mary Puffer at Wrentham, 26 Dec. 1705, d. at Wrentham, 12 Apr. 1766, ae. 85 y.
ABIGAIL 1st, b. at Wrentham, 12 Jan. 1684, d. at Wrentham abt. 1690.
JONATHAN, b. at Wrentham, 21 March 1686, m. ————, d. at Wrentham, 7 June 1759, ae. 73 y.

SUSANNAH, b. at Wrentham, m. ————, mentioned in her father's will of 1721, d. ———.

ABIGAIL 2nd, b. at Wrentham, 1 Jan. 1693, m. Thomas Skinner at Wrentham, 4 Jan. 1720/1, d. ———.

PUFFER FAMILY.

POFFER George,[1] Braintree, was granted land by Boston on the 24th of Feb. 1639/40 for five heads, that is, twenty acres, at Mount Wolleston now Braintree. Of him nothing more is known but the family was continued under the name of Puffer by two persons who may confidently be called his sons, and the widow Puffer who died at Braintree 12 Feb. 1677 was undoubtedly his relict. Mary Puffer, " an aged woman," who died at the same place, 22 July 1700, is perhaps more likely to have been his daughter than the widow of his eldest son.

CHILDREN:

James, b. abt. 1624, m. **Mary Swalden,** 14 Feb. 1656, d. at Braintree, 25 July 1692, ae. abt. 68.

MATHIAS, b. ———, m. (1) 12 March 1662, Rachel Farnsworth, d. ———; m. (2) 11 April 1677, Abigail Everett, d. 27 Dec. 1685; m. (3) 14 May 1697, Mary Crehore, d. ———; d. at Dorchester, 9 May 1717.

MARY, b. ———, m. ———, d. at Braintree, 22 July 1700.

PUFFER James[2] (*George*[1]) was probably the oldest son, born about 1624. Married at Braintree, 14 Feb. 1656, Mary Swalden (? Spaulding). He died at Braintree, 25 July 1692, aged about 68. Nothing further is known of him.

CHILDREN:

Richard, b. 14 March 1657/8, m. at Dorchester, **Ruth Everett,** 23 Mar. 1681, d. in Wrentham, 3 Aug. 1723, ae. 66 y.

MARTHA, b. 28 Dec. 1658, m. ———, d. ———.

MARY, b. 12 Jan. 1660, m. ———, d. ———.

JAMES, b. 5 May 1663, m. at Braintree, Mary Ellis of Dedham, 25 Sept. 1690, removed to Sudbury, d. 11 Nov. 1749, a. 86.

RUTH, b. 25 Jan. 1667, d. 29 Jan. 1667.

RACHEL, b. 25 Jan. 1667, m. Eleazer Isgate of Braintree, 7 Jan. 1695, d. ———.

JABEZ, b. 4 Feb. 1672, m. at Braintree, Mary Glazier, 3 Dec. 1702, d. ———.

EVERETT FAMILY.

EVERETT Richard.[1] I know nothing of the date or place of his birth. He married for his first wife, Mary. Who she was and date of her death I know not. He married second, 29 June 1643 at Springfield, Mary Winch, who came in the ship " Francis " to Ipswich, April 1638, age 15, a member of the family of Rowland Stebbins.

The first positive record we have of him is at Agawan (now Springfield), on 15 July 1636, when he witnessed a deed from the Indians transferring land to William Pynchon and others. He is described in the History of Springfield as " Mr. Pynchons trader." On 18 Aug. 1636 he was at Watertown and attended the first recorded meeting of the proprietors of the new town called Contentment, name afterwards changed to Dedham. His name was then spelled and for several years after " Richard Evered." He was admitted freeman in 1646 and was Selectman of Dedham in the year 1660–1 and the town records there give a complete description of the town offices held by him, together with his church membership, the christening of his children, the amount of his yearly taxes, together with the date of his death which occurred on the 3 July 1682. His will was made 12 May 1680 and probated 25 July 1682; bequeaths to wife Mary, sons Jediah, John and Samuel, daughters Abigail Puffer and **Ruth;** James, Daniel and Mary, children of deceased daughter Mary and James Macherwithy; and grandchild **Sarah Fisher.** The inventory of his estate is given as £277 : 15 s. 11 d. His wife Mary lived for several years after.

CHILDREN:

First wife:

JOHN, b. abt. 1636, m. Elizabeth Pepper, 13 May 1662, d. 17 June 1715.

ISREAL 1st, b. ————, d. 4 April 1646.

MARY, b. 28 Sept. 1638, m. James Macherwith, Nov. 1662, d. 13 June 1670.

SAMUEL, b. 31 March 1639, m. Mary Pepper, 28 May 1669, d. 26 June 1718.

SARAH 1st, b. 14 March 1641, d. 1 April 1641.

JAMES, b. 14 March 1643, d. 21 April 1643.

Second wife:

Sarah 2nd, b. 12 June 1644, m. **Cornelius Fisher,** 25 July 1665, d. 28 Feb. 1675/6.

ABIGAIL, b. 19 Nov. 1647, m. Matthias Puffer, 11 Apr. 1677, d. 27 Dec. 1685.

ISREAL 2nd, b. 14 July 1651, m. Abigail, d. 23 Dec. 1678.

Ruth, b. 14 Jan. 1653/4, m. **Richard Puffer,** 23 March 1681, alive 1727, age 74 years.

JEDEDIAH, b. 11 July 1656, m. Rachel, d. abt. 1698/9.

PUFFER Richard[3] (*James,*[2] *George*[1]) was the oldest child of James and Mary (Swalden) Puffer, and he was born at Braintree, 14 March 1657/8. He married at Dorchester, 23 March 1681, Ruth, daughter of Richard and Mary (Winch) Everett of Dedham. She was born (probably at Dedham) 14 Jan. 1653/4. He is credited with military service under Capt. John Holbrooke and was paid 02–01–00 on 23 Sept. 1676. He lived in Wrentham and died there 3 Aug. 1723 in his 66th year. On the 21 Feb. 1727, when his son William was appointed to administer on his estate, both were then called of Wrentham, and his widow Ruth was then about 74 years old.

CHILDREN:

Ruth, b. at Dedham, 17 March 1682, m. **John Day** of Wrentham, 12 Dec. 1706, d. at Wrentham, 17 March, 1768.

MARY, b. at Dedham, 21 Jan. 1684, m. Ralph Day of Wrentham, 26 Dec. 1705, d. at Wrentham, 30 Dec. 1769, ae. 87 yrs.

WILLIAM, b. at Wrentham, 17 July 1686, m. Elizabeth Guild of Wrentham, 25 May 1710, d. ———.

RICHARD, b. at Wrentham, 17 July 1689, m. Anna Hawes of Wrentham, 11 July 1719, d. at Wrentham, 12 Feb. 1758, ae. 69 yrs.

RACHEL, b. ———, m. Edward Gray of Wrentham, 14 June 1722, d. 17 May 1754.

SARAH, b. abt. 1696, m. Samuel Morse of Wrentham, 2 May 1741, d. 8 Feb. 1772.

BENONI, b. at Wrentham, 4 Jan. 1698, d. at Wrentham, 16 Jan. 1698.

DAY John[3] (*John,*[2] *Ralph*[1]) was the eldest child of John and Abigail (Pond) Day, born in Dedham, 11 Oct. 1679. He married at Wrentham, 12 Dec. 1706, Ruth, daughter of Richard and Ruth (Everett) Puffer. She was born at Wrentham, 17 March 1682. His house, according to a map of Wrentham, published in 1735, was located on the road to Franklin, to the east of what is now called Whitings Pond. (See illustration, page 21.) He died at Wrentham, 2 April 1758, age 79 years, his widow died there also on 17 March 1768.

CHILDREN:

RUTH, b. 1 Oct. 1707, m. John Hill, 15 Nov. 1733, d. ———.

JOHN, b. 1 Mar. 1708/9, m. ———, d. ———.

CALEB, b. 9 Apr. 1711, m. Bethiah Ware, 24 Jan. 1737/8, d. ———.

ISREAL, b. 2 Nov. 1713, m. Maria Heaton, 23 May 1739, d. ———.

Ebenezer, b. 28 June 1716, m. **Bathsheba Hall,** about 1746, d. in Keene, N. H., 12 Jan. 1776, a. 60 y.

HANNAH, b. 14 May 1718, did not marry, d. in Wrentham, Mass., 30 Oct. 1755.

DANIEL, b. 6 Dec. 1720, m. ———, d. ———.

ICHABOD, b. 27 Aug. 1723, m. Elizabeth Davis, 23 Nov. 1749, d. in Wrentham, Mass., 3 Nov. 1769, a. 47 yrs.

HALL FAMILY.

HALL Edward,[1] probably freeman 1636 at Salisbury. He was at Duxboro, Mass., 1636-7-8; at Braintree, Mass., 1640; at Taunton, 1641; at Duxboro again 1642 and 3; a proprietor at the settlement of Bridgewater in 1644, when allotment was made to him in 1645, March 28, and withdrew from the jurisdiction in 1652. Edward Hall had a family in Braintree from 1650 to 1655. He removed to Rehoboth in 1655. On 26 May 1668, lots were drawn for meadow lands in the North purchase (now Attleboro), Cumberland, R. I., and part of Norton and Mansfield. He made his will 23 Nov. 1670, died 27 Nov. 1670. His estate was valued at £84. The name of his wife was Esther or Hester, who survived him. The proprietory records of Rehoboth credit him with a fifty-pound right of commonage in 1658 and the widow Hester Hall with the same right in 1671 and John Hall with the same in 1685, and with only one half of that from 1697 to 1715. " Married in Rehoboth, 24 Dec. 1674, Thomas Jorden and Esther Hall." It is possible this was his widow.

CHILDREN:

JOHN, b. at Braintree, 28 Jan. 1651, m. Mary Newell, 18 Nov. 1684, d. 1721.

ESTHER, b. at Braintree, 23 Oct. 1654, m. John Kindrick of Boston, 23 Oct. 1672, d. at Newton, 10 Sept. 1723, ae. 70 yrs.

SAMUEL, b. at Rehoboth, 24 Oct. 1656, m. Elizabeth Brown, 14 Apr. 1686, had a family at Taunton.

JEREMIAH, b. at Rehoboth, 24 July 1658, m. ———, d. ———.

THOMAS, b. at Rehoboth, 31 March 1661, m. ———, d. ———.

PRESERVED, b. at Rehoboth, 20 or 30 March 1663, m. (1) 25 Jan. 1698/9,
Lydia Levitt; m. (2) 3 Dec. 1730, Mrs. Hannah May; d. at Hingham,
5 Aug. 1740, ae. 77 yrs.

ANDREW, b. at Rehoboth, 10 May 1665, m. (1) 1691, Susan Capen, d.
18 Aug. 1736; m. (2) 1737, Mary Bennit; d. at Newton, Dec. 1756.

Benjamin, b. at Rehoboth, 7 Aug. 1668, m. **Sarah Fisher,** 9 Jan. 1691/2,
d. at Wrentham, 26 Aug. 1726.

FISHER Cornelius[2] (*Anthony*[1], son of Anthony and Mary
Fisher. He married 1st at Dedham, 22 Feb. 1653, Leah, daughter
of Nathaniel and Elizabeth Heaton. She died at Wrentham
12 Jan. 1664 and he married 2nd at Dedham, 25 July 1665, Sarah,
daughter of Richard and Mary (Winch) Everett, who was born
at Dedham, 12 June 1644 and died at Wrentham, 28 Feb. 1675/6.
He joined the Dedham church 6 Feb. 1648, was made freeman
2 May 1649 and admitted a " townsman " at Dedham, 3 Jan.
1652/3. He was a carpenter by trade, Constable in Dedham,
1668, and Pound-master 1672. Was one of the 13 Wolonopaug
proprietors who signed 27 Feb. 1662/3 and was in Wrentham
when they were established as a separate town in 1673, having
gone there with the first settlers. On the 12 Jan. 1674, the
Dedham Selectmen " agreed with Cornelius Fisher to ring the
bell and sweep the Meeting House; and for his pay he is to
receive fifty shillings for one holle year, and as his property is
next to the cemetery he is required to keep the fence in repair."
He was Representative to the General Court in 1692. He died
at Wrentham, 2 Jan. 1699 " the first head of a family died in
the town of a natural death for thirty years." In his will
dated 3 Feb. 1697, he mentions his eldest son Cornelius,
daughter Elizabeth, son-inlaw **Benjaman Hall,** Eleazer and four
daughters. The inventory was filed 20 June 1699 and totaled
£249 : 9 : 8.

CHILDREN:

First wife:

ELIZABETH, b. 20 June 1654, d. 14 Sept. 1665.

LEAH, b. 5 May 1656, m. William Goddard of Sherborn, 10 Dec. 1685,
d. 10 Sept. 1720.

EXPERIENCE, b. 10 Jan. 1658; was living in 1699 and unmarried.

CORNELIUS, b. 8 Feb. 1660, m. (1) before 1691 Ann Whitney, d. 6 March
1701; m. (2) 27 March 1702, Mercy Colburn; d. 20 Sept. 1726; m.
(3) 13 Feb. 1726/7, Mary Ware; d. 6 Jan. 1743, a. 84 y.

GRAVESTONES OF EBENEZER AND BATHSHEBA DAY
North Cemetery, Keene, N. H.

ANN, b. 22 Aug. 1661, m. (1) 2 Feb. 1681, Isaac Heath, d. 22 Dec. 1684; m. (2) 2 Dec. 1685, Francis Youngman; d. after 1701.

ELEAZER, b. 8 July 1663, m. (1) 21 Mar. 1688, Hannah Leonard; m. (2) 2 June 1718, Mary Maccany; d. ———.

Second wife:

DOROTHY, b. 17 Apr. 1667, d. 10 April 1668.

Sarah, b. 1668, m. at Wrentham, **Benjamin Hall,** 9 Jan. 1691/2, d. at Wrentham, 2 Nov. 1756.

JONATHAN, b. 28 Oct. 1671, d. 9 Feb. 1675, the 3rd death on Wrentham record.

HALL Benjamin[2] (*Edward*[1]) was the youngest child of Edward and Hester Hall, born at Rehoboth, Mass., 7 Aug. 1668. He married at Wrentham, 9 Jan. 1691/2, Sarah, daughter of Cornelius and Sarah (Everett) Fisher. She was born probably at Dedham in 1668. He removed to Wrentham prior to his marriage there and was absent from Wrentham a year or two before 1699 and a year or two next after 1710. He died in Wrentham, 26 Aug. 1726 and his widow died there also 2 Nov. 1756.

CHILDREN:

JOSIAH, b. at Rehoboth, 15 Jan. 1694, m. ———, d. ———.

SARAH 1st, b. at Wrentham, 20 Feb. 1696/7, d. at Wrentham, 6 May 1697.

EDWARD, b. at Wrentham, March 1698, m. Hannah Fisher, 7 Feb. 1721/2, removed to Uxbridge, d. bet. Nov. 1764 and 65.

DOROTHY, b. at Wrentham, 20 May 1700, m. Samuel Ellis, 14 Sept. 1720, d. ———.

Jeremiah, b. at Wrentham, 8 May 1703, m. **Dorothy** ——— before 1722, d. after 1759.

BENJAMIN, b. at Wrentham, 8 May 1703, m. Betty Blake, 15 Nov. 1727, d. ———.

PRESERVED, b. at Wrentham, 28 Nov. 1706, m. Abigail Whiting, 10 Sept. 1729, d. after 1758.

SARAH 2nd, b. at Wrentham, 15 March 1708/9, m. Peter Lyon of Walpole, 22 Aug. 1734, d. ———.

There may have been two other children not born at Wrentham.

HALL Jeremiah[3] (*Benjamin,*[2] *Edward*[1]), son of Benjamin and Sarah (Fisher) Hall of Wrentham, Mass., was born on the 8 May 1703; married Dorothy; who she was and where she came from we know not. He was one of the original proprietors of Upper

Ashuelot (now Keene, N. H.), was one of the leaders in settling the township and one of the first party of eight persons that came here in 1734, and began the settlement and again in 1735, 36 and 37, was the "Standing Moderator" of the proprietors' meetings and was paid for having represented the proprietors at the general court. His name is first on the list of members at the original organization of the church in 1738. He was designated in the records of 1738 as "Capt.," and was also a physician, the first in town and is called "Dr. Hall of Keene," as given in the Annals, that caused the capture of Pierre Raimbault near Northfield 1747. When the place was abandoned by the families in the spring of 1747, he and several others of the settlers joined the military company of Capt. Josiah Willard, which was stationed here that year and next; was clerk of that company. He buried his wife Dorothy here 15 Jan. 1753 and soon afterwards removed to Pembroke, Mass. We find him a practising physician in that town in 1756; and he was appointed surgeon's mate, afterwards surgeon of Col. Joseph Thatcher's regiment in the expedition to Crown Point in 1757. In 1758 from March to November he was surgeon of Col. Thomas Doty's regiment for the reduction of Canada; and in 1759, March 31 to Dec. 31, surgeon of Col. John Thomas's regiment at Halifax.

CHILDREN:

JEREMIAH, b. 11 June 1722, m. Elizabeth, d. at Pembroke, Mass., 1 Oct. 1807, ae. 85 yrs.

DOROTHY, b. 15 Sept. 1724, m. ———, d. ———.

Bathsheba, b. 12 Aug. 1726, m. Ebenezer Day abt. 1746, d. at Keene, N. H., 5 Sept. 1798, ae. 73 yrs.

KEZIAH, b. 13 March 1728/9, d. at Keene, N. H., 7 Oct. 1744, ae. 16 yrs.

SAMUEL, b. 5 Jan. 1731/2, m. (1) before 1754, Amity, d. after 1757; m. (2) before 1767, Susanna; d. at Keene, N. H., 17 May 1790, ae. 58 y.

JESSE, b. 21 April 1734, m. Achsah before 1755, d. at Keene, N. H., 13 July 1808, ae. 74 y.

BENJAMIN, b. 1741, d. at Keene, N. H., 29 Sept. 1744, ae. 3 y.

DAY Ebenezer[4] (*John*,[3] *John*,[2] *Ralph*[1]) was the fourth son of John and Ruth (Puffer) Day. He was born at Wrentham, 28 June 1716. He married at Wrentham about 1746, Bathsheba, daughter of Jeremiah and Dorothy Hall; she was born 12 Aug. 1726 at Wrentham. He was one of the early settlers of Keene,

BATHSHEBA BLAKE
63 years old
1818

N. H., an original member of the church at its formation in 1738. Served in Capt. Willard's company of soldiers at Keene in 1747/8. He lived on the farm recently known as the " Carpenter farm," the last but one in Keene on the old road to Surry, east side of the river, where he and his sons kept tavern for many years. When the Indian war broke out in 1755 he, hurriedly warned of an attack by the Indians at Upper Ashuelot, hastily gathered his family and started at once for the fort, which was reached in safety. He died at Keene, N. H., 12 Jan. 1776 and his wife died there also 5 Sept. 1798. (See illustration, page 51.)

CHILDREN:

DOROTHY, b. at Wrentham, 18 Apr. 1747, m. Josiah Ellis, 7 Jan. 1768 at Keene, d. ———.

EBENEZER, b. at Wrentham, 27 Mar. 1749, may have married at Keene, N. H., Hephzibah Browne, 3 March 1789, d. ———.

RUTH, b. at Keene, N. H., 24 Apr. 1751, m. ———, d. ———.

Bathsheba, b. at Keene, N. H., 27 March 1754, m. **Nathan Blake Jr.,** 1 May 1777, d. at Chelsea, Vt., 4 June 1820, ae. 66 yrs.

HANNAH, b. at Keene, N. H., 26 Feb. 1758, m. Adin Holbrook, 2 Feb. 1780, d. at Keene, 29 July, 1824, ae. 66 yrs.

DANIEL, b. ———, m. ———. Kept a tavern at Keene and was living in 1829.

ENOS, b. 30 July 1760, m. ———, d. ———.

KEZIA, b. 10 Aug. 1763, m. Joseph Brown, 9 Feb. 1786, d. at Keene, 3 Jan. 1836, ae. 72 yrs.

SABRA, b. 11 Feb. 1766, did not marry, d. at Keene, 2 Sept. 1840, ae. 74 yrs.

BLAKE Nathan[6] (*Nathan,*[5] *Robert,*[4] *John,*[3] *John,*[2] *William*[1]) was born in Keene, N. H., 1 May 1752, fourth child of Nathan and Elizabeth (Graves) Blake. He married at Keene, N. H., 1 May 1777, Bathsheba, daughter of Ebenezer and Bathsheba (Hall) Day. She was born at Keene, N. H., 27 March 1754. It is interesting to look back and recall the stirring times into which he came, his father at this date being active in all town affairs, in church work and working with others for a charter and interceding with Gov. Wentworth for this and a separate township to be called Keene. He doubtless spent many nights as a child in the Fort (and it is recorded of his wife Bathsheba when a baby in 1755: " upon an alarm of Indians coming, Mr. Day (her father) hastened home, saddled his horse and told his wife to

quickly make ready to ride to the Fort. Mr. Day taking little
Ruth in his arms, Mrs. Day on the pillion behind, tightly grasped
a meal sack, into which they had thrust the one year old baby
Bathsheba, rode four miles at great speed to the Fort; the meal
sack dangling from the saddle; reaching the Fort in safety, upon
opening the sack the baby was found to be head downwards," but
fortunately my grandmother suffered no serious injury from this
perilous escapade). Young Nathan was enjoying the school
privileges for which the pioneers had labored; for during the
decade from 1660 to 1670 much money was raised for this purpose,
and the township divided into four districts. In 1773, we find
him on the Muster Roll of the Foot company; thus at 21 he
was among the fighting forces; on the Association Test, 1776, and
one of Capt. Howlett's company who went to the relief of Ticon-
deroga in 1777. Nathan Blake 2nd and his wife Bathsheba
resided in Keene, where eight children were born to them, two
dying in infancy. He with his brothers were owners of cloth
dressing, wool carding and dyeing mills, grist and lumber
mills, and much land. We find in 1785 much interest and enthusiasm manifested in the erection of a new Meeting House,
the pews being sold at auction in advance of the construction of
the building; Pew No. 61, price £10. 6 s. to Nathan Blake 2nd.
I enjoy this definite bit of information and love to think of my
father with his two brothers and three sisters as sitting in Pew 61,
imbibing at this early age the principles of religious training and
loyalty which were leading traits in his character. In the year
1800, he and his wife with three sons and three daughters removed to Chelsea, Vermont, where they were among the early
settlers — had mills, stores and other business enterprises. He
died at Chelsea, Vt., 10 Jan. 1813 and his wife died there 4 June
1820, both buried in Chelsea, Vt.

CHILDREN:

AMPLIAS, b. Keene, N. H., 27 Nov. 1778, m. (1) 25 July 1802, Sarah
Hall, d. 29 March 1810; m. (2) 8 Aug. 1811, Mary Paine, d. 2 Dec.
1823; m. (3) 11 May 1824, Fanny Lamb, d. 3 Nov. 1856; d. at
Chelsea, buried at Montpelier, 30 July 1855.

ROXANNA, b. at Keene, N. H., 2 Oct. 1782, did not marry, d. at Montpelier and buried at Chelsea, 20 Apr. 1865, ae. 83 y.

Nathan, b. at Keene, N. H., 15 Oct. 1784, m. **Susan Torrey,** 6 Sept.
1815, d. at East Corinth, Vt., 31 Jan. 1849.

TEASPOON, CUP AND SAUCER, BATHSHEBA DAY BLAKE

BATHSHEBA, b. at Keene, N. H., 10 March 1787, m. Asanel Dennison, d. at Chelsea, Vt., 5 Sept. 1845, ae. 57 yrs.

ELIJAH 1st, b. at Keene, N. H., 3 Sept. 1789, d. at Keene, N. H., 5 Apr. 1790, ae. 7 m.

ELIJAH 2nd, b. at Keene, N. H., 8 Apr. 1791, m. Hannah Huntley of Topsham, Vt., d. at East Topsham, Vt., 17 Oct. 1828, ae. 36 y.

ROSELINDA, b. at Keene, N. H., 29 June 1793, m. Dyer Throop Hinckley, 6 March 1807, d. at Orford, N. H., 3 Feb. 1836.

PARLEY, b. at Keene, N. H., 15 June 1797, d. at Keene, N. H., 31 July 1797, ae. 6 w. 4 d.

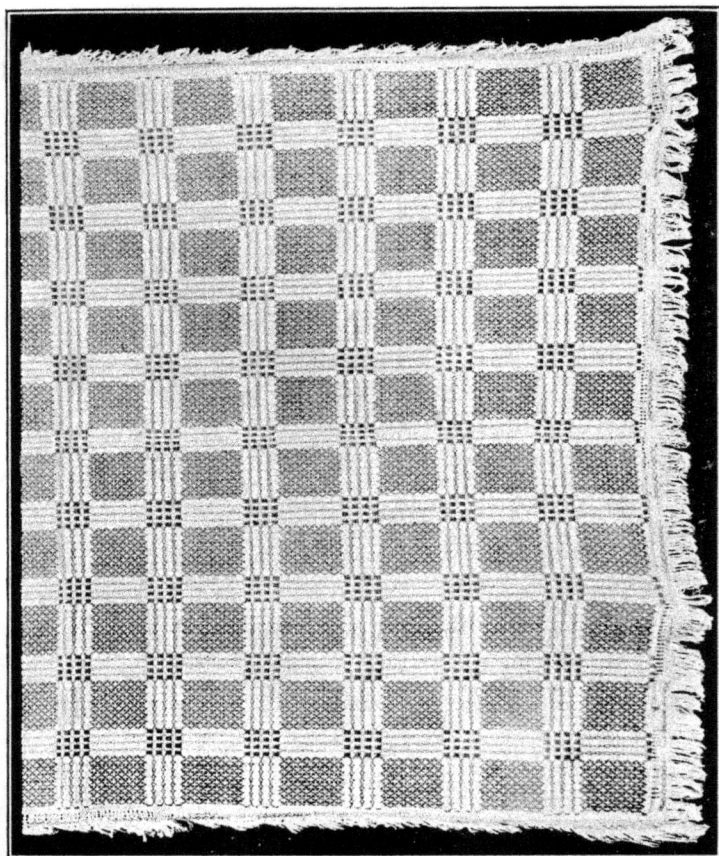

COUNTERPANE, BATHSHEBA DAY BLAKE

PART II.

ANCESTRAL LINE OF TORREYS AND BRANCH
FAMILIES IN ENGLAND AND AMERICA.

CONTENTS

TORREY COAT-OF-ARMS

ANCESTRAL LINE OF TORREYS AND BRANCH FAMILIES IN ENGLAND AND AMERICA

TORREY GENEALOGY.

TORREY is a Baronial Norman name, and the English families of the name are descended from the De-Tury, Turi or Turri family of Normandy; Henry and Richard De-Tury were in Normandy in 1180–95; Barony and Castle of Tury in Normandy; Jordan and Simon Turri in England in 1189.

Torry Coat-of-Arms — A Horse, passant, P. Pr. Furnished Gu. —

Motto — Turris Fortissima Deus:
"God is a most strong Tower."

TORREY FAMILY IN ENGLAND.

TORRY William[1], who died June 1557 in Combe St. Nicholas, in the diocese of Bath and Wells, by his Will dated 7 Oct. 1556 and proved June 18, 1557, we read, "My body to be buried in the church-yard of Combe St. Nicholas; To the church of St. Andrews, in Wells twelve pence — To the church of Combe St. Nicholas 6 shillings, eight pence — To Elizabeth Screvyn, my servant a Chilver Sheep — To John Morys my servant a Chilver Sheep — To every of my children ten sheep — The residue of my goods not given in other bequests I give and bequeath to Tomasyne, my wife, whom I make and ordain sole executrice."

Witnesses of Will William Gollopp & Thomas Torry
(two of the overseers)

Will of Henry Cookney of Hawkschurch, Dorset, dated 13 May 1593, Will proved 23d Jan. 1601, mentions in this will his wife Emmett, and his brothers-in-law Phillip Torry & William Torry & John Cookney to be overseers.

CHILDREN:

Phillip, b.————, married Margaret————, died leaving a will proved
31 Aug. 1604.

EMMETT, b. ————, m. Henry Cookney, was living in 1593.

WILLIAM, b.————.

TORRY Phillip[2], son of William and Thomasyn, in his Will,
made the last day of August 1604 we read, " Phillip Torry, late
of Wadbrook, in the parish of Hawkschurch, Dorset, husbandman, etc., did make his last Will and testament, in his manner and
form following, or the like in effect, viz.: *To his son William
Torry* he did bequeath ten young sheep, and not any other
chattel or goods whatsoever. He bequeaths all the rest of his
goods to Margaret, his wife, and Dorothy, his daughter. And
last of all he appoints his forenamed son William Torry the sole
executor of his last Will and testament."

Witnessed by Henry Holcombe, John Cookney, with others.

Will proved 23d February 1604/5.

CHILDREN:

William, married and was living in 1621.

Dorothy, married, living in 1604.

TORREY William,[3] son of Phillip and Margarit, married and
had a son Phillip whom he outlived.

Phillip, b. ————, married Alice, died 1621.

See will of Philip Torry[2] of the 31 Aug. 1604. Who mentions his son
William Torry.[3]

See will of Philip Torry[4] of the 16 April 1621. Who mentions his
father William Torry.[3]

TORRY Phillip[4], of Combe St. Nicholas, Somerset, husbandman, by will dated 16 April 1621 and proved 27th June 1621,
we read, " To be buried in the churchyard of Combe — to the
relief of the poor of Combe three shillings four pence — Ann
Torry, mine eldest daughter shall have threescore pounds when
she shall accomplish the age of sixteen years, to be paid my
overseers who shall take the government of it until she shall
accomplish the age of one and twenty years — To her the
biggest brass pan, to be delivered to her at the time of her marriage, and not before — To my daughter Mary Torry twenty
pounds at sixteen — to be held (as before) until she is twenty one,
and the second brass pan; to Sarah Torry, my daughter three

INTERIOR OF CHURCH, COMBE ST. NICHOLAS, SURREY, ENGLAND

Which was restored by Torrey ancestors

and thirty pounds six shillings eight pence at sixteen (as before) and the second best brazen pot; to James Torry, my son thirty pounds at 16 (as before) four silver spoons when he is one and twenty — To my son Phillip Torry 20 lbs. at 16 (as before) and he shall be put at some trade, as apprentice, as soon as he is able — I give unto *William Torry my son* the biggest brazen pot, the furnace kettle, table &c with condition his mother shall have the use of it so long as she doth keep herself widow and dwelling in the house — To Joseph my son ten pounds — all the rest to my wife, whom I make sole executrix — *My father William Torry*, my cousin John Fry, John Richards, Robert Sellecke & Thomas Lambert to be overseers, & I give them 5 shillings apiece " —

Proved by Alice Torry, the widow —

Will of Alice Torry, widow of above Phillip — in Bettam, parish of Combe St. Nicholas, Somerset, widow, dated 24 April 1634 — " To be buried in church yard of Combe — to the parish church 11 1s–4d; for the poor of the parish VIs VIId — To son James Torry, so much of mine own estate as to make his father's bequest and his sister Maries by 3 score pounds, and the same to be paid unto him within three months after my decease — A similar bequest to my son Phillip Torry, to be paid him when he shall attain the age of one and twenty years, and not before — To Joseph Torry a similar bequest of three score pounds — To Samuel, the son of *my son William*, one Book, in the house, Mr. Perkin's works. — I give to him also one ewe and lamb the best of all the flock — All the rest of my goods, not given nor bequeathed, my debts and legacies paid, and my funeral debts discharged, I give and bequeath to William Torry, my son, whom I do make whole and sole executor, and for my sons assistance in the performance of the trust I do intreat Mr. Joseph Greenfield, my cousin John Blake, Henry Dunster and Hugh Sheppard to be my overseers, for the good of my children " —

Wit. Henry Dunster and signed John Clarke.

Memo: 13lbs. 10s. due from my brother-in-law Thomas Lombard. " The seal seemed to be a chevron between three Crescents — H. F. W. — "

" All the foregoing Torry ' Wills,' with the exception of that of Henry Cookney and Alice Torry were gathered by me early in Oct. 1884. I was accompanied in the search by the late Hon.

Alphonso Taft, then U. S. minister to Austria or Russia, who kindly gave me not long after the abstract of the Alice Torry will, found by him in the district Register at Wells.   H. F. W. — Also in a letter to H. F. Waters, dated Nov. 6, 1884, Hon. Alphonso Taft says: ' The line as I find it is William, who died in 1557, leaving a will.   Phillip, his son who died in 1604, leaving a will — William, his son, who survived his son Phillip, but the date of whose death we have not — Phillip, who died in 1621, leaving a will, named his four sons who emigrated to America.'   Mr. Taft also furnished, from the Bishop's Register at Wells, the following for Combe St. Nicholas: "

> 1608, **William,** son of Phillip Torrie was bapt. 21 day of December.
> 1608, Agnes, daughter of Joseph Combe was baptized the 4th of January.
> 1629, **William Torry** was married unto Agnes Combe the 17 of March.
> 1639, **Jane, wife of William Torry** was buried the 27 day of April.

Hon. Alphonso Taft was father to Ex-President Wm. H. Taft, Henry F. Waters, author of " Gleanings in England," was an authority of high rank — being sent by Harvard College on research work for historical purposes.   He died in 1913, Salem, Mass.

From authentic record 'tis proved that the above Agnes Combe lived only one year after marriage.   Wm. Torry then married Jane Haviland who died 1639, was mother of two sons brought to America — Samuel, b. 1632, William, b. 1638.

The photographs of the church of Combe St. Nicholas, which we fortunately secured, were taken by Prof. William Torrey Harris of Washington, D. C.   (See illustration, pages 62–64.)

CHILDREN:

> **William,** CAPT., bapt. at Combe, 21 Dec. 1608, m. (1) 17 March 1629, Agnes Combe, d. abt. 1630; m. (2) 1630 or 31 **Jane Haviland,** d. 27 Apr. 1639; m. (3) ———; d. at Weymouth, Mass., 10 June 1690.
> JAMES, LIEUT., b. ———, m. Anne Hatch at Scituate, Mass., 2 Nov. 1643, d. at Scituate, 6 July 1665.
> PHILLIP, b. ———, m. Mary, widow of John Scarborough, 1 Oct. 1647, d. at Roxbury, 12 May 1686.
> JOSEPH, LIEUT., b. abt. 1615, was married, d. at Newport or Westerly, R. I., 1676.
> ANN, oldest daughter.
> MARIE or MARY, d. before 1634.
> SARAH.

CHURCH, COMBE ST. NICHOLAS, SURREY, ENGLAND
Torrey ancestors buried in the graveyard

HAVILAND FAMILY IN FRANCE.

Near Barfleur on the north coast of France, the river Saire enters the English Channel and but three flights of an arrow above the river mouth, lies the strong Castle of Haverland. (A historian of 1160 tells us, and goes on to describe its attack from the Norse Vikings during King Alfred's reign, 888 A.D.) Early French records at St. Lo in Normandy, and an old document states that this castle " d'Abellent " was the cradle of the Haveland family, and that the names of the Seigneurs of that house have been written in numbers of ways. Old seals attached to early charters and documents of the 11th, 12th, 13th, 14th and 15th centuries show the name spelled Abellant, Avilland, Haverland, Havellant, etc., etc. — but they surround the same device, a three-turretted castle which was the Haviland Coat-of-Arms. But a more definite introduction seems to come from Guernsey, one of the Channel Islands just across the peninsula from the Castle de Heverland. Near that castle lived a Norman Lord (which we will call *No. 1* Haverland of the first generation), who in 1061 was dispatched by Duke William, to the relief of Isle of Guernsey which had been attacked by pirates. Success was rewarded by a grant to him and his followers of one-half of the Island. From the fact that five years later, records prove the Havilands to be property owners in Guernsey, it is surmised that they were numbered with the " Dukes " followers. This was at the time of the Conquest of England by William the Conqueror. The changes brought about by William resulted in the Saxon nobility being deprived of their rank and their estates and titles and Coats-of-Arms, and given to the Normans. All lands were held directly from the King on condition of military or other service. These large apportionments of land carried with them the titles of Baronet or Lord, and their houses were called Manor Houses.

From another source we learn that " The ancient Guernsey family of De Havilland derived its name from the fiefs of Haverland situated near Valognes* in Normandy, of which they were lords in A.D. 1050." In Guernsey they were tenants, in Capite, as early as 1176 of another fief to which they had given the name, and by which it is still known. In the " Haviland Chronicles,"

* Valognes is 22½ miles southwest of Barfleur.

the following name is counted No. 3 in line of descent. (No. 2 seems to be missing.) Among those accompanying Duke William across the Channel in 1066, when he so successfully asserted his claims to the English throne was one (No. 3) *Sieur de Haverlain.* No. 4 is missing. The next on record is *Robert[5] baron of Haverland.* His name appears in 1130 A.D. as a witness to a deed. *Robert de Haverland[6]* was in 1179 A.D. Deputy Governor of Guernsey. *Robert Baron de Haverland[7]*, whose name appears as a witness in 1219 to a charter of Philip d'Aubigne, granting lands in Guernsey to the Monastery of St. Michael's Mount. *William[8]* 1233 *Lord of Haverland* accompanied Richard Cœur de Lion to Palestine, and in memory of this crusade added two martlets to his paternal arms. *Peter[9] Lord of Haverland* eldest son of *William[8]* ceded some land to a Monastery of Montisbourg, 1 Feb. 1260. His green seal is attached to the charter, a castle triple tourred, and on each side turret a martlet, surrounded by "S. Petri de Haviland." *Bernard de Haverland[10] William de Haverland[11]* son of Bernard, 1299. *Thomas de Haverland[12]. William de Haverland.[13] Bernard de Haverland.[14]* The last four names are in 1331, mentioned as being tenants of the king in Guernsey, under Edward III. *Thomas,[15] Sieur de Havilland* is a notable figure in the family history. From him all who are recognized as belonging to the family are descended. From his eldest son, Thomas,[16] the Guernsey line derives, and from James[16] and his wife, Helen de Bevoir, the two English branches of Dorsetshire and Somerset are descended. Thomas Sieur De Haviland, fought with distinguished gallantry at the siege of Mont-Orgueil Castle, Jersey, 1467. He received in reward for his services on that occasion, a patent conferring certain commercial privileges to avail himself of which he established his second son, *James,[16]* at Pool, County Dorset, England, from whom were descended the Havellands of Wilkswood House in the isle of Purbeck, now extinct.

HAVILAND FAMILY IN ENGLAND.

de HAVILLAND James[16], second son of Sieur Thomas[15], was born about 1440 and married before leaving Guernsey, built up a thriving commerce which outlived him more than a century. The coat-of-arms he brought with him shows a third change in the Haviland coat-of-arms, and three triplet turreted castles appear " to difference the several branches of the family, also a motto Dominus Fortissima Turris," had been added (no crest). The absence of a crest is evidence that the family was noble before 1484 A.D. The variation in the name de Haviland from generation to generation is curious, the prefix " de " was dropped by the English branch about 1500.

In 1502 he added at his own charge, the north Aisle of the Church of St. James, which was and continued to be the burial place of the Havilands, so long as any of them resided in the town. The church was Romanist and had four altars with attendant priests, James and his wife supporting the service for that aisle, and after their death the eldest descendant living became trustee.

In the north aisle over the arches cut in the stone in large letters are these inscriptions with the Havilland and de Beauvoir arms at either side: — " These six arches were made at the charge of James de Havelland[16] and Helene his wife on whose souls God have mercy. Anno Domini 1503."

At the east end of this aisle is a stone retaining marks of effigies, lables and coats-of-arms. It was for James de Havelland[16] and his wife, but the brasses are gone, although in 1749 the arms were to be seen there, and also in the glass of the windows.

In 1494 he was Mayor of Poole.

CHILDREN:

RICHARD, b. ———, m. Eleanor Chrek. The death of Richard's only son, made James[17] the second son, the head of the house.

James, b. ———, m. Julia, she d. 4 June 1550.

JOHN, b. ———. Settled on the Island of Purbeck.

WILLIAM, b. ———. Was a staunch Romanist and contended for the following of the ritual in the Church of St. James in Poole.

HELENE or ELEANOR, b. ———, m. William Pitt. From these were descended the Earl of Chatham and James Russell Lowell of America.

HAVELAND James[17] is mentioned only as having a wife Julia and an only son *Christopher*.[18] The wife Julia was buried at Pool the 4 June 1550.

HAVILAND Christopher[18], was the only son of James[17] and Julia Haveland, born at Pool, Dorcet, 1512. He married at Pool, 16 Sept. 1544, Cecilia Mann. (She was the daughter of

"John Mann of the Westgate House, Canterbury." This aldermanry of the gates was an honored position. It demanded the furnishing of five knights for its defense, and it is interesting to know that the arms of that family shows five spears issuing from battlement.) He settled in Pool and was Mayor for the year 1569. He was the ancestor of "Haviland-Burke" the famous English "Genealogist," the Haviland of Ditton Hall and De Havilland of Langford Court, County Somerset. His wife Cecilia was buried at Pool 26 Aug. 1586. He was buried in the same place 24 Jan. 1589/90.

THE POOL PARISH REGISTER COMMENCES 1538.

Births

Ao 1546.

Thomas Havelland ye sonn of Xpoffer Havillande was bapt. [. . . . . .]

1548. Richard Havylland son of Xopoffer Havylland, babt. X days of [. . . . . .]

Matthew Havelland[19] son of Mr Xpoffer Havellande[18] bapt 15 of Junii 1550

1551. John Havelland son to Cristofer Havelland bapt. 26 Oct.

1553. James Havelland, son of xpofer Havellande bapt. [. . . . . .]

1555. Margaret Havelland dau. Christofer Havelland, bapt. 17 April

1560. Elinor Havellande, dau. of Christopher Havellande bapt. 15 Dec.

1563. William Havellande son of Christopher Havelland bapt. 30 May.

1564. Cysselye Havellande dau. of Christopher Havellande bapt. 7, Feb.

1566. Nathannell Havelland son Christopher Havelland, bapt. 25, April.

Marriages

An. 1544.

Mr **Christoffer Havylland**[18] and **Cecyly Manne,** xvj Sept.

Deaths

1547. Thomas Havylland son of Xpofer Havelland was buryed the Vth day of Oct.

1550. *Julyan Havelland*[17] my mother was buryed the iiij day of June.

1550. Richard Havellande son of Xpofer Havellande buryed XXX Aug.

1557. John Havylland son Xystoffer Havylland, buryed 6, Oct.

1571. William Havylland son of Mastre Xistopher Havylland buryed 27, Oct.

1586. Aug. 26. **Cysley Havilland** was buryed.

1589. Jan. 24. **Master Christopher Havilland**[18] the son of James Havilland[17] was buryed

CHILDREN:

THOMAS, bapt. 1546, buried 5 Oct. 1547.

RICHARD, bapt. 10 [?] 1548, buried 30 Aug. 1550.

Matthew, bapt. 15 June 1550, m. (1) 9 May 1575, **Mary Kechin, d.** 20 Nov. 1583; m. (2) Joyce [?], d. 28 Oct. 1607; m. (3) Thasia [?]; d. 11 March 1619.

JOHN, bapt. 26 Oct. 1551, buried 6 Oct. 1557.

JAMES, bapt. [?] 1553, was Mayor of Salisbury in 1598–1601.

MARGARET, bapt. 17 April 1555, m. Sir Peter Buck.

ELEANOR, bapt. 15 Dec. 1560, m. Rev. William Hiley, d. 1639.

WILLIAM, bapt. 30 May 1563, buried 27 Oct. 1571.

CYSSELYE, bapt. 7 Feb. 1564.

NATHANNELL, bapt. 25 April 1566.

KYTCHIN FAMILY.

Monument of Robert Kytchin and Joan* Sacheville his wife.

From Pryce's History of Bristol.

" On a monument over the vestry door in the East end of the South aisle of St. Stephen's church are represented a man and his wife kneeling at a desk with hands upraised as in prayer, and shields of Arms over their heads, that over the man bears Argent, on a Cheveron quarterly, gules and azure, between three Birds, proper, three Fleur-de-lys. Or. for Kytchin, — that over the woman, Azure, three crossbows bent, and each charged with five arrows. Or. for Sachville, — beneath them is inscribed as follows.

Deceased the 5ᴴ Septᵐber Ano Dominii 1594.
Robert Kitchin Alderman & his wife
Lieth neere this place, closed in Earth & clay:
Their Charities Alike in Death & Life,
Who to the Poore gave all their goodes away
Leaving in trust such men to act the same,
As might with truth preforᵐᵉ their good intent
So that the Poore indeed, and eke in name,
To lasting Ages in this Citie meant,
And other places of this Kingdom faire,
As Kendalltowne & Stuckland field both have.
With Bath, the native Place of her first Ayre,
The bountie of their gviftes they to them gave."

* This family of Sackeville or Sicca-villa, was of great antiquity and distinction in Devonshire.

KECHIN Robert, will reads: " Merchant one of the Alderman of the city of Bristol dated 19 June 1594 proved 10 Jan. 1594/5. Body to be buried in parish of St. Stephen in Bristol near the place where my first wife Johane was buried. — To *Robert Havyland son of Matthew Havyland* of Bristol three tenements; remainder to William Havyland, then to John Havyland son of Matthew Havyland of Bristol, merchant. — Wife Justyne, and other bequest to the sons of Matthew Haviland. — To brother Matthew Ketchin; to sister Agnes. — To Robert Ketchin of London, being son of brother Matthew. — To niece Agnes, daughter of Matthew. — To niece Elizabeth, wife of John Friend of Bristol hooper. — To niece Margaret Ketchin daughter of brother Matthew. — To niece Elizabeth Ketchin daughter of brother John, deceased. — To Jane Ketchin his other daughter. To niece Marriam Nottingham, wife of John of Bristol. — To Robert Nottingham son of John Nottingham of Bristol " hullior " and of Marriam his wife, and to William their youngest son. — John Barker, Matthew Haviland, John Rowberoe and Abel Kitchen to be executors and trustees."

HAVILLAND Matthew[19], son of Christopher and Cecilia (Mann) Havilland, was baptized at Poole June 15, 1550, settled in Bristol where he was mayor in 1607–8. He married 1st Mary, dau. of Robert Ketchen; 2nd Joyce; 3rd Thasia. He was a strong supporter of the Protestant cause and contributed largely toward the equipment of the fleet sent against the Spanish Armada. In 1616 he was Master of the Society of Merchants and was Alderman until his death. He possessed the Manor of Hawkesbury and estates in Glostershire and Somersetshire and of Charlinch and various other manors in Co. Somerset.

He composed a curious Broadside which explains itself.

A

MONUMENT

OF

GOD'S most gracious preservation of England from
Spanish Invasion, Aug. 2, 1588, and Popish
Treason, Novem. 5, 1605.

To my Posterity.

God's ancient Church two solemn feasts did keep,
  On two set days, by his own Word directed.
a When Pharaos's Hoste was drowned in the deep,
b And proud Haman's treason were detected.

Two works of equell grace, but greater wonder,
The Lord hath done for us, past all man's reason;
When Papists did attempt to bring us under,
c By Spanish huge army and damn'd d Percie's treason.

I, and my house these e great things will remember,
And in remembrance sanctifie two days,
In August one, the other in November;*
f Both made by God, for us to give him praise.

Dear children, charge your children after you
Still to observe these feasts as I now do.

MATTHEW HAVILAND

a Exod. 12.2 : 3.   b Esth. 9.17.   c Aug. 2, 1588.   d Nov. 5, 1605
        e Sam. 12.14   f Psal. 118.24.
        Luk. 1.49   Psal. 78.4, 6, 7.

His mansion still stands in Small Street, and his monument is to be seen at St. Warburghe. He was one of the early merchant princes whose counting-house was the four bronze pillars, called " the Nails," which now stands in front of the exchange. — The fact of his life spanning the event connected with Spain's defeat and the failure of the gunpowder plot explains his interest in their commemoration.

The will of Mathew Haviland dated 2 March 1619 and prob. 22 May 1620.   Extracts which follow: " I Mathew Havyland of the cittye of Bristoll, merchant and one of the Alderman of the sayed Cittye, being of the age of three score and nyne years or there about, etc.   Body to be buried in Warborowes churchyard, even in the grave in which my wife Joyce was laied in."   A legacy of 5 pounds is given " To Mr. Yeaman, preacher to make him a gown, soe as will preach at my funeral, and his texts to be on the 12 Chapter of Ecclesiastes 7th vese, in the church of St. Warborrows (St. Warburgh).   Also a yearly payment of four pounds to the city of Bristol, that twelve sermons may be preached yearly for ever at the Common Goale of said city. — To grand child Matthew Havylande, son of Robert. — To my son buildings in Hawkesbury, Gloucester, for maintainence of son William etc.   Grand child Bartholomew Havyland son of said William, etc.   Son John to have certain land in Somerset. — To my son Matthew ⅛ part of wine. — The portion Tacie my wife shall be

* The second feast was still observed in Plymouth, England, in 1708.

fifty £ per year. — To my son Matthew my house & tenement in
Small St. — To *Son Robert's children*: Matthew, Mary, Florence,
Jane & Elizabeth. — Daughter Anne Lorte's children: Sampson
& Joyce. — Reference to bond of father Sampson Lortt.— I give
unto my daughter Mary Holworthie's children, Mathew, Mary,
Richard, Anne & John, one hundred nobles. — To my son-in-law
Mr. Richard Holworthie the sum of one hundred nobles. — To
my Sister Elionor Helye, 5 pounds and a gown. — Son Robert
and all his heirs shall pay yearly forever out of my lands called
the 'Grange' in or by Kingswood, Wiltshire. — My kinsman
Mr. William Pitt draper, Mr. William Pitt merchant and Edward
Batter gent. to be overseers."

HAVYLANDE Matthew, of Bristol (son of the preceding Matthew and brother to Robert), merchant, will dated 16 May 1623,
proved 29 April 1624.— " To Mr. John Farmmomster of parish of
St. Warburge 5£. — To my niece Joyce Lorte daughter of Sampson Lorte, late of Bristol, Merchant, one hundred £ and my estate
& messuage dwelling, situated near the 'Crowde' door of St.
Nicholas church. — To Joyce Lorte & one of my neices, Mary
Holworthy one of the daughters of Richard Holworthy, merchant. — To my nephew Matthew Haviland, son of brother
Robert; my household stuff etc. in the dwelling house of the
said Robert at Hawkesberry, Gloucester.   To my kinsman Peter
Helge of Bristol. — To my brother-in-law Mr. Richard Holworthy of Bristol merchant. — Where as my dear father Matthew
Haviland, late of the city of Bristol, Alderman, deceased; gave
me 500£ to pay yearly to Mrs. Thasia Haviland, his then wife,
50£ per annum; and for better security I leave it into the hands
of Richard Holworthy and appoint brother Robert to pay 100£
said sum to be distributed as follows:— to Matthew Holworth
and Mary Holworthy, Ann Holworthy, Richard Holworthy &
John Holworthy children of said Richard & Mary, his late wife,
my sister deceased: To Prudence & Thomas Holworth two other
children of said Richard. — To each of the *children of brother
Robert*, namely, Matthew, Mary, Florence, *Jane*, and Elizabeth
Haviland. — Residu to my brother-in-law Richard Holworthy,
whom I constitute my sole and only executor."

HOLWORTHIE Richard, Alderman of Bristol, will dated
10 Oct. 1643, proved Dec. 9, 1645. — " To *brother Robert Haviland,*" etc. etc.

COLSTON Ann, in her will dated 13 July 1603, proved 28 Feb. 1603/4. Calls herself a " widow." " Body to be interred in St. Nicholes Crowd; in city of Bristol; where my mother or my good husband Mr. Richard Hentley lieth. Mr. *Matthew Haviland's* three eldest sons *Robert*, William and John, — Matthew Haviland and his sisters Anne and Mary Haviland, Mr. Matthew Haviland to be executor: My loving daughter-in-law Mrs. Joice Haviland his wife " —

BAPTISMS, MARRIAGES AND BURIALS, EXTRACTS FROM THE PARISH REGISTERS OF ST. STEPHEN AND ST. WERBURGHS, BRISTOL

Marriages at St. Stephen

Master **Mathew Haviland**[19] and **Mary Kytchin** were married 9 May, 1575.

Burials at St. Stephen

1583. Nov. 20. Mary, wife of Master Mathew Haviland.

In the Register of Baptisms at St. Werburghs.

1577. Feb. 11. **Robert**,[20] son of Mathew Haviland was baptized.
1579. Aug. 20. John, son of Mathew Haviland & Mary his wife, was baptized.

Marriages at St. Werburghs

1607. Aug. 30. Richard Holworthie & Mary Haviland were married.

Burials in St. Werburghs

1607. Oct. 28. Joyce, wife of Mathew Haviland, "Mayor."
1616. Jan. 9. Mary,* wife of Master Alderman Haviland.
1648. July 19. **Robert Haviland,** Esquire of Christ Church Parish.
1643. Richard Holworthy died. He married Maria daughter of Master Matthew Haviland.

CHILDREN:

First wife:

Robert, bapt. 11 Feb. 1577, m. Elizabeth Guise, buried 19 July 1648.
WILLIAM, m. ———, had a son Bartholomew; living in 1619.
JOHN, b. 20 Aug. 1579, m. (1) 13 May 1623, Elizabeth Everard; m. (2) Anastalia Blake; d. 10 Aug. 1663.

Second wife:

MATTHEW, m. ——— (?) (may have m. Mary, who d. 9 Jan. 1616), was Mayor of Bristol at time of Gunpowder plot, d. leaving a will, proved 29 Apr. 1624.
ANN, m. Sampson Lorte.
MARY, m. Richard Holworthie 30 Aug. 1607, d. between 1619 and 1623.

* It is possible this Mary may be the wife of Matthew Haviland's son Matthew.

GUISE FAMILY.

GYSE DE John,[1] who married Tacy, daughter of Lord Gray de Ruthyne, had two sons Anslme and William. William, the younger son of John, inherited the estates of his father at the death of his elder brother Anslme (1563) and from him descended Sir William Guise of Kent of Elmore.

GYSE William,[2] younger son of John De Gyse[1] was father undoubtedly of the following children and of whom we are inserting some Wills to prove relationship.

GUYSE John[3] of Elmore, Gloucestershire, gent., will dated 31 March 1614, proved 24 Oct. 1614. " To brother William Guyse, the younger, one hundred £. To *sister Havyland* for life the use of 50£ and after her decease to William Guyse the younger. To brother Charles Guyse 30£. — To my sister Perrye 20 shillings: the rest of my goods etc. to brother William Guyse the elder, whom I make my executor."

GUISE William,[3] of Gloucester, Esqre, will dated 22 July; codicil, dated 30 Dec. 1640, proved 31 May 1641. — " To my beloved brother Sir William Guise, knight, 20 shillings to buy him a ring. — To the Lady Elizabeth his wife and my kind sister whom I have ever found loving to me and mine, the like sum of 20 shillings to buy her a ring. — To my dearly beloved wife my house at Gloucester, where in I lived, and the garden for one and thirty years if she lives so long. — To my daughter Anne Guise toward her marriage 300£. — To my daughter Elizabeth Guise, 300£ toward her marriage. All the rest to my wife Elizabeth, who I make sole executrix." The codicil is as follows: — " I give to my kind *brother Haviland* and *sister* and my nephew Matthew Haviland, to each 20 shillings to buy them a ring. In presence of *Robert Haviland* and *Matthew Haviland*."

CHILDREN:

    WILLIAM, SIR,* b. ———, m. Lady Elizabeth Ken, d. between 1640 and 1650.

    JOHN, b. ———, d. leaving a will proved 24 Oct. 1614.

    Elizabeth, b. ———, m. **Robert Haviland.**

* Sir William Guise had a son William who married Ciscilia Dennis, by whom he had Christopher, Elizabeth, Ellinor and Frances. Elianor married Lawrence Washington and after Sir William Parigiter of Gretworth, Knight. Lawrence Washington is one of the Ancestors of George Washington.

CHARLES.
SISTER, b. ————, m. (?) Perrye, living in 1614.
WILLIAM, b. ————, m. Elizabeth (?), had daughters Anne and Elizabeth; d. leaving a will proved 31 May 1641.

HAVILAND Robert,[20] was baptised at St. Stephen, Bristol, 11 Feb. 1577 and was son of Matthew and Mary (Kytchin) Haviland. He married Elizabeth, daughter of William Guise of Elmore and lived in Bristol and was of Hawkesberry, Gloucester. He, according to the " Visitations of Gloucestershire " in 1623, had five children: " Matthew Haviland, 15 years old. Mary, Florence, *Jane* and Elizabeth." He was a member of Christ Church Parish. He died at Bristol and was buried on the 19 July 1648 in the Parish of St. Werburghs.

Will of *Matthew Haviland* of London, clerk (i.e. Minister), dated 6 April 1667 proved 4 Feb. 1670/1. — " Reference to instrument dated 1663, between me the said Matthew and Constance my wife, and Fulke Wormelayton of Wapping, Middlesex, distiller, on one part and Lewis Roberts of city of Gloucester, gent., Benjamin Albin citizen and skinner of London and Samuel Baiylye citizen and cordwinder of London, on the other part. — After the decese of my wife: — they shall permit my sister Mary Davyes, of London, widow, etc. — then sell, proceeds to go to children of *my four sisters.* — The said Mary Davyes. Florence, late wife of Robert Culme of Bristol. — *Jane, late wife of William Torry of New England* and Elizabeth, late wife of George Offield, late of Bristol, gent. — My wife to enjoy the goods that was my late father Mr. Robert Haviland of Hawkesbury, Gloucester. — Then to Elizabeth, Hannah and Sarah Davyes daughters of my said sister Davyes, and Elizabeth Culme, daughter of my said sister Culme. — To my cousin Thomas Offield 10£. — To my brother-in-law Samuel Sprint all those books I lent him and my cousin Richard Sprint all those books I lent him. — To my brother-in-law Robert Culme. — To my loving aunt Mrs. Elizabeth Guise and her daughters my cousins, Anne & Elizabeth, and my Sister-in-law Mrs. Sarah Andrews widow and my sister-in-law Mrs. Anne Sprint 20 shillings apice."

Will of *Sarah Andrews* of St. Leonards, Shoreditch, Middlesex, widow, dated 20 Sept. 1669. " I give & bequeath unto my loving *brother Matthew Haverland*, clerk my dimond ring to wear in rememberence of me. — To my loving sister Constance Haverland, my silver watch, as a token of my love. To my cousin Samuel Bayley of London, mercer, the sum of ten £, To my cousin Rebecka Sprint, widow ten £. To husband Richard Andrew citizen & scrivener of London. — My loving brother and cousin Samuel Sprint clerk, Zachariah Sprint, clerk, Richard Sprint, clerk, and Samuel Sprint, bookseller, Sister Barbara Barnes of Hackney, widow, Cousin Benjamin Andrews."

Henry F. Waters in his "Gleanings in England," says " Rev. Matthew Haviland was rector of Trinity church, London from which he was ejected under the Bartholomew Act. He was born about 1608 and was the son of Robert and Elizabeth (Gyse) Haviland of Hawkesbury, Gloucestershire."

CHILDREN:

MATTHEW, REV., b. 1608, m. Constance; d. leaving a will, proved 4 Feb. 1670/1.

MARY, b. ———, m. ——— Davyes; was living in 1667.

FLORENCE, b. ———, m. Robert Culme; d. before 1667.

JANE,[21] b. ———, m. **William Torry** abt. 1630 or 31; d. at Combe St. Nicholas, 27 April 1639.

ELIZABETH, b. ———, m. George Offield; d. before 1667.

CONTENTS

TORREYS IN AMERICA

ORIGINAL TORREY EMIGRANTS.

Previous records have shown the genealogy of this family from 1500 to 1640 in England and well authenticated dates prove that the William Torrey born in 1608 was the 5th in line in this record, but for convenience we now assume the numeral (1) for him and his brothers as the first of this name in America. Will also state that all the records of the family here for the first two decades used the name " Torry." Then we find the letter (e) introduced to read " Torrey " on all documents and tombstones. In the year 1640 *William*,[1] with his two young sons of 8 and 2 years of age, also his three brothers, James,[1] Philip[1] and Joseph[1] and Cousin George Fry came to New England. William and Joseph first located in Weymouth, Mass., James in Scituate and Phillip in Roxbury.

James[1] married Ann the daughter of Elder William Hatch, 2 Nov. 1643 at Scituate, Mass. In " Davis Ancient Landmarks of Plymouth" is found the statement that " the first clothing mill in Plymouth Colony was erected in 1643 by James Torrey on the first herring brook in Scituate." He was in military life and a lieutenant, was a man of great usefulness and respectability, was accidentally killed by an explosion of powder in Scituate 6 July 1665, leaving five sons and five daughters.

Phillip[1] settled at Roxbury, Mass., and married Mary, widow of John Scarborogh, 1 Oct. 1647. In the Suffolk Deeds dated 5 March 1673/4, he made deposition that reads " Phillip Torrey age 59 years or ther about heretofor of Combe St. Nicholas in the County of Somersett untill the year 1640 (yeoman) in that year removeing to New England with William Torrey & Samuell his son both of the Sd Comb, St. Nicholas with whom hee Lived for severall years, & beeing arived in New England Settled & hath ever since Lived in Roxbury, in the County of Suffolk in New England, etc." — He died at Roxbury, 12 May 1686, and it is not known that any of his direct descendants are now living.

Joseph[1] came to America with his three brothers and settled at Weymouth, Mass. Although not in our line of descent his work should be included as it is one more life record of able and patriotic devotion to the colonies, and shows of what moral and mental fibre were the pioneers. He removed to Rehoboth, Mass., in 1643, and then to Newport, R. I., in 1644, and on the 3 July 1644, he with 29 others signed a compact for Good Government. In 1647 he and Obidiah Holmes were released from paying part of their bonds for good behaviour for not attending Court. Was a Juryman in 1647–8 and Freeman 7 June 1648. " On 2 Oct. 1650, He & wife were prosecuted by the Grand Jury for holding of Meetings upon the Lords day from house to house contrary to orders of the Court." Doubtless the feuds and schisms of the seventh Day Baptists with the bodies calling themselves Baptists, Antimonians and Memonites, made the life of the new colony one of strife at that period; in which Joseph Torrey and his friends took an active part.

In 1652 at Newport a Samuel Hubbard writes, " I and my wife had hands laid on us by brother Joseph Torrey." From 1652 to 1674 we find his name constantly as either Commissioner, or General Recorder, or holding some important office in the Colony. 26 May 1664, Joseph Torrey writes to Samuel Hubbard. Misquamicut (Westerly), Dear and much respected brother Hubbard and brother Robert and Sister Ruth; though yor condition be at present a lonesome condition with respect to that fellowship and communion that sometimes you have enjoyed, yet I hope you are under such fruitful seasons with respect to the drops of Heaven, that your actions that you are necesitated to be laboring about, will put you in mind of that building that shall never decay; The object your eyes behold are good; it is spring time, the earth is putting forth its strength, the trees blossom and bud, and that which hath long been kept down by the winter cold doth now receive life and vigour anew from the shinings of the sun. I hope it is so with your hearts. I rest and remain yours in any service of love, in the best relation, Joseph Torrey." — 1667, May 13, he and three others were ordered to go forth from house to house throughout Newport and the villages and precincts thereof to take a precise and exact account of all the arms and ammunition and weapons of war each person is furnished with. At the same date he was a committee with two others, required with all possiable speed to mount the great guns on carriages. He held the office of Lieutenant some years. 1670, June 29, he and two others were allowed the sum of £10. 10s. for service as commissioner to Conn. — 1671, Jan. 30, he was allowed £6.8s.8d. for several services — We gain much light upon the exact state of affairs by a letter of Samuel Hubbard who writting 1671, Dec. 16, to his family in Westerly alludes to the difference between those who held Seventh Day views and the rest of the congregation. Mr. Hubbard gave his views in favor, " Brother Torrey said they required not my faith, they replied fiercly, it was a tumult, J. Torrey stoped at last." — In 1671 and '72 Joseph Torrey was Attorney General of Rhode Island. A bit of history may prove very helpful at this point, showing exactly the affairs of Rhode Island.

In 1636 Roger Williams was banished from the Salem Puritan Colony for his free religious beliefs, — he fled and by boat landed at the spot and founded what is now Providence — later he was joined by John Clarke, a physician who left England and came to America with a party of whom Ann Hutchinson was one, was banished from Boston, he settled in Newport, R. I., and became a preacher and leader there; Joseph Torrey was an Elder in his church, and evidently a working factor in all the stirring events of that stormy period — for in the year 1675 came the famous King Phillip War which is the key to a letter sent by Samuel Hubbard to Dr. Edward Stanett of London, dated 29 Nov. 1676, saying " In beginning of those troubles of the wars Lieut. Joseph Torrey, elder of Mr. Clark's church having but one daughter, living at Squamicut, Misqamicut, and his wife being there, he said unto me, ' come let us send a boat to Squamicut, my all is there and part of yours.' We sent a boat so as his wife and daughter, and his son-in-law and their children and my two daughters and 11 children and an apprentice boy all came and brother Crandall and his family with as many others could possibly come, etc." He also alludes to the death of Mr. Torrey as having occurred this year (1676).

FIRST GENERATION.

WILLIAM TORREY AND JANE HAVILAND.

TORREY Capt. William,[1] who is 5th in line of descent in England and of the 1st generation in America, was born at Combe St. Nicholas, Somerset, England, and baptized there 21 Dec. 1608 the son of Phillip and Alice Torrey. He married for his first wife, Agnes, daughter of Joseph Combe, 17 March 1629. She died about 1630. (For the following is found on record.) " 1630, Feb. 14. Was issued a commission to William Torrey late husband of Agnes Torrey, als. Combe deceased, whilst she lived of Combe St. Nicholas." He then married for his second wife, *Jane,* daughter of Robert and Elizabeth (Guise) Haviland about 1630 or 31. She died and was buried 17 April 1639, being the mother of Samuel, born 1632 and William born 1638. He again married a third wife, and neither her name, place or date of marriage are known, the latter, however, occurred before 1641. She was the mother of all the children born in America, he having come here in 1640 and settled at Weymouth, Mass. In him centers our chief interest and direct line of descent. He was a man of strong character and evidently a leader of men, for we find constant records of his activities in the town affairs. In 1641 he was a member of the Artillery company (later known as the " Ancients & Honorables "); in 1642 a Freeman. From 1642 to 1649 excepting 1646 & 1647 was representative to the General Court from Weymouth and again from 1649 to 1666, he was clerk of the deputies. In Johnson's History of New England, it is said " he was a good penman and was usually clerck of the deputies " — also " he had great qualifications for the place." We find many records of payment made him for these duties and in 1650 he was given a grant of " Slate Island " (just off Weymouth Neck), later in " 1683 a grant of 500 acres of land for his patriotism and loyal service." His place of abode in Weymouth is still known, although the dwelling is demolished; yet from well described boundaries still existing, we place it on the east side

CAPT. WILLIAM TORREY FARM

Weymouth, Mass.

of neck road, opposite " Capt. Torrey's Cove," now called
" Sampson's Cove," North Weymouth; Bridge Street, the direct
road to Hingham, passes through his home lot, this is a well
located and sightly point, giving a view of the shore and Back
River. (See illustration.) Many most interesting records
show him an active factor in colony and town affairs,
in which he is always called Capt. William Torrey, being a
captain of Weymouth militia. He was a deputy in 1679 and
80. Was invariably chosen a selectman of the town; was
magistrate and accorded the power to marry, by the General
Court for many years. He was chosen deputy in May 1690
after the overthrow of Andros; but his death occurred June 10,
following.

He had received in England a liberal education and was profi-
cient in the Latin tongue; which here in the colony placed him
in the front rank of importance and service. He educated and
fitted his son Samuel for Harvard College. He was constantly
serving on Committees pertaining to schools and educational
matters; was chosen among others to pass upon the merits of
John Eliot's translation of the Indian Bible — also one of others
to judge of the merit of " The First New England History " by
William Hubbard in 1679. In 1687 he wrote a " Discourse on
Futurities or Things to Come," a curious essay on the speedy
coming of the Messiah, which later, in 1757, was published by his
family, and is commented upon as showing a great knowledge of
scripture; the only copy now known to exist is in the Public
Library of Boston. The record and name of wife and date
of his third marriage are not to be found, but entries of the birth
of 5 children, born in Weymouth are to be seen, among them being
a son Angel, the progenitor of Ex-President William H. Taft on
his mother's side. In his will they are all named, and interesting
extracts follow which show him to have been a man of wealth
and of goodly intent to this third wife and his numerous family.
He died in Weymouth 10 June 1690 — and probably buried in old
cemetery Weymouth. Although the tombstones of many of the
Torrey name are still in excellent condition, among them his sons,
their wives and children, we fail to find Capt. William Torrey,
but in the group of these graves, high on the sightly hill, is one of
marked distinction, of costly aspect, but the nameplate is missing,
which we, as well as some historians believe to be his last resting

place. (See illustration.)   The research and study involved
to find these early records leaves one with a glow of enthusiasm and inspiration for " plain living and high thinking "
which is involved in the great sacrifices of these early settlers;
with a sense of profound reverence and deep gratitude that of
such were one's ancestors.   His will of 15 May 1686, follows:
" I William Torrey Sr. of Weymouth, in New England, etc.,
first to Samuel Torrey my eldest son, shall have the 500 acre
lot lately granted to me by the General Court.   Second, my
Wife to enjoy my dwelling house $\frac{1}{2}$ of the land, and $\frac{1}{2}$ meadow
fresh and salt in the lower Plantation.   Third, *William Torrey*
my second son shall have $\frac{1}{2}$ orchard $\frac{1}{2}$ upland meadow mow-
ing grass.   I have given him 3 acres of land, whereupon he
hath built a house.   My will is that she (my Wife) retain so
much and what remains over and above to hand over to her
sons Josiah and Angel Torrey, to be improved for her.   My
Will is that my grand daughter Haywood and Micihijah to
have one part of Books, Josiah another and Angel a third."
" Wm. Chard and Joseph Dyer made oath that they did see Capt.
Wm. Torrey late of Weymouth, sign will."   The Inventory of
Capt. Torrey's property amounted to £360-10s-6, proved 17 July
1690.

CHILDREN:
First wife not known to have had children.

Children by second wife:
SAMUEL, REV., b. in England, 1632, m. (1) 15 May 1657, Mary Rawson,
    d. 10 Sept. 1692; m. (2) 30 July 1695, Mary, widow of William Sym-
    mes, d. 12 Mar. 1720/1; d. at Weymouth 21 April 1707, ae. 75 yrs.
William, b. in England, 1638, m. **Deborah Greene** of Warwick, R. I.,
    before 1670; d. at Weymouth 11 Jan. 1717/18, ae. 80 yrs.

Third wife:
NAOMY, b. at Weymouth, 3 Dec. 1641, m. John Lowell (?) of Boston,
    before 1665; d. after 1680 and before 1686.
MARY, b. at Weymouth, Aug. 4 or Dec. 3, 1642, m. William Downe.
MICAJAH, DEACON, b. at Weymouth, 12 Oct. 1643; d. at Weymouth,
    20 Jan. 1710/11, a. 67 y.
JOSIAH, b. ———, 1650, m. Sarah (Wilson) Batt, at Medfield, 5 May
    1680.
ANGEL, b. at Weymouth, 10 June 1657, m. Hannah; lived at Mendon,
    Mass., d. at Bristol, R. I., 1725.

ADDENDA TO FACE PAGE 84

Since the printing of this Genealogy we learn from well authenticated records the name of the third wife of Capt. William Torrey to have been Elizabeth Fry, born in Combe St. Nicholas, England, daughter of Edward Fry and sister to George Fry who came to America on the same ship. They were married before immigrating to America in 1640. She was the mother of six children, all born in Weymouth.

The fact that in his will of 1686, Capt. William Torrey did not name any of his daughters, led me into the supposition of their early death, but I now find records to the contrary.

Naomi Torrey, according to one record, married John Lowell of Boston. The "Savage" and Lowell Genealogies claim it to have been a Naomi Sylvester, who was born in 1649. John Lowell married a "Naomi" before 1665, probably about 1664, making Naomi Sylvester 15 years of age, a possible but not probable alliance, while the date of birth of Naomi Torrey is 1641, rendering her of a more suitable age. In Rev. Samuel Torrey's Will of 1706, comes much evidence, and we read this item: "I give to Ebenezer Lowell my Kinsman 30£." John and Naomi Lowell of Boston had a son Ebenezer, and only through the marriage of Naomi Torrey to John Lowell could Ebenezer Lowell be kinsman to Rev. Samuel Torrey.

Again, from an authentic, and a very interesting Probate document, comes this information:

"John Lowle, Bond.

"Know all men by these presents That we Naomi Lowle widow & William Griggs, Cooper both of Boston in the county of Suffolke & Josiah Torrey of Mendon in sd. County of Suffolke within their Majesties Province of the Massachusetts Bay in New England are holden and stand firmly bound and obliged unto William Stoughton Esqr. in full sum of one hundred and Fifty pounds current money of New England. To be paid unto the sd. William Stoughton his Succesors in the office of Judge of Probate of Wills and granting Administrations within the sd. County of Suffolke or assignes to the true payment where of we do bind ourselves our heirs Execrs and Adminrs jointly and severally firmly by these presents. Sealed with our Seales Dated the Twenty seventh day of September 1694."

The natural inference must be that only a sister would call upon Josiah Torrey in Mendon, to assist her in the settlement of her husband's estate. We know that Josiah Torrey of Mendon of that date was son of Capt. William Torrey of Weymouth.

The grand daughter Haywood, mentioned in Capt. William Torrey's Will of 1686, is supposed to have been one of the two daughters, Ruth or Margaret, of John and Naomy Lowell, born 1665 and 1667, and one of whom may have married a Haywood before 1686.

We learn of the marriage of Mary Torrey by Rev. Samuel Torrey's Will of 1706 in which he mentions "To sister Mary Downs," also "To Kinsman, William Downs."

By a clerical error in the birth tables, the name of one daughter, Judith, was omitted, which we here insert and who was mentioned in Rev. Samuel Torrey's Will of 1706 as follows: "To my Kinsman John Hunt son to my sister Judith Hunt deceased." In a Hunt Genealogy we find under Thomas Hunt of Boston, anchor-smith, that he had a wife Judith, and a son John, and on the gravestone of his wife Judith is inscribed, "died 18th Oct. 1693, age 38 years: daughter of William Torrey of Weymouth."

The tables of Capt. William Torrey's children by his 3rd wife should read:

NAOMY, b. at Weymouth 3 Dec. 1641, m. John Lowell of Boston before 1665. Was living in 1693 and died before 1706.
MARY, b. at Weymouth 4 Aug. or 3 Dec. 1642, m. William Downe of Boston before 1682, died after 1706.
MICAJAH, Deacon, b. at Weymouth 12 Oct. 1643, m. Susanna —— before 1673, d. at Weymouth 20 Jan. 1710/11, a. 67 y.
JOSIAH, b. [?] 1650, m. Sarah (Wilson) Batt at Medfield, 5 May 1680.
JUDITH, b. abt. 1654, m. Thomas Hunt of Boston before 1674, d. 18 Oct. 1693, a. 38 y.
ANGEL, b. at Weymouth 10 June 1657, m. Hannah ——; lived at Mendon, Mass., d. at Bristol, R. I., 1725.

Tombs of Rev. Samuel and Mary Torrey   Supposed grave of Capt. William Torrey

HEADSTONES OF THE TORREY FAMILIES

Weymouth Heights Cemetery

REV. SAMUEL TORREY.

It is interesting at this point to diverge enough from the line of descent to give a brief record of *Samuel Torrey*,[2] William,[1] as showing the type of character inherited by the Torrey family. Being sent by his father to Harvard College, he had passed through the first prescribed course of study for the three years and would have taken his A.B. in 1650, yet because the term was lengthened to four years he and others left the college; his father had given him his first classics, but he had so improved his opportunities, that he had great repute as a Minister, and was ordained 14 Feb. 1665, to succeed Thomas Thatcher as pastor of the church in Weymouth, to the great satisfaction of the father. He had previously preached at Hull. He was chosen to preach the election sermons in 1674 and 1683 and again in 1695, an honor in no other instance conferred in Massachusetts. He was so highly esteemed for his discretion as to be chosen President of Harvard College in 1681 upon the death of Oakes, and again after the death of Rogers, 1684, but he declined in both instances. The Weymouth town records give abundant proof of his activities as a faithful and devout Minister for more than thirty years.

Reverend T. Prince, writing on 2 April 1757, wrote of him in this wise. "And as my Parents had high Veneration for Him, and he had receiv'd them into his Friendship for the Benefit of Learing and Religion, when I was 10 years of Age, they sent me 45 miles from their House in Sandwich to injoy the great Privilege of living with Him; and he afterwards always kindly received me at his House where I us'd to call in my Going to and Returning from College I can write of Him from my personal Acquaintance with him Being of a tall and proper Stature, excellent intellectual Powers and Accomplishments and of great and Stead Sanctity, Solidity and Majesty in his Countenance and Conversation. He struck all about Him with singular Reverence; tho' at seasonable Intervals, as at the Table and when his Friends came to visit Him, He would be innocently

witty and cheerful; but ever mixed agreable Instruction with
other Entertainment and Diversion.   He seem'd superior to all
the Ministers who came to see him, who behaved towards Him
with distinguishing Deference, And he was a Person of such deep
and extensive Views that in Public Affairs of great Difficulty, the
Governer, Dep. Governor and Council of the Colony us'd to send
to him, tho' 15 miles off (with some other elderly and judicious
Ministers in and near Boston) to help them with his wise Obser-
vations and Advice. — His Prayers both in the Family and
Public and his Sermons were very Scriptural, experimental,
pathetical, sensible, flowing from a warm and pious Heart, and
with wondrous Freedom and Variety. When He treated on
awful Subjects, it was with most awakening Solemnity; but
otherwise, He usually express'd Himself with the most tender
and moving Affection, when he saw any Fault in any of his
Family, He would first only look with a holy and awful Dis-
pleasure neither exposing nor rebuking. — I believe He never
struck any Person in his life — a look was Terror and Reproof
enough, — but then take us alone into his Study and speak with
such Tenderness and Tears as to melt us down in a Moment.
In his Family Worship, He would often Pray affectionately for
every person by name, or by such Description as we all knew,
extremely suitable to our various Cases, which wonderfully
bound us to Him: as also for others occasionally there, and in a
very striking Manner, And I shall never forget the moving
Exortation, Prayers and Tears He us'd to pour out among the
Children, at their Catechizing a Monday Mornings at Sun-rise
in the Meeting House.   Nor had he any affected Tone; but all
his Pronunciation was perfectly agreable to the Nature of the
Things delivered, and so as to engage the most lively Attention, —
In Conversation with the late Honourable and learned Lawyer,
John Read, Esq., as I happened to speak of my living with the
Rev. Mr. Torrey of Weymouth; He immediately said. — ' Mr.
Torrey! that was the most wonderful Man in Prayer I ever heard;
When I was Senior Sophister at College in 1696 there being a
Day of Prayer kept by the Association at Newtown, upon some
extraordinary occasion, in the House of Public Worship; I and
several others went from College to attend the Exercise; where
two Prayers made by two ministers beside a Sermon by a third
in the Forenoon and the like in the afternoon: and then Mr.

Torrey stood up and pray'd near Two Hours; But all his Prayer so intirely new and various without Tautologies, so exceeding pertinent, so regular, so natural, so free, lively and affecting; that towards the End of his Prayer, hinting at still new and agreable Scenes of Tho't we cou'd not help wishing Him to enlarge upon them; but the Time obliged Him to close to our Regret, and we could have gladly heard Him an Hour longer: His Prayers so wonderfully enlivened and mov'd the Congregation, that we seem'd not to be sensible of the Time's elapsing till he had finished.' — And such extraordinary Talants were the Reason, why as I have heard, the Association used to appoint Him to bring up in the Rear of their Religious Exercises both in Public and Private. The wife of his Youth was the Daughter of Mr. Secretary Rawson; and tho' He never had any offspring yet over Her Grave He erected a handsome Monument. There was as I remember a singular Esteem and Intimacy between Him and Lieut. Governor Stoughton, the Honourable chief Justice Samuel Sewall, Esq; the Rev. Mr. Joshua Moody, the Rev. Mr. Vice President Willard, the Rev. Mr. Hobert of Newtown and the Rev. Mr. Thacher of Milton."

At the Weymouth Height cemetery we find two impressive tombs of classic form such as were used by people of distinction, bearing the following inscriptions: " Here lyes intered ye body of the Rev. Mr. Samuel Torrey pastor of the church of Christ in Waymouth aged 75 years — died April ye 21st 1707." — The other inscribed thus: " Mrs. Mary Torrey age 50 years died on 10th Sept. 1692 " — both situated upon a hill of great beauty of form and location, with tall savin trees marking boundaries and standing as sentinels over their graves. This old cemetery is truly of unique beauty, and if any descendants of the Torrey name have a love for the beautiful they may be sure 'tis a rightful inheritance — for in every spot chosen by these early comers either for residence or burial they have selected sightly spots with grand views. (See illustration, page 84). His 2nd wife was Mary, widow of Captain William Symmes.

SECOND GENERATION.

WILLIAM TORREY AND DEBORAH GREENE.

GREENE FAMILY.

GREENE Robert, gentleman of Bowridge Hill, Gillingham, Dorsetshire, England, taxed on the Subsidy Rolls of Henry VIII, 1543, Edward VI, 1547, Elizabeth, 1558. Date of birth and 'death unknown. His son *Richard Greene, Sr.*, of Bowridge Hill, England, second son of Robert, died May 1608. His only son *Richard Greene, Jr.*, of Bowridge Hill, England, married Mary Hooker, daughter of John Hooker, member of Parliament from Exeter — their fourth son, *John Greene* was the first generation in America.

GREENES IN AMERICA.

GREENE John,[1] surgeon, was the son of Richard and Mary (Hooker) Greene, born 1590, married 1st at St. Thomas church, Salisbury, 4 Nov. 1619, Joanna Tattershall. She died 1643. His 2nd wife was Alice Daniels, a widow, and his 3rd wife was Philip. According to Savage, " John Greene was from Hampton in the ship " James," 6 April 1635, and arrived at Boston with wife and five children 3 June 1635, had been of Salisbury, was at Providence in 1636." As the name of John Greene does not appear in Massachusetts Colonial Records in the period intervening between his arrival at Boston and his settlement at Providence it is to be presumed that he made no settlement in Boston or elsewhere in Massachusetts. We know, however, that he was at one time in Salem, where he probably was associated with Roger Williams. On 1 Aug. 1637, he first appeared in Massachusetts Colonial Records in this wise: " Mr. John Greene of New Providence, bound to Quarter Court, first Tuesday of 7th month next for speaking contemptuously of Magistrates, stands bound in 100 marks" (Mass. Col. Rec. Vol. 1, p. 200). On which the action taken is as follows: " John Greene of New Providence fined 20£ and forbidden the jurisdiction on pain of fine and imprisonment for speaking contemptuously of Magistrates, 19 Sept. 1637" (Mass. Col. Rec. Vol. I, p. 203), and 12 March 1638 a letter from him being received by the court of Massachusetts, "wherein the court is charged with usurping the power of Christ over the church and mens consciences, etc. He was ordered not to come into that jurisdiction under pain of imprisonment and further censure."

On 8 Oct. 1638 he was one of twelve persons to whom Roger Williams deeded land bought of Cononicus and Miantomomi, 1639, was one of the twelve original members of the 1st Baptist church. Nov. 1642, he bought land called "Occupassuatuxet" of Miantomomi; this land remained in occupancy of his heirs until 1782, and is now called "Spring Green Farm." Jan. 12, 1643, he and ten others bought of Miantomomi for 144 fathoms of wampum, a tract of land called Shawomet (Warwick), and on 12 Sept., 1643, he with others of Warwick was notified to appear at Boston to hear complaint of Pomham and Socconocco, "as to some unjust and injurious dealing toward them by yourselves." They refused to obey the summons, declaring that they were legal subjects of the King of England and beyond the limits of Massachusetts authority. Soldiers were soon sent, who besieged the settlers in a fortified house. In a parley, it was now said, "that they held blasphemous errors, which they must repent of" or go to Boston for trial, and they were soon carried there, except John Greene who fortunately escaped. His companions were imprisoned till the next March and then he and they were banished. His first wife, the mother of his children, died at Conanicut in 1643, having taken refuge there when the Massachusetts troops under Captain Cooke made their raid, on the defenceless and inoffensive inhabitance, of Warwick or as it was then call, Shawomet. In 1644, he and Samuel Gorton and Randall Holden went to England to obtain redress for their wrongs, being obliged to take ship at New York. He and Holden returned successful in their mission, landing in Boston, Sept. 13, 1646.

In the years 1654–55–56–57, we find him a Commissioner, and Freeman in 1655. "His will is dated Dec. 28, 1658, and proved Jan. 7, 1659, his wife Phillip to be executor (except in matters in difference between testator and William Arnold; which son John was to attend to). To wife that part of building now erected, containing "large hall and chimney, chamber, garret and little dairy room which butts against the old house etc. All to her for life as also half the orchard and swamp and 2 heifers. — *To son John*, neck of land called ' Ottupashatuxet ' and meddow belonging thereto and also a right of land in purchase of Providence. To son Peter, that other house adjoining etc. also Peter to have yoke of steers and half of the oxen, he providing wife of Testator with thirty loads of wood per year, etc. — To son James, six acres and my great lot with rights at Warwick Neck. To son Thomas meddow and six acre lot etc. To four sons right as purchaser of Warwick. — To four sons and daughter Mary Sweet, what money can be gotten by law or otherwise from William Arnold in the case depending betwixt me and him also my Son John hath recovered half of it for his use according to my former promise. To grand-child Ann Hade a heifer and yearling calf, to be disposed of by her uncle James Greene for her profit. To friend Samuel Gorton 40 shillings." In 1668 Aug. 27. " His widow Phillip deeded to son-in-law (i.e., stepson) John Greene considering her desolate condition and to free herself of many troubles attending it my dwelling house lot and all the rest of estate, household goods etc. except a cow and some small things already given my grand daughter Phillip Greene reserving also wearing apparel. He engaged to provide her with meat, drink, lodging etc. and six pounds per annum and to transport said pay to Newport at his own cost by Sept. 29 annually." He died at Warwick, R. I., about the first week in Jan. 1658/9.

CHILDREN:

Children by first wife:

John, b. in England, bapt. 15 Aug. 1620, m. **Anne Almy** of Portsmouth, R.I., before 1649; d. 27 Nov. 1708, a. 88 yrs.

PETER, b. in England, bapt. 10 March 1621/2, m. Mary Gorton of Warwick; d. Feb. 1659.

RICHARD, b. in England, bapt. 25 March 1623/4; d. young in England.

JAMES, b. in England, bapt. 21 June 1626, m. (1) 1658, Deliverence Potter of Warwick, d. 1664; m. (2) 3 Aug. 1665, Elizabeth Anthony of Portsmouth; d. 27 Apr. 1698, ae. 71 yrs.

THOMAS, b. in England, bapt. 4 June 1628, m. Elizabeth Barton of Warwick, 30 June 1659; d. 5 June 1718, ae. 90 yrs.

JOAN, b. in England, bapt. 3 Oct. 1630, m. John Haye (or Hade or Hayden).

MARY, b. in England, bapt. 19 May 1633, m. James Sweet abt. 1654.

ALMY FAMILY.

ALMY William,[1] of Saugus (Lynn), perhaps as early as 1631, went home and came again 1635, in the ship " Abigail," age given as 34 years, wife Audrey 32, and children, *Annis* 8, and Christopher 3; Removed 3 April 1637 to Sandwich, Mass., where he had land granted to him there, for " he and nine others were given liberty to view a place to set down and have sufficient land for three score families." Removed and sold his Sandwich lands on 22 June 1642, to Edmund Freeman. On 14 Nov. 1644, he had land granted him at " Wading River " (Portsmouth, R. I.) and was certainly freeman there in 1655, was a Juryman 1656, and in the years 1656–57–63, was a Commissioner. In the year 1668 was Foreman of Jury. In his " will dated 28 Feb. 1676/7 and prob. 23 Apr. 1677, he makes sons Christopher and Job, his executors. He first requested that his body be buried beside his son John, if testator's wife outlived him, she to have all the estate for life. To son Christopher at death of wife: the half of farm next the land which I gave to son John. To son Job, the other half of farm with dwelling house, two orchards etc. To daughters *Anna* and Catharin each two parts of cattle and movables and to sons Christopher and Job, each one part. To Grandchild Bartholomew West £20, at twenty one years of age." He died 1677.

CHILDREN:

> Annis, b. in England abt. 1627, m. **John Greene** before 1649; d. at Warwick, R. I., 6 May 1709, a. 82 y.
>
> CHRISTOPHER, b. in England abt. 1632, m. Elizabeth Cornell, 9 July 1661; d. 30 Jan. 1713.
>
> JOHN, CAPT., b. ———, m. Mary Cole; d. 1 Oct. 1676.
>
> JOB, b. ———, m. Mary Unthank; d. 1684.
>
> CATHARINE, b. ———, m. Bartholomew West.

GREENE John[2] (*John*[1]), Deputy-Governor of Rhode Island, was the son of John and Joanna (Tattershall) Greene. He was born in Salisbury, England, and baptized 15 Aug. 1620, came to New England with his father; he married Ann, daughter of William and Audray Almy before 1649. She was born about 1627.

In 1651, Feb. 3rd, he and three others agree with the town to build a mill at own cost and to grind the town corn at 2 quarts in a bushel; the town granted for their encouragement a lot of land that was formerly Mr. Gorton's.   In the years 1652 to the year 1663, he was Commissioner, from 1652 to 1654 General Recorder. In 1655 was a Freeman, also General Solicitor.   From 1657 to 1660 was Attorney General, 1658, Warden.   In 1660, Apr. 30, he was appointed by town " to write to the President & Assistants about the Indians pressing in upon our lands and spoiling our timber, desiring their assistance to suppress their violence." In 1664–74–75–77–80, a Deputy.   1670, June 29, he and John Clarke were chosen agents to go to England for vindication of charter before his Majesty, and redeem the same from the injurious violation thereof by the colony of Connecticut.   1671, Jan. 30, he was allowed £10 for his charge and pains in going to the treaty at New London, etc.   1676, Apr. 4, it was voted " that in these troublesome times and straits in this colony, this Assembly desiring to have the advice and concurrence of the most judicious inhabitants, if it may be had for the good of the whole, do desire at their next sitting the company and counsel of Mr. Benedict Arnold and fifteen others among whom was Capt. John Greene."   In 1679, Feb. 3, he and Randall Holden being in England were called upon to give information as to Mount Hope; they valued it at £4000 consisting of 4000 acre.   1679, Aug. 1, the Assembly ordered £60 paid him and Randall Holden disbursed by them in England, etc.   1680, May 5, he and two others were empowered by Assembly to purchase a bell " for the public use of this colony and for given notice or signifying the several times or sittings of the Assemblys and Courts of Trials and General Councils."   The bell was purchased for £3. 10s. of Freelove Arnold, daughter of Governor Benedict Arnold.   1683, Sept. 17, he and Randall Holden sent a letter to King Charles II, concerning Governor Cranfield of New Hampshire and Commissioners, who would show no commission from the King. 1683–84–85–86–90–91–96, Major for the main.   1686, Dec. 22, he was notified by Gov. Andros of his appointment as a member of his council. 1690, Jan. 30, he, with others, sent a letter of congratulation to William and Mary on their accession to the crown and informing them that since the deposing of Andros, the former government under the charter had been reassumed, mentioning also the seizure of Andros in Rhode Island, on his flight from Massachusetts.

HEADSTONE OF MRS. DEBORAH TORREY
Weymouth Heights Cemetery

1691, June 27, he was voted 10s. by the Assembly for his encouragement for drawing up an address to their Majesties; for drawing up a letter to Governor of New York and transcribing it, for writing six commissions and setting the seals to them for the military officers on the main land. 1690–1700, he was Deputy-Governor. 1706, Dec. 20, he made his will — proved 1708, Dec. 20, Exs. sons Peter, Job, Richard and Samuel. " He called himself inhabitant of Greene Hole, alias Occupasituxet, in his eighty-seventh year, and for as much as his wife is in eightieth year of her age and exercised with lameness in her left side wholly incurable, which notwithstanding the good help of our children, is like to prove chargeable therefore in case it should please God she should survive me, I ought to have the better care to leave her the better supplied. To her that part of son Richard's house we now by agreement dwell in during our lives and use of household goods and provisions, three cows, kept for her by Richard, as also fuel provided by him and £5 paid her by son Samuel, yearly for life. To son Samuel the north side of Green Hole to a certain line, with privilege of fowling, fishing, etc., etc. To son Richard rest of the neck with island near adjoining and housing, barn, orchard etc. he paying £20 per year to my lame beloved wife till her death. To son Peter, all right in undivided lands at Coweset, except 100 acres. To son Job, all right in land belonging to seven purchasers. To daughter *Deborah Torrey* £16. To daughter Phillip Dickerson's children £16, to be improved till they are of age. To daughter Ann Green £16. To daughter Catharin Holden £16. To daughter Audry Spencer £16. To grand daughter Mary Dyer £16. To four sons land undisposed of, and all stock of cow kind and horse kind." He earnestly charges his children to care for his wife " to manifest their love to me and her in lending their help unto her, and so I take leave, commending my wife and children to the fear of God, in whose fear I rest, in assured hope of Salvation."

Inventory, £167. 9s., viz., 15 cows, 2 oxen, 3 steers, 5 horses kind, flagon, tankard, porringer, beaker, candle stick, sconce, chafing dish, brass scales, stillyards, 2 cases of bottles, razor, hone, 3 beds, cabinet, desk, 2 guns, pair of pistols, belt, rapier, cane, book £6, silver plate, 2 cups and spoons £8. 5s., money £14, table, chairs, etc. Receipts for legacies were given by *William* and *Deborah Torrey*. John and Audray Spencer, Edward and Mary Dyer, Charles and Catherin Holden and Ann Greene.

On their " Old Homestead Farm " at Warwick, R. I., we find a family graveyard with stones reading:

" Hear lyeth the	" Here lyeth the body.
body of John Greene Esq.	of Ann ye wife of
& late deptie Govern^r	Major John Greene.
he departed this life.	She deceased in the
in ye 89 year of his age.	82nd year of her age.
November ye 27. 1708"	May ye 6th 1709"

CHILDREN:

Deborah, b. 10 Aug. 1649, m. **William Torrey** before 1670; d. at Weymouth, Mass., 7 Feb. 1728/9, a. 80 y.

JOHN, b. 6 June 1651.

WILLIAM, b. 1 March 1652, m. Mary Sayles, 11 Dec. 1674; d. 1679.

PETER, b. 7 Feb. 1654/5, m. Elizabeth Arnold, dau. of Stephen; d. 12 Aug. 1723.

JOB, b. 27 Aug. 1656, m. Phebe Sayles, 22 Jan. 1685; d. 6 July 1745.

PHILIP, b. 7 Oct. 1658, m. (1) Caleb Carr of Jamestown; m. (2) Charles Dickerson.

RICHARD, b. 8 Feb. 1660, m. Eleanor Sayles, 16 Feb. 1693; d. 24 May 1711.

ANNE, b. 19 March 1662/3, m. Thomas Greene, son of Thomas.

CATHERIN, b. 15 Aug. 1665, m. Charles Holden; living in 1717 at Masapaug, R. I.

AUDREY, b. 27 Dec. 1667, m. Dr. John Spencer; d. at East Greenwich, R. I., 17 April 1733.

SAMUEL, b. 30 Jan. 1669/70, m. Mary Gorton, dau. of Benjamin.

TORREY William^2 (*William^1*), son of William and Jane (Haviland) Torrey, born in England, 1638. Came to Weymouth with his father in 1640. He married Deborah, daughter of John and Anne (Almy) Greene before 1670. She was born 10 Aug. 1649. He was a Freeman, 1672. His father gave him a good education and we find by the will of his father, dated 1686, that he had been given three acres, upon which he had built him a house, and it is probable that he acquired most of his father's " Home-Farm." In his will dated 20 Sept. 1715, he calls himself a husbandman of Weymouth, and names his wife Deborah and son John to be executors. To wife Deborah £10, also one-half of West End of Dwelling house. Mentions his five sons John,

HEADSTONE OF MR. WILLIAM TORREY
Weymouth Heights Cemetery

Samuel, *Joseph*, Phillip and Haviland, also daughter Jane. (Note the recurrence of the Haviland names.) One item of his will reads: " I give to my son John, £20 in money to be leived out of part of my real estate as is hereafter expressed after my wife's decease, provided he bring up one of his sons to learning (Viz) at the Collage." The Inventory of his estate, dated 23 April 1722, is recorded as being £1336. 8s. 8d. He died at Weymouth, 11 Jan. 1717/18, age 80 years, and his wife died there also, 8 Feb. 1728/9, age 80 years; both are buried in the Weymouth Heights Cemetery. (See illustrations, pages 93–95.)

CHILDREN:

WILLIAM, b. 14 Sept. 1670; d. young.

JOHN, b. 23 June 1673, m. Mary Symmes, 26 Dec. 1700; d. at Weymouth, 7 Jan. 1729/30, ae. 57 yrs.

SAMUEL, b. abt. 1675, m. Abigail Bridge, 29 June 1699; d. 6 Sept. 1748.

Joseph, Ensigne, b. abt. 1678, m. **Elizabeth Symmes,** 24 March 1704/5; d. at Weymouth, 22 April 1723, ae. 45 yrs.

PHILLIP, b. 2 May 1681, m. Mary Marsh, 3 Jan. 1708/9; d. at Weymouth, 13 March 1754, a. 73 y.

HAVILAND, b. ————, m. Elizabeth Croade before 1716 (lived at Plymouth, Mass.); d. 1750.

JOSIAH, b. 19 Sept. 1686, d. at Weymouth, 16 Aug. 1706, ae. abt. 20 y.

JANE, b. abt. 1689, m. William Reed, 13 Dec. 1716; d. at Weymouth, 24 Jan. 1729, ae. 40 y.

THIRD GENERATION.

JOSEPH TORREY AND ELIZABETH SYMMES.

SYMMES FAMILY.

SYMMES William, and his wife were truly religious and firm protestants in the reign of Bloody Queen Mary, 1553 to 1558. Their son, *Rev. William Symmes*, was ordained to the ministry in 1588; he had two sons, *Zechariah* and William.

SYMMES FAMILY IN AMERICA.

SYMMES Rev. Zechariah[1] was born 5 April 1599 at Canterbury, County Kent, England. He was educated in Emanuel College at the University of Cambridge and graduated with an A.B. 1620. He first preached as a lecturer at the church of St. Atholines in London in July, 1621. In 1625, he removed to Dunstable for nonconformity, where he remained eight years as rector. He married in England; and owing to religious persecutions, he with his wife and seven children came to America on the ship " Griffin," 18 Sept. 1634, in company with Rev. John Lothrop,William Hutchinson and his wife, the famous prophetess. He and his wife were admitted to the church of Boston, 5 Oct. 1634; afterwards to the church at Charlestown, 6 Dec. 1634, and was invited to become teacher of the church there; was ordained 22 Dec. 1636 and filled that position until 1670. He married a second wife Sarah, " whoes goodness exceeded her stature." He was a man of high character, a strong upholder of the truth; very serviceable to the parish and Colony. There was granted to him 300 acres of land on both sides of the Aberjona river, composed of a 279 acre farm " located southwest of Mistic Pond; west from Increase Nowell, since owened by Gov. Everett; to the north was Woburn and to the north-west was E. Converse etc, 11 acres at Barr Medow " in south part of what is now Stoneham. The farm in 1753 was annexed from Charlestown to Medford. Now it is a part of the town of Winchester.   He died at Charlestown, 28 Jan. 1670/1.

CHILDREN:

Children by first wife:

A SON, according to "Mather," b. abt. 1623.

SARAH, b. in London, abt. 1625, m. (1) Rev. Lemuel Haugh, d. 1648; m. (2) 13 Nov. 1662, Rev. John Brock, d. 18 June 1688; d. 27 April, 1681.

William, Capt., bapt. Dunstable, Eng., 10 Jan. 1626/7, m. (1) before 1652, Sarah (?) (d. 1653 at Cambridge ?); m. (2) before 1677, **Mary** (?), d. at Weymouth, 12 March 1720/1; d. suddenly, 22 Sept. 1691.

MARY, bapt. Dunstable, Eng., 16 April 1628, m. (1) 15 Sept. 1652, Thomas Savage, d. 14 Feb. 1681/2; m. (2) Anthony Stoddard, d. 16 March 1687.

ELIZABETH, bapt. Dunstable, Eng., 1 Jan. 1629/30, m. Hezekiah Usher, 2 Nov. 1652; d. after 1654.

HULDAH, bapt. Dunstable, Eng., 18 March 1630/1, m. William Davis, before 1656; d. after 1665 and before 1667.

HANNAH, bapt. Dunstable, Eng., 22 Aug. 1632; d. early.

REBECCA, bapt. Dunstable, Eng., 12 Feb. 1633/4, m. Humphrey Booth.

Second wife:

RUTH, b. at Charlestown, Mass., 18 Oct. 1635, m. Edward Willis, 15 June 1668; d. after 1698.

ZECHARIAH, REV., b. at Charlestown, Mass., 9 Jan. 1637/8, m. (1) 18 Nov. 1669, Susanna Graves, d. 23 July 1681; m. (2) 26 Nov. 1683, Mehitable Dalton; d. at Bradford, Mass., 22 Mar. 1707/8, a. 70 y.

TIMOTHY 1st, b. at Charlestown, Mass., 7 Mar. 1640, d. at Charlestown, 25 Sept. 1641.

DEBORAH, b. at Charlestown, Mass., 28 Aug. 1642, m. Timothy Prout, 13 Dec. 1664; d. 13 March, 1716.

TIMOTHY 2nd, b. at Charlestown, Mass., 1644, m. (1) 10 Dec. 1668, Mary Nichols, d. 18 Sept. 1669; m. (2) 21 Sept. 1671, Elizabeth Norton; d. of smallpox, 14 July 1678, ae. 35 yrs.

SYMMES Capt. William[2] (*Zechariah*[1]), son of Zechariah Symmes by his first wife, was baptized at Dunstable, County Bedford England, 10 Jan. 1626/7.   He had two wives, but date of marriage of either is not known.   He married the first wife Sarah about 1650, (died 1653 at Cambridge (?)), and married the second wife Mary, about 1676.   He inherited his father's farm, which was located in what is now Winchester.   His daughter Sarah was child of his first wife, as his servant John Warner testified that his master was a widower, when this daughter married in 1672. Farmer's Register says that his second wife Mary, when his widow, married the Rev. Samuel Torrey, 30 July 1695. This Mary Torrey, in her will dated 20 March 1720, names Nathaniel Symes as her son. Mentions eldest son, William Symmes of Charlestown, Timothy Symmes of Scituate. She bequeathed " a small Tichen Bed," " a green rugg," " a pair of Sheets," " My Oldest brass kettle, now lent to *my Son-in-Law Joseph Torrey.*" " To my daughter Mary Torrey." " To my daughter *Elizabeth Torrey.*" These are named for various bequests.

According to a Middlesex Probate record William Symmes died suddenly on 22 Sept. 1691.

CHILDREN:
First wife:
SARAH, b. 1652, m. Rev. Moses Fiske of Braintree, 7 Nov. 1672; d. 2 Dec. 1692 ?.

Second wife:
MARY, b. 1677, m. John Torrey of Weymouth, 26 Nov. 1700; d. at Weymouth, 14 Feb. 1758, ae. 81 yrs.

WILLIAM, b. 7 Jan. 1678, m. Ruth Convers, 7 Dec. 1704; d. at Medford, 24 May 1764, ae. 86 yrs.

Elizabeth, b. abt. 1682, m. (1) 24 March 1704/5, Joseph Torrey, d. 22 April 1723; m. (2) 6 Aug. 1724, William Calder.

TIMOTHY, b. 1683, m. Elizabeth (Collomorn) Rose, 31 July 1710; lived at Scituate, d. possibly after 1758, the year of his wife's death there.

ZECHARIAH, b. 168[?], d. 19 Jan. 1707.

NATHANIEL, b. abt. 1690, m. Lydia Holbrook, 10 Dec. 1714; lived in Weymouth, d. after 1731.

TORREY Joseph[3] (*William,*[2] *William*[1]), fourth son of William and Deborah (Greene) Torrey, born (place is not known by me) about 1678. He married 24 March 1704/5, Elizabeth, daughter of William and Mary Symmes of Charlestown. She was born about 1682. He was on record as being " Ensign," and was a trader and active in Weymouth, for he with his brother John and others (according to Weymouth town records of 7 March 1715) " were granted land at Hunts Hill, the lowlands and beach adjoining at the mouth of Fore River, for the carrying on of their Fish Trade to Cape Sable." It is of interest to note that his wife's mother married his uncle the Rev. Samuel Torrey as his

HEADSTONE OF MR. JOSEPH TORREY
Weymouth Heights Cemetery

second wife. This household also had high ideals and were people of culture, learning and piety. In his Will dated 15 April, 1723, he calls himself a " Yeoman." Mentions his wife Elizabeth and further says: " Also I give to my *son Joseph* for his Learning at Collage til he takes his first Degree, that is to say, I give to him one hundred & fifteen Pounds to be pay'd out of my moveable estate, twenty five Pounds per Annum the three first Years & thirty five Pounds ye fourth year of his being at Collage " and also mentions son Zachary and two daughters, Mary and Deborah. The inventory of his estate is dated 5 Aug. 1723 and totals £1240. 9s. 1d. He died 22 April 1723, and is buried at Weymouth Heights Cemetery next his father. (See illustration.)

CHILDREN:

Joseph, b. 19 Oct. 1707 in Weymouth, m. (1) 15 May 1730, **Elizabeth Wilson,** d. 6 May 1746; m. (2) abt. 1748, Elizabeth Fisk, d. 5 July 1780; d. at South Kingston, 25 Nov. 1792, age 85 yrs.

MARY, b. 16 Aug. 1709 in Weymouth, m. John Reed at Weymouth, 20 June 1734; d. at Weymouth, 3 Feb. 1790, age 78 yrs.

DEBORAH, b. 9 Oct. 1711 in Weymouth, m. David Nash at Weymouth, 4 April 1733.

ZACHARIAH, b. 10 May 1717 in Weymouth, removed to Middletown, Conn.

FOURTH GENERATION.

JOSEPH TORREY AND ELIZABETH WILSON.

TEFFT FAMILY.

TEFFT John,[1] was of Portsmouth and Kings Town, Rhode Island, married Mary, whose maiden name is not known. 1655, was a Freeman. 1662, Nov. 22, he and wife Mary sold 7 acres to Robert Skint of Newport, R. I. 1671, in May, was in Kings Town, his name being recorded as an inhabitant of Pettaquamscott. 1674, Nov. 30, he made his will; he names as Executor his *son-in-law Samuel Wilson.* "To son-in-law Samuel Wilson, my now dwelling house and 2 acres in Pettaquamscott. To wife Mary, all cattle vis. two oxen, two cows, two yearling steers, eight swine kind, a ewe and a lamb and all other moveables. To son Samuel Tift 2.s. To son Joshua 1.s. To daughter Tabitha Tift 1.s. and an iron pot after wifes deceas. Debts to the sum of £1.3s to be paid equally by son-in-law Samuel Wilson and son Joshua Teft." 1679, Nov. 19, his widow signed in satisfaction of her third, her signature being witnessed by Tabitha Gardiner. He died Jan. 1676.

CHILDREN:

> **Daughter, name unknown, m. Samuel Wilson.**
> SAMUEL, b. in Providence, 1644, m. Elizabeth Jenkes; d. 1725.
> JOSHUA, b. ———, m. Sarah ———; d. Jan. 14, 1676.
> TABITHA, b. 1653, m. George Gardiner, Feb. 13, 1670; d. in 1722.

WILSON FAMILY.

WILSON Samuel,[1] born 1622, married (1) ——— *Tefft*, daughter of John and Mary Tefft; (2) Elizabeth Sweet, widow of John. He was of Portsmouth and Kings Town, R. I. 1644, May 27, had an addition to his lot granted. 1653, Aug. 2, was on a jury found in the case of Thomas Bradley. 1655, was made a Freeman. 1657, Jan. 20, was in Kings Town, he and others bought of certain Indian Sachems a large tract of land called Pettaquamscut Purchase. 1669–70–78, Conservator of the Peace. 1669, Aug. 19, he and two others were empowered to require Suckquash and Ninecraft to appear before Council Wednesday next at Newport, to give satisfaction, touching the alarm of the country upon suspicion of the Indians plotting to cut off the English. 1670, June 21, he had a letter sent to him by the Commissioners of Connecticut, sitting at Wickford, requesting the delivery of two of their men detained by Thomas Mumford, they being messengers of Connecticut inoffensively riding on the King's highway. he complied and released the men on July 13, 1670. 1684, June 30, an agreement was made by the orphans of Samuel Wilson, with consent of Jired Bull, executor. The eldest brother Samuel Wilson was to have three lots adjoining the housing, with said housing, etc. — part of the land of his father-in-law Tefft. The rest of the land was to go equally to the children, including Samuel and so all of them a share. The agreement was signed by Samuel Wilson and Robert and Mary Hannah. 1694, March 15, a partition of estate was made at this date, signed by Thomas Mumford as guardian of James Wilson, Robert Hannah and wife Mary, John Potter and wife Sarah and by Hannah and Potter in behalf of orphan *Jeremiah*, brother of James. He died in 1682, age 60 years.

CHILDREN:

SAMUEL, b. ———; d. at South Kingston, 1690.

MARY, b. 1663, m. (1) Robert Hannah, d. 1706; m. (2) 1708, George Webb, d. 1735; d. 1737.

SARAH, b. 1666, m. John Potter; d. 1739.

JAMES, b. 1673, m. Alice Sabeere; d. Feb. 1706.

Jeremiah, b. 1674, m. (1) 8 Dec. 1700, Ann Monoxon; m. (2) **Mary;** d. at South Kingston, 2 June 1740.

WILSON Jeremiah[2] (*Samuel*[1]), of New Shoreham, Newport, South Kingstown, R. I., was the son of Samuel Wilson, born in 1674; married 1st Ann Manoxon, 1 Dec. 1700; 2nd Mary (?). His marriage and the births of his three first children were recorded at New Shoreham. " 1706 March 12, calling himself now of Block Island, for future maintaining of love and good will between myself and near relatives, confirms 448 acres that

Robert and Mary Hannah had by deed of partition in 1694, being part of portion that fell to said sister Mary and of which a deed of gift had been given to Robert Hannah and Mary, by Samuel Wilson: elder brother of Jeremiah. Now, therefore, Jeremiah conveys all rights he has either from his father Samuel or brother Samuel or brother James, which are deceased, and privilege of fishing, fowling, hawking, and hunting etc., so long as wood groweth and water runneth." In 1722 was in Newport and made a Freeman the same year. 1740, May 19, he made his will and it was proved June 9, 1740. Executors, wife and son Samuel. " To daughter Mary Robinson wife of Edward of New London Ct., merchant £50. To daughter Ann Mumford wife of William £50. To daughter Sarah Fanning wife of William 20s. and confirmation of house and lot in Newport given by deed, and release of mortgage, but if she die without issue then house and land to my sons Jeremiah and John equally. To *son-in-law Rev. Joseph Torrey* land in South Kingstown and £100. To daughter Judith Wilson £300. To son Samuel, east half of my farm where my dwelling house stands, south part of dwelling house, blacksmith shop two yoke of oxen six cows and two breeding mares, at age. To sons Jeremiah and John all lands in Providence purchased of Daniel Abbott, when they are of age. To sons James and George west half of homestead farm at age, they paying my daughter Alice Wilson £300. To dear and loving wife; north part of dwelling house; garden, and liberty of cutting firewood for life, Negro man Virgie and Woman Phillis, and six cows. To sons Jeremiah and John one hundred sheep, a riding beast to each, and negro Caesar to be sold and Money put at interest for use of Said Jeremiah and John at age. To wife Mary, power to sell certain lands. To daughter *Elizabeth Torrey wife of Rev. Mr. Torrey,* 20s. To Mary Pollock wife of William 20s. To sons Samuel, Jeremiah, John and James and daughters Judith and Alice, rest of the estate equally."

"Inventory: — £1778. 19s. 11d., viz., wearing apparel, £17, plate £4, firelock, £4, books £1. 10s., stillyards, lime kiln £7, 22 cows, 8 calves, 8 oxen, 4 three year, 11 two years, 10 yearlings, 10 horse kind, 14 swine, 5 sucking pigs, 280 sheep, 152 lambs, 2 negro and women £240, 6 years time in mulatto servent Jacob, £35 worsted comb etc."

He died 2 June 1740.

CHILDREN:

MARY, b. 13 Sept. 1701, m. Edward Robinson of New London, Conn.

ANN, b. 7 Dec. 1702, m. William Mumford.

SARAH, b. 5 March 1707, m. (1) William Fanning; m. (2) 1 July 1744, Dr. William Gould, d. 29 Jan. 1757; buried at New London.

Elizabeth, b. 1712, m. **Rev. Joseph Torrey,** 15 Oct. 1730; d. at Kingston, 6 May 1746, ae. 34 yrs.

JUDITH, b. ———. Was not married in 1740.

MARY, b. 13 Nov. 1721, m. William Pollock.

SAMUEL, b. 23 March 1723.

JEREMIAH \
JOHN   } twins, b. 11 May 1726.

JAMES, b. 2 Sept. 1728.

GEORGE, b. 7 Feb. 1730.

ALICE, b. 15 June 1733.

TORREY Rev. Dr. Joseph[4] (*Joseph,*[3] *William,*[2] *William*[1]), first child of Joseph and Elizabeth (Symmes) Torrey, born at Weymouth, Mass., 19 Oct. 1707 and married on 15 Oct. 1730, Elizabeth, daughter of Jeremiah and Mary Wilson, at the home of her father in South Kingston, the ceremony being performed by Rev. Mr. McSparren of the Episcopal Church. His first wife Elizabeth Wilson, from whom comes our line of descent, left six children — she died 6 May 1746. He later married Elizabeth Fisk, who also left children. A probate record of 1725 shows that Joseph Torrey (a minor) appointed John Torrey of Weymouth his uncle to look after his interest in his father's estate. He graduated from Harvard College as an A.B. in 1728. Doubtless he was employed in educational matters, for in May, 1730, he was hired at Weymouth as schoolmaster at £50 per year. Soon he was in South Kingston, R. I., as a practising physician and also filled the church pulpit temporarily. In a deed dated 8 June 1738, he and his brother Zacharia sell a " Tract of land and dwelling house and barn thereon standing situated lying and being in Weymouth, there being 2 acres." He is called " of South Kingston Colony of Rhode Island and Providence Plantation in New England Clerk " (i.e., Minister). Further he states, " having power to sell as will appear in the last Will and Testament of our Honored *Father Joseph Torrey late of Weymouth Dec.*" *Memorandum.* " That *Elizabeth* the wife of the above Joseph Torrey surrendered her right of Dower." Dr. Torrey preached in the church which was founded in 1695, seemingly maintained as a Mission Church by contributions from other churches, the Old South Church of Boston being the principal donor. On 4 Dec. 1731 a committee of four gentlemen wrote to the authorities in Boston requesting that Dr. Torrey be settled over them as a minister. On 17 May 1732 a Congregational Church was organized and on the same day Dr. Torrey was ordained by Rev. Samuel Niles of Braintree who had formerly preached in this parish. I will quote from records of Old South Church giving a glimpse of the early trials of church and pastor. " There was a collection I remember in many of the congregational churches in 1737 to defend a lawsuit unjustly brought against Dr. Torrey to recover the parsonage estate possesed by Mr. Torrey. The estate was left by a gentlemen for the support of an orthodox minister in Kingston, and I remember one Dr. McSparren a church minister took it into his head that no minister was orthodox unless he was ordained by a bishop etc. etc. so by the help of some no better than himself, he brought an action to recover the estate for himself and successors, but he failed in his unjust prosecution. Mr. Torrey received £35. 10s." It is also recorded that Dr. Torrey annually received money from the Old South Church, also from 1731 to 1736 Kings Chapel aided in the maintenance. This church was on " Tower Hill," and the site of the old home is still called " the Torrey Lot." In the Kingston church records copied from " Early Narragansett history," we find a resolution of thanks to Samuel Holden of London for his aid in the lawsuit. Doubtless this as many other colonial affairs had to be settled in England and it is to be inferred that Dr. Torrey gave this name to his son, born at this period, in gratitude for his aid. Miss Caroline Hazard in " Collage Town," her book, remarks: " This Dr. Torrey was an interesting man, a physician both of the body and the soul. The old Presbyterian had a uniform way of reproving his son, a very naught boy, to whom he would say with great emphasis when he behaved amiss. Why! I am ashamed of you John! I am ashamed of you!" And here for 61 years this grand and lovable man lived and worked for the good of his parish and people, leaving a name most honorable in history. His will, made 18 July 1788, is a long and interesting document. He directs his executors to sell his mansion house at Tower Hill

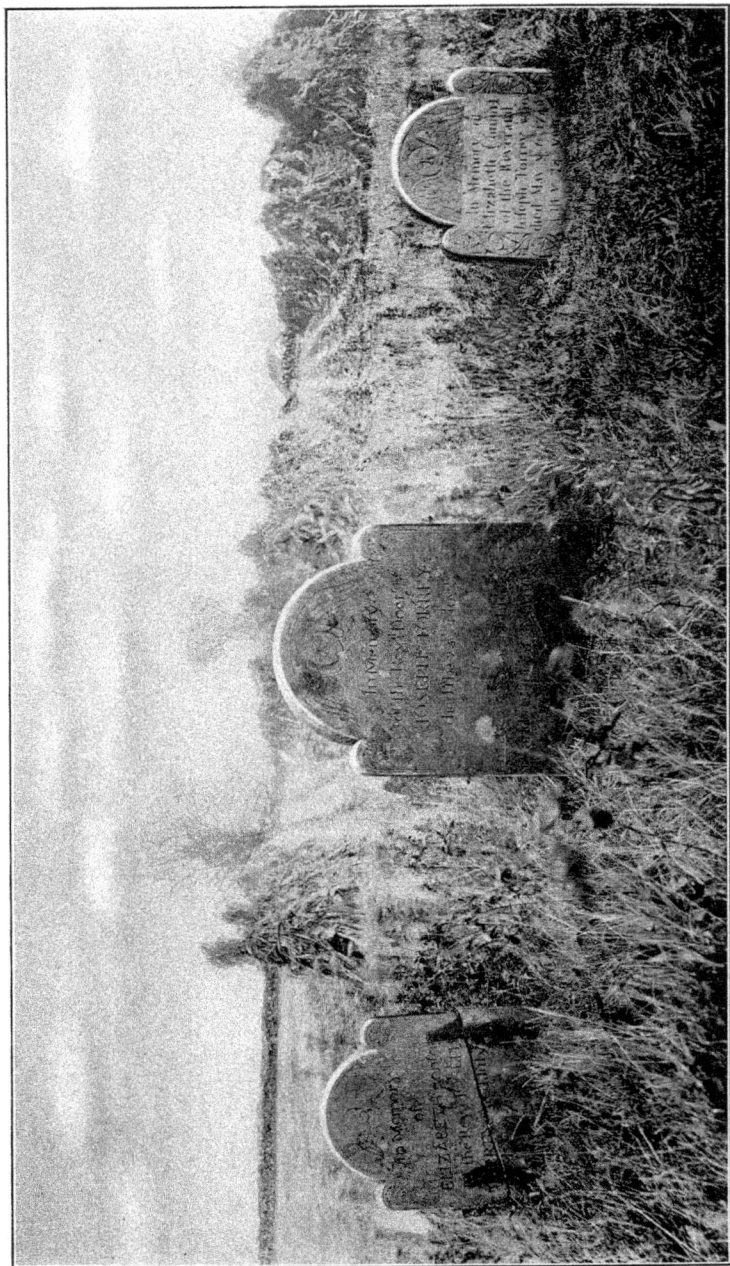

GRAVESTONES OF REV. DR. JOSEPH TORREY

Who died "1791 in the 85th year of his age and the 61st of his ministry," with his two Consorts. Tower Hill, Kingston, R. I.

as soon as possible, gives one half his estate to son Joseph of Killingly, Conn., to his granddaughter Ann Hawkins, 20 milled Spanish dollars, Elizabeth Torrey all his household furniture, John Fisk Torrey, horse, saddle and 50 acres of land in Killingly. His son Joseph he made executor. This shows he left a goodly amount of property and he must have been a thrifty parson. Dr. Torrey died at South Kingston, R. I., 25 Nov. 1792 and lies in the little cemetery upon " Tower Hill," and here we looked with great interest upon the glorious view over the rolling country from this high plateau, and at our feet among the apple trees we found his headstone, with those of his two consorts one upon each side. (See illustration.)

CHILDREN:

First wife:

ELIZABETH 1st, b. 19 July 1731, m. Edward Adams of Killingly, Conn.

JOSEPH JR., b. 4 Feb. 1732/3, m. Hannah Fisk of Killingly, Conn., Dec. 1757; d. at Killingly, 19 Feb. 1804, age 72 yrs.

OLIVER 1st, b. 14 Feb. 1734/5, prob. did not marry; d. at South Kingston, 11 May 1755, age 21 years.

ANN, b. 13 May 1737, m. Thomas Hawkins.

Samuel Holden, b. 1738, m. **Ann Gould** of Branford, Conn., 3 April 1760; d. at Killingly, 1 Dec. 1786, age 48 yrs.

MARY, b. ———, m. Capt. William Pollock.

LUCY, b. ———, m. Rev. John Fisk Osgood at Boston, 11 Oct. 1770.

Second wife:

JOHN FISK, b. abt. 1750, did not marry; d. at Killingly, 1 July 1816, ae. 66 yrs.

OLIVER 2nd, b. 24 March 1756, m. Tamer Davis, 13 Sept. 1784; d. at Killingly, 7 March 1843, age 87 yrs.

WILLIAM, b. 21 Jan. 1764, m. (1) Hannah Plank, d. 5 Aug. 1800; m. (2) Zilpha Davidson, d. 10 Jan. 1866; d. at Killingly, 25 Aug. 1847, age 84 yrs. 7 m. 4 d.

ABIGAIL, b.———, m. ———Wilson, ⎫ Brothers, both removed to Ohio
SARAH, b. ———, m. ——— Wilson ⎭ and both died shortly after.

ELIZABETH, 2nd, b. ———, did not marry; d. at South Kingston, 30 Nov. 1808.

FIFTH GENERATION.

SAMUEL HOLDEN TORREY AND ANN GOULD.

GOULD FAMILY.

Bradfield, Whitehead and Bishop Families.

GOULD Dr. Richard[1] was born in or near North Taunton, Devonshire County, England, 28 April 1662, where the family had valuable estates. Was the first of this family to come to America. Nothing is known of his wife except that her name was Cruft, nor of his children, save William, who later followed his father to America. He settled in Branford, Conn., and quoting from the " Annals of Branford ": " was there in 1700. It is probable that he was the first permanent physician in town. He was much esteemed as is evident from his being elected Tythingman in 1728." Only the most dignified and trusted were chosen to this office in that day. From a manuscript left by his son William we read: " Richard Gould, my honored Father departed this life 23rd April 1746 in the 84th year of his age."

CHILDREN:

William, b. 11 Feb. 1692/3, m. (1) 11 June 1718, Abigail Farrington, d. 25 May 1725; m. (2) 9 Dec. 1725, **Mary Whitehead**, d. 18 Nov. 1743; m. (3) 1 July 1744, Sarah (Wilson) Fanning, d. at New London; d. at Branford, 29 Jan. 1757, a. 64 y.

He may have had other children in this country.*

BRADFIELD FAMILY.

BRADFIELD Lesly.[1] This name is mentioned in the Wethersfield, Conn., records in 1643, and may have been there earlier, and in 1644 settled at Branford, Conn., locating near the shore. He died 26 July 1655, leaving a family. His widow Mary married 2nd George Adams. This is the first marriage on the

---

* A Lieut. Thomas Gould, b. abt. 1689, m. Mary (?), and d. at North Guildford, Conn., 17 June 1746, a. 57 y. May have been a son of Dr. Richard Gould (?).

record. There was a son Samuel and a daughter Maria or Martha. In the records of the Court of Magistrates at New Haven 30th, 4th Mo. 1657, this item is found. " Goodman Addams a man that came to worke at the iron worke who is in treaty of marriage, wth widdow Bradfield of Branford, whose husband dyed aboute two yeares agoe and left her wth two chilldren and an estate amount to some-what above ninety pounds."

CHILDREN:

SAMUEL, b. ——, m. Sarah Graves, 27 June 1667.
MARIA or **Martha**, b. ——, m. **John Whitehead**, 9 March 1661; d. prob. at Branford after 1711.
A DAUGHTER, b. ——, d. 29 July 1655.

WHITEHEAD FAMILY.

WHITEHEAD John,[1] of New Haven and settled in Branford, Connecticut, where he married Martha, daughter of Leslie Bradfield, 1661, March 9 (Branford Land Records), was with his brother Thomas, brought to this country when a mere child by Francis Hall of New Haven at the request of Deacon George Alcocke of Roxbury, Mass., who was uncle to the Whitehead boys; this was in the year 1639. We find in the New Haven records, under date of 1647, Feb. 1, as follows: " John Thompson, atturney for Thomas Allcote in the Baye requirreth youthes of Francis Hall wch he brought from England long since, that is to saye John Whitehead and Thomas Whitehead and saith he hath order to send them to the said Thomas Allcote whoe is ther unkell. Francis Halle saith at the desire of their unkell Mr. Allcote of Roxberey, since deceased, hee brought these youthes over, and was at great charges with them for their passage and other occasions, wch he saith Mr. Allcote promised to paye, to his satisfaction when he came heare, but when he came ther unkell was deade and knew not of whom to seeke his money. — iff the boyes had dyed he should have lost it, for ought he knows, for he knew of no other unkell they had, but he was blamed that he had not used that meanes to find oute ther unkell or send to ther mother as he might have done (thoughe he saith he hath sent), but he acquainted the Courte then wth it and wth ther approbation, one of them was disposed to Mathias Hitchcoke, the other he kept himselfe till they might have further light to dispose of them."

Pope's " Pioneers of Massachusetts," under Thomas Alcock says: " His sister Elizabeth Whitehead of Lemington Priors wrote him 1647, 25, 8 month concerning her sons John and Thomas Whitehead then with Francis Hall of New Haven." The notebook of William Aspinwall is Mr. Pope's authority. The appearance of Mr. Alcock's attorney in New Haven was evidently the result of the said letter.   George Alcock of Roxbury, who died Dec. 30, 1640, was brother of Thomas Alcock who resided at Boston, Mass., in 1647.   Francis Hall's statement, that when he arrived here Mr. George Alcock was dead, is contradicted by the record which shows that Mr. Hall was in New Haven more than a year and a half before George Alcock died.

According to the revised copy of the church records, John Whitehead and Martha B. Whitehead became members of the church in 1653, but of course her name must have been Martha Bradfield at that time, thus showing that the record has been changed since 1653.   He was also one of the parties to the new church covenant in 1667.   He was nominated Freeman 1669, Jan. 19.   In 1682, he with others made choice of their plow land in Branford.   He owned a house and upland at Indian Neck. He died at Branford before the second Monday of June, 1695, when his widow Martha exhibited the inventory of the estate to the county Court at New Haven and was appointed administrator on his estate and the name and age of the eight surviving children were given as follows: *John Whitehead*, oldest, Samuel 23, Eliphalet 21, Thomas 14, Hannah Whitehead 31, Mercy 27, Damaris 25, Elizabeth 18.

The said inventory amounts to £231.-14.-00.   On March 16, 1707, Martha Whitehead " widdow and administrator of the estate of my late husband John Whitehead of Branford, deceased, deeds to her three sons-in-law, Peter Tyler Senr. of Branford, William Luddington of East Haven and Benjamin Howd of Branford two thirds of the homestead.   On March 1, 1707–8 she deeds land to her son-in-law Micah Pamer for part of his wife's portion.   On 3 Jan. 1708, John and Thomas Whitehead, Peter Tyler Senr in right of Hannah his wife, Micah Pamer in right of Dameris his wife, and Benjamin Howd in right of Elizabeth his wife all of Branford and William Luddington of New

Haven in right of Mary his wife, in consideration of our near Love, Goodwill and Dutifull affection to our Dear Mother Martha Whitehead, deed her their right in the house etc." On May 21, 1709, Martha Whitehead deeds land to Hannah Tyler in " Considertion of great care and relief which I have had from my Daughter Hannah, In my long weak desolate condition." 4 Dec. 1711, she deeds land to her son Thomas. Several other deeds appear of record from Martha Whitehead. The names of the children appear both in the land and church records of Branford, the date of the baptism, with one exception, being the same as the date of birth.

CHILDREN:

MARY, b. 6 May 1662. Not included in the names of children appended to the inventory of her father's estate in 1695.

HANNAH, b. 10 March 1664, m. Peter Tyler of Branford, 25 Dec. 1688.

John Jr., b. 20 Feb. 1665/6, m. Mehitable Bishop, 9 Aug. 1704; d. after 3 Jan. 1707/8, before 1st Monday in March (1), 1707/8.

MARTHA, changed to MERCY, b. 10 Jan. 1667/8, m. William Luddington of East Haven, Conn., June, 1690; d. 23 Nov. 1743, a. 75 y.

DAMARIS, b. 20 Jan. 1669/70, m. Micah Pamer of Branford, 14 Feb. 1693; d. before 29 Oct. 1714.

SAMUEL, b. 24 Nov. 1672. Had been absent about 8 years in 1708 and "not known to be living," but was included in his brother John's estate in 1714.

ELIPHALET, b. 27 Sept. 1674, m. left no issue; d. after 2nd Monday in June (10), 1695, before 1st Monday in March (1st), 1707/8.

ELIZABETH, b. Oct. 1677, m. Benjamin Howd of Branford, 1 Oct. 1705.

THOMAS, b. 27 Feb. 1680/1.

BISHOP FAMILY.

BISHOP John[1] came in the first ship (" St. John ") that came direct from England to New Haven, Conn. He was at Guildford, 1639, and died there before 7 Jan. 1661, when the inventory of his estate was taken. The will of his wife Ann is dated 20 June 1673. She calls herself " widow, notices her son John Bishop; grand-daughter Elizabeth Hubbard; noticed her old servent Tho's Smith." She gave most of her estate to be " divided betwixt her three children John and *Stephen* Bishop and James Steele," and made James Steele, her son-in-law, sole executor and gave him " £6 over and above his third part of all her estate in this country and in England." The inventory of her estate was dated 1 May 1676, and amounted to £81. 9s. 7d. A part of her property was at Hartford, but the larger share of it was at Guildford at her decease.

CHILDREN:

JOHN, b. in England, m. Susanna Goldham, 13 Dec. 1650; d. prob. at Guildford, Oct. 1683.

Stephen, b. in England, m. **Tabitha Wilkinson,** 4 May 1654; d. at Guildford, 1 Aug. 1690.

A DAUGHTER, prob. Bethia or Ann, b. ———, m. James Steele, 18 Oct. 1651.

Possibly another daughter, b. ———, m. (George ?) Hubbard.

BISHOP Stephen[2] (*John*[1]) was the second son of John and Ann Bishop; he was born in England and married Tabitha Wilkinson, 4 May 1654. He died at Guildford, 1 Aug. 1690, and his widow died 21 Dec. 1692. The six living children being mentioned in the wills of both father and mother.

CHILDREN:

STEPHEN, b. 20 Dec. 1655.

TABITHA, b. 14 Sept. 1657, m. Nathaniel Foot, before 1696; d. 1715 a. 57 y.

CALEB, b. 24 Jan. 1660.

David, b. 8 Dec. 1663; d. young.

Mehitable, b. 12 Sept. 1668, m. **John Whitehead,** 9 Aug. 1704; d. after 1707/8.

HANNAH, b. 27 March 1671; d. young.

JOSIAH, b. 20 March 1674; d. young.

EBENEZER, b. 5 Aug. 1675.

JAMES, b. 18 Aug. 1678.

WHITEHEAD John Jr.[2] (*John*[1]) was the son of John and Martha (Bradfield) Whitehead, and was born at Branford, Conn., 20 Feb. 1665/6. He married *Mehitable,* daughter of Stephen and Tabithe (Wilkinson) *Bishop,* 9 Aug. 1704. She was born 12 Sept. 1668. He was the eldest son and died before the estate of his father was settled, as is shown from the following, dated the first March 1707/8. " Administration on the estate of John Whitehead, late of Branford deceased granted to Mehitable, widow, relict of the dec'd XXX ordered to make an inventory — by reason that her said husband being eldest son, and Thomas Whitehead have not recd. their portions of their father's estate John Whitehead senr. Formerly of said Branford decd XXX. The court being certified by receipts under ye hands of Peter Tiler, Benjamin Howd, William Luddington, and Michael Pamer in right of their wives, that they have received their full portion of the inventoried estate of their father said John Whitehead Senior deceased, and also their portion of their brother Eliphalet Whitehead since deceased do order; that all the residue of the real inventoried estated (except the widow's dower sett off and lands allotted to said four daughters) be divided by three free-holders of Branford, a double share thereof to the heirs of *John Whitehead decd., son of John Whitehead Senior*, and one single share to said Thomas Whitehead, and for as much as Samuel Whitehead, son to sd. John Whitehead Senr. decd. hath been absent about 8 year and not known to be living or dead, if he happen to return must be considered by an equal portion with the rest, etc." The final distribution of the estate of John White-head Jr. is recorded under date of " 29 Oct. 1714, John Russell, Uzall Wardwell and Edward Frisbie dividers, when Thomas, Samuel, Elizabeth Howd, Hannah Tyler and Mercy Luddington are given their portion direct, the remainder being given to the legal representatives of John and Damaris." He died at Branford after 3 Jan. 1707/8 and before the 1 March 1707/8.

Prob. only child:

Mary, b. at Branford, 3 Nov. 1705, m. **William Gould** at Branford, 9 Dec. 1725; d. at Branford, 18 Nov. 1743.

GOULD Dr. William[2] (*Richard*[1]). Quoting from a manuscript in the handwriting of Dr. William Gould,[2] we read that he was " born 11 Feb. 1692/3 in North Taunton, of the family of Cruft, in the Parish of Oak Hampton in the County of Devon or Devonshire Old England." He married for his first wife, Abigail Farrington (born Dennison), 11 June 1718 and they also came to America, but several years later than the father, and also settled in Branford, Conn. This wife died 25 May 1725, aged, 26 years, and is buried at Branford. He then married 2nd *Mary*, daughter of John and Mehitable (Bishop) *Whitehead*, 9 Dec. 1725. She was born at Branford 3 Nov. 1705, and was the mother of all his children. She died 18 Nov. 1743. He married for 3rd wife widow Sarah Fanning (born Wilson), 1 July 1744 and she it was who reared the younger children.

Dr. Gould was a man of much learning and a respected physician and during the early years of his medical practice in Branford was contemporary with his father, Dr. Richard Gould.[1]   He became the owner of much landed property in Branford; tracts of land on Pave Street and Hopyard Plain, once owned by him, still bear the family names as owners.   In his last Will and Testament, probated at Guilford, Conn., 4 April 1757, by his wife Sarah and his son William, his property is put down as £3257. 8s. 11¼ d. £1151 being personal estate.   In the cemetery at Branford on his tombstone we read:

> " In Memory
> of Dr William
> Gould Esquire
> Who departed
> this Life Jan[r] 29
> 1757 Aged 63
> Years 11 Months
> & 18 days."

CHILDREN:

JOHN, b. 2 Oct. 1726, m. and had issue; d. at sea, 6 April 1754, a. 28 y.

WILLIAM, DR., b. 17 Nov. 1727, m. (1) Mary———, d. 8 July 1750; m. (2) 11 Dec. 1751, Mary Maltbie, d. ———; m. (3) a dau. of Richard Gray of Branford, Conn.; d. at Branford, 29 July 1805.

THOMAS, b. 14 April 1730.

MARY, b. 27 June 1732, m. Joseph Brockway, 11 Jan. 1753.

ABIGAIL, b. 29 July 1734.

WHITEHEAD, b. 13 Feb. 1736.

ANNA 1st, b. 1 May 1738; d. 16 June 1738.

Anna 2nd, b. 9 Jan. 1740, m. **Samuel Holden Torrey,** 3 April 1760; d. at Killingly, Conn., 4 Nov. 1822, a. 83 y.

MEHITABLE 1st, b. 6 Aug. 1741, d. 13 Aug. 1741.

MEHITABLE 2nd, b. 10 Jan. 1742, d. 2 May 1742.

We here divert from the direct line of descent to introduce **Dr. William Gould,**[3] (*William*[2], *Richard*[1]), born 17 Nov. 1727, who followed the profession of his father, and was a man of great influence in his native town, had a commission from the Government to conduct a Smallpox Hospital, — wishing to record the life of his third son **James Gould,**[4] (William,[3] William,[2] Richard,[1]) by his third wife, daughter of Richard Grey of Branford,

Conn. James Gould was graduated from Yale College in 1791, on which occasion he delivered the Latin Salutatory, then the highest honor for the graduating class. In 1793 he was appointed Tutor of Yale College. Among his pupils were the Hon. Henry Baldwin, Judge of the Supreme Court of the United States, the Rev. Lyman Beecher, etc. In May 1816, Mr. Gould was appointed Judge of the Superior and Supreme Court of Errors of Connecticut, with the title of LL.D. Judge Gould was one of the most finished and competent writers who have ever treated upon the subject of Jurisprudence. As a lawyer he was one of the most profoundly philosophical of his age. He, with his associate Judge Tappen Reeves, founded the " Litchfield School of Law," and to them flocked from every part of the Union the youths who were to shape the Jurisprudence of their respective States. Here might be seen Calhoun, Clayton, Mason, Loring, Woodbury, Hall, Ashley, Phelps, and a host of others who were preparing themselves for the high places of the Cabinet, the Senate, and the bench. Judge James Gould married Oct. 1798, Sally McCurdy Tracy, eldest daughter of the Hon. Uriah Tracy of Litchfield, Conn., by whom he had eight sons and one daughter.

The above graphic paragraphs were copied from the Gould records and sent me by John C. Morgan of Rushville, N. Y., to whom I am also indebted for much valuable data.

TORREY Dr. Samuel Holden[5] (*Joseph,*[4] *Joseph,*[3] *William,*[2] *William*[1]), son of Joseph and Elizabeth (Wilson) Torrey, was born at South Kingston, R. I., 1738, and married Anna, daughter of William and Mary (Whitehead) Gould, 3 April 1760. Their first home was doubtless in Branford, Conn.; to substantiate this assumption I here insert extracts of copies of deeds of land found among old family papers and loaned me by Clara Morgan. " Deed of land Branford, County of New Haven, Colony of Connecticut. To Samuel Holden Torrey, From Philemon Robbins and Hannah Robbins, sum £150 dated 27 March 1761," and another " Deed of land in Branford in New Haven County; Colony of Connecticut. To Anne Torrey wife of Samuel H. Torrey, from William Gould sum £178:15 shillings dated 17 Sept. 1761 " — evidently adjoining lands to make the Branford home. They soon removed, however, to Killingly, Conn., as shown by deed from Isiah Cady, dated 6 April 1767. Quoting from " The History of Windham County, Conn.," by Richard M. Baylies, published in 1889. " The Joseph Cady Farm, east of Putnam Village (now owned by Eli Davis), was noted for producing a remarkable variety and quantity of medicinal herbs and roots much used by the Medicine Men of the Indians. — It is traditionally reported that Indians came from a great distance to gather these herbs, and that in consequence this locality was made a sacred haven, where no bloodshed was lawful, and tribal foes might meet in safety." Again, from the same authority we read: " Killingly Hill has now received another practising physician, Doctor Samuel Holden Torrey, son of the famous Dr. Joseph Torrey of South Kingston, R. I. His young wife Anna Gould of Branford, brought with her four slaves as part of her marriage portion." Family tradition gives mention, that when she went for an airing in her chaise they trotted by its side. My mother used to relate as one of her choicest bits of history, that " Grandmother Ann Gould was attended at church by a woman slave to carry her Fan and fan her." Ann Gould was born in Branford, Conn., 9 Jan. 1740, being the eighth of the ten children born to William Gould,[2] by his second wife Mary Whitehead; his first wife was Abigail Farrington, who died very soon after marriage and of whom our only souvenir is the Old Hair Trunk with steel nail letters, " A. F.," and date " 1710 " thereon, which is now in our possession, having been cherished as a precious souvenir in the home of Ann Gould Torrey. From her comes the tradition that it was used as a medicine chest and more than once was sent to England and returned with said commodities. We also have a handsome Highboy, of the Jacobean period (see illustration), which constituted a part of her marriage outfit, used by her during her long life in Killingly, and bequeathed to us in the will of one of her immediate family. The Gould family was one of much wealth and culture and doubtless Ann Gould received an excellent education and the advantages of good society in a home of refinement. Dr. Torrey was endowed with a much more thorough medical training than was common at that period, having studied several years with his father-in-law, Dr. William Gould of Branford, who had received his training in England. Dr. Torrey was an esteemed and successful physician in Killingly, where he lived on the " Home Farm," and at his early death, which occurred 1 Dec. 1786, in his 48th year, he left his widow

HIGHBOY AND HAIR TRUNK, ANNA GOULD TORREY

with six sons and much property. We can in no better way give accurate glimpses of customs and conditions of the period than by inserting the following " Lease and Contract," also her will in her own hand writing.

"Anne Gould Torrey (widow of Dr. Samuel Holden Torrey) and her son William Gould Torrey," who lived on the " Home Farm." " Ann Torrey leases it to William her son, with stipulation that all Farming Tools, Horse or Mare, oxen etc. shall be kept in good order, he to have use of one half of farm. To give to said Anne $7\frac{1}{2}$ pounds of good Marketable Sheeps Wool before 10 June 1798, — also to let said Anne have one Hog to kill, also one good fat sheep to be killed in the fall of the year for her sole use, also to find said Anne with fire-wood, cut fit for the fire at the Dore, — also to assist in making fires, — also Ten dollars in money — also enjoins said William to improve said farm according to the Rules of good Husbandry. — To return all as per Inventory prevsiously mentioned without fraud. Killingly 5 April 1798, signed William Gould Torrey, Anne Torrey. witness Erastus Torrey. — " In her will which is of much interest to us and dated Killingly, 15 Jan. 1817, we read: " After my decease then I give to my son Samuel's daughter Anne, my black damask Gown and russet Petticoat. Then I give to my son William G. Torrey's son Holden, one silver spoon and one large pewter Platter and (Mr. Gare's ?) Sermons — I give to my son Oliver's daughter Anne my Red cloak, to Sukey* my black silk Gown, and diaper Tablecloth. Then I give to my Son Erastus my best bed counterpane and curtains and large hammared Platter and six Plates, — I likewise give his daughter Gracia a gold necklace, one silver spoon and my blue cheniel Gown, togeather with (Nanrs ?) Dialogues, — Then I give my son Augustus my looking Glass, and to his son Augustus one silver spoon: Then I give to my son William Gould Torrey my second bed and bedding, — The remainder of my property to be divided by my heirs as they think proper. — William, Augustus, and Erastus, I consider as my proper heirs to that part of my estate not now befor disposed of, signed Anne Torrey. Witnesses, Hannah Bishop, Susan T. Bishop, Olivers daughter Clarissa, purpal (Wrlebove ?) Gown." Ann Gould Torrey died 4 Nov. 1822.

In 1875, visiting the old Killingly Cemetery, after much search

* "Sukey," was my mother.

we found two old headstones, overturned and buried in weeds and brambles; they were to the memory of Dr. Samuel and Mrs. Anna Torrey.   It was my pleasure to put in perfect order and condition, these two headstones, reset with cement in a new base and they doubtless will endure for many years.   They proved to be very costly and elaborate stones and I felt fully repaid when I reflected that Anne Gould would be grateful to " Sukey's " daughter for this slight act of filial love.   (See illustration.) We visited the old Farm, but another house had replaced their home and I gazed reverently over the scenes where was spent the lives of these my immediate ancestors, convinced that in no way could we better realize their former being and existence, than to in person visit their lands, homes, and their graves.

CHILDREN:

SAMUEL HOLDEN, JR., b. 21 Jan. 1761, m. Judith Larned abt. 1785; d. at Killingly, 12 Jan. 1813, age 52 years.

OLIVER 1st, b. 15 Feb. 1764; d. prob. at Branford, Nov. 1766.

WILLIAM GOULD, b. 1 June 1766, m. (1) Sarah ———, d. 10 Dec. 1799; m. (2) Lois Holms, d. 13 March 1816; d. at Killingly, 9 Sept. 1849, age 84 yrs.

Oliver 2nd, b. 18 Dec. 1768, m. **Sabra Freeman**, 10 June 1792; d. at Hopewell, N. Y., 14 Aug. 1820, age 52 yrs.

JOSEPH 1st, b. 9 Feb. 1771; d. prob. at Killingly, 25 Oct. 1773.

JOSEPH 2nd, b. 12 Nov. 1775; d. at Killingly, 17 Aug. 1792, age 17 yrs.

AUGUSTUS, DR.,* b. 4 May 1778, m. (1) Mercy Freeman, 11 Oct. 1807; m. (2) Mrs. Susan Gates; removed to Canandaigua, N. Y., and died there 5 Dec. 1858, age 80 yrs.

ERASTUS, DR.,* b. 13 Feb. 1780, m. Gracia Chase, 1805; d. at Winsor, Vt., 10 Nov. 1828, age 48 yrs.

* These two brothers graduated from Dartmouth College.

HEADSTONES OF DR. SAMUEL HOLDEN AND ANNA TORREY
"Old Killingly Cemetery," Putnam, Conn.

CONTENTS

SIXTH GENERATION.

OLIVER TORREY AND SABRA FREEMAN.

NOYES FAMILY.

NOYES Peter,[1] born in England, about 1591, was of Sudbury 1639. Came in the ship "Confidence," 24 April 1638, from Southampton, aged 47 with son Thomas age 15, daughter Elizabeth and three servants, is called a "yeoman" in the customhouse records, but after arrival here is called "gentleman." He was of Penton in County Hants, which is near Andover, England. Went home after a short visit or exploration here; well pleased with what he saw at Watertown and next year he came again in the "Jonathan" with Nicholas, Dorothy, Abigail and Peter, all probably his children and also with possibly three more servants as he paid for their passages. He and his son Thomas are found on a list in the Sudbury town records, as being early granters or settlers who went to the Sudbury Plantation about 1639. He is mentioned as highway surveyor, 1639. He had shared in the first division of lands in the town, and again in second and third, that were made in 1640. He was a Freeman, 1640. In 1642 the records show that he was maintaining a Ferry; the same year, with others, "are impowered to build a bridge across the river." In 1648 " was to see people joyne in Marriage in Sudbury" — and was Selectman 18 years. Representative 1640–41 and 1650, and was Deacon of the church there. In the Will of "Peeter Noise" of Sudbury, dated 22 Sept. 1657, proved 6 Oct. 1657, mentions "lands lying in the Parish of Andevoe in the county of Southm, called the Breaches," are "settled on eldest son Thomas Noyse," also mentions "two sons Peeter Noys and Joseph Noyse," and "three daughters, *Elizabeth*, wife of Josiah Haynes, *Dorothy*, wife of John Haynes and Abigail, wife of Thomas Plimpton," and "To Mary Noyse, my daughter-in-law the wife of my son Thomas," and "Kinsman Shadrach Habgood." He died at Sudbury, 23 Sept. 1657.

CHILDREN:

THOMAS, b. in England, 1623, m. Mary Haynes before 1657; d. at Sudbury, 7 Dec. 1666.

Elizabeth, b. in England; m. (1) abt. 1643, **John Freeman,** d. abt. 1648; m. (2) 13 Nov. 1649, Josiah Haynes, d. 1698; d. between 1669 and 1698.

NICHOLAS, b. in England. Not mentioned in his father's will of 1657.

Dorothy, b. in England, m. **John Haynes,** 13 Oct. 1642; d. at Sudbury, 8 Apr. 1715.

ABIGAIL, b. in England, m. Thomas Plympton.

PETER, b. in England, m. Elizabeth Darrel at Sudbury, 30 Nov. 1654.

JOSEPH, DEACON, b. ———, m. (1) at Sudbury, 12 Nov. 1662, Mary Darvell, d. 24 Sept. 1677; m. (2) at Sudbury, 14 July 1680, Mary Willard, d. 28 Dec. 1715; d. at Sudbury, 16 Nov. 1717.

FREEMAN FAMILY.

FREEMAN John.[1] By the English admiralty records it appears that there were several bearing the name of John Freeman registered as intending passage in the ship "Abigail," 1635. The "John, husbandman, ae. 35, Jo ae. 9 and Sycillae ae. 4," mentioned there were children of said John and that the "Maria ae. 50," also mentioned was his sister. It has been conjectured, with a probability amounting nearly to certainty, that it was he who is reported as original proprietor of Sudbury, 1639. Who he married we are unable to say, except her Christian name was Elizabeth, as found by the Birth Records of Sudbury (perhaps daughter of Peter Noyes of Sudbury ?),* and she may have been a second wife. In 1643 John Freeman is mentioned in the Sudbury town records in connection with taking the invoice of the Meeting House. He died about 1648 and we find the marriage of Elizabeth Freeman to Josiah Haine at Sudbury, 13 Nov. 1649. This is no doubt John Freeman's widow.*

CHILDREN:

First wife:

JOHN, b. in England abt. 1626.

SYCILLAE, b. in England abt 1631.

* In the will of Peter Noyes dated 1657 and proved 1657 he mentions "My daughter Elizabeth Haines wife of Josiah Haines," while in the Will of Josiah Haynes, his wife is not mentioned but refers to her two children by her first husband (John Freeman) viz., "Joseph Freeman and Elizabeth Gates wife of Thomas Gates" and calls them "Son and daughter-in-law."

Second wife:

Joseph, b. 29 March 1645 at Sudbury, m. **Dorathy Haynes,** 6 May 1680; d. at Preston, Conn., 2 Feb. 1697/8.

James, b. 10 June 1647 at Sudbury; d. 18 June 1647.

Elizabeth, b. 23 June 1648 at Sudbury, m. Thomas Gates, 6 July 1670; d. prob. at Preston, Conn.

HAYNES FAMILY.

HAYNES John. His marriage to Alice Lambert 23 Oct. 1575 is found on the Sherburn, Dorcet register and which may be the marriage of Walter Haynes' parents. The following is a copy of the Will of Alice Haynes, widow of Semley, Co. Wilts, England, and dated 20 March 1620. "It: I give to Suffraine Hayne my best bore cloth and an apon and Marie Hayne a pillow-ber and one Pewter dish, and Elizabeth Hayne a Pewter dish and Suffraine a Pewter dish. It: My Sonn *Walter Hayne* shall have the use of my bigest brass pann during his life, wch pann I give to Thomas Hayne his sonn and my silver spoon. It: I bequeth to Walter Hayne my sonn the half years p'fitt of my tenement after my decease whom I make and ordaine to be my whole Executor to whom I bequethe all the rest of my goods." Inventory is dated 1623.

HAYNES Walter.[1] The following, dated "Southamton 24 April 1638," is from a list of names of passengers of the ship "Confidence," intended for New England. "Walter Haynes, Sutton mandifield, Co. of Wilts, Linnen Weaver, age 55, Eliza his wife, Thomas, John, Josiah, their sonnes under 16 years of age, Suffrance, and Mary, their daughters, beside 3 servants." Most of the passengers of the "Confidence" settled at Sudbury, Mass. He is found in a list from the town records of Sudbury, as being of the early granters or settlers who went to the Sudbury Plantation about 1638 or 1639. He was a prominent person in the community and had a house by the meadow margin when in 1676 it was used as a garrison and which early in town history was called " Mr. Haynes old house." He was made a freeman 13 May 1641, and was a Representative for the years 1641–44–48–51, Selectman for ten years. His will of 25 May 1659 and Proved 4 Apr. 1665 mentions his wife Elizabeth, son Thomas, who is away from home, and never married; *John*, who is made executor; and Josiah, daughters Suffrance, wife of Josiah Treadaway;

Mary, wife of Thomas Noyes, beside a daughter, Goard and son-in-law Roger Goard to which he devises a tenement at Shaston in Dorsetshire. This family uniformly spell the name with an *i* instead of a *y*, thus, "Haines." The Inventory of his estate amounted to £495:18:10. His wife died at Sudbury, 15 June 1659. He died probably at Sudbury, 14 Feb. 1664/5.

CHILDREN:

SUFFRANCE,* b. in England before 1620, m. Josiah Threadway.

MARY,* b. in England, before 1620, m. (1) before 1657, Thomas Noyes, d. 7 Dec. 1666; m. (2) —— Bacon.†

ELIZABETH,* b. in England before 1620, m. Roger Goard in England, d. prob. in England.

THOMAS,* b. in England before 1620. Never married.

John,‡ b. in England about 1621, m. **Dorothy Noyes**, 13 Oct. 1642; d. 6 March 1697.

JOSIAH,‡ b. in England; m. Elizabeth (Noyes ?†) Freeman, 13 Nov. 16[49]; d. between 31 Jan. and 4 July 1698.

HAYNES John² (*Walter¹*), son of Walter and Elizabeth Haynes, born in England about 1621, was brought to this country by his father in 1638. He married at Sudbury, Mass., Dorothy, daughter of Peter Noyes, 13 Oct. 1642. She was born in England. He was a Freeman in 1646, was a representative in 1669. John Haynes was selectman 18 years and Deacon of the church at Sudbury, he lived and died there, and I believe all of his children were born there. His will is dated 1 Oct. 1692 and prob. 19 April 1697 in which he mentions by name his married

---

* All these children were born in England before the Will of Alice Haynes (mother to the above Walter Haynes) was drawn in 1620.

† In the Will of Josiah Haynes dated 31 Jan. and Prob. 4, July 1698. He mentions "Son-in-law" (i.e., Step-son) Joseph Freeman and daughter-in-law Elizabeth Gates, wife of Thomas Gates, and also refers to land in Preston. His wife is not mentioned. It has been conjectured that she was the widow of John Freeman; this would seem to me to prove it. (See Articles on John Freeman and Peter Noyes.) He also mentions sister Mary Bacon, which gives us the added information that his sister Mary had married again after the death of Thomas Noyes in 1666.

‡ These two boys were born in England between the year of Alice Haynes Will 1620 and 1638 the date of the above Walter Haynes' arrival in America.

children: John, Peter, Elizabeth, Mary, *Dorothy* and Son James, also mentions "My now wife Dorothy," Son David and two daughters Rachel and Ruth. Administration granted to Dorothy Haines and David Haines, dated 29 March 1697. The inventory of the estate of Deacon John Haines, "who died ye six^t of March Anno Domo 1697," and the total amounted to £556 : 15 : oo.

CHILDREN:

ELIZABETH, b. 19 July 1644, m. Henry Balcom of Charlestown, 12 Aug. 1666. A widow Balcom d. at Sudbury, 20 Nov. 1715.

JOHN, CAPT., b. 6 May 1649, m. Ruth Roper at Sudbury, 19 June [16]83, d. at Sudbury, 11 Dec. 1710.

MARY, b. ———. A Mary Haynes married Josiah How at Sudbury, 18 May 1671.

Dorothy, b. 1651, m. **Joseph Freeman**, 6 May 1680; d. at Preston, Conn., 26 Jan. 1697/8.

PETER, b. 7 April 1654, m. Elizabeth Rice, 2 Jan. 1677.

RACHEL, b. 12 Feb. 1655, m. John Lochard of Sudbury.

JOSEPH, b. 7 Sept. 1656. (Killed in youth by a fall from a tree.)

THOMAS, b. 1658; d. at Sudbury, 30 May 1683.

JAMES, b. 17 March 1660/1, m. Sarah Noyes, 21 Dec. 1689; d. at Sudbury, 15 Oct. 1732.

DANIEL, b. 16 May 1663. He died a soldier in 1688.

RUTH, b. 7 April 1668, m. Joseph Noyes at Sudbury, 20 Dec. 1693; d. at Sudbury, 20 May 1727.

DAVID, b. 4 May 1670, m. Tabitha Stone of Framingham.

FREEMAN Joseph (Sergt.),[2] (*John*[1]), was the son of John and Elizabeth (Noyes) Freeman, born in Sudbury, Mass., 29 March 1645. He married 6 May 1680 at Sudbury, Dorothy, daughter of John and Dorothy (Noyes) Haynes. She was born 1651. He became a prominent man, first settled at Stow, Mass., and afterward at Preston, Conn. The first record we find of him dated 26 March 1677 in the Sudbury Town Records, is as follows: "Jos. Freeman with others are given liberty to build a saw-mill on Upper Hop Brook." He was a Freeman in 1678. From a document dated 1681, we learn that he with others were owners of twelve original lots drawn in the town of Stow. On 9 April 1683 he with four others were chosen the first Selectmen of Stow. In 1684 he is on a committee to purchase a tract of land " for them selves and for all the rest of the English proprietors therof;

giving them the full power to treat with and purchase the same of the Indians; proprietors of the said tract of land to satisfy & pay them for their natural ancient & hereditary rights title & interest therunto." He was representative to the General Court from Sudbury 1691.

He soon removed to Preston, Conn., that part now called Griswold, and bought a farm, a description of which now follows: " The Old Freeman Farm, in Griswold, Conn. — On 5 May 1692 the heirs of Christopher Huntington, deceased, of Norwich Conn. sold to Joseph Freeman, better known as Sergeant Joseph Freeman, and Josiah Haynes both of ' Sudbrough,' Mass., a tract of land in Preston, Conn. bounded on the west by the Norwich line, containing 250 acres. This tract was nearly in the form of a square with the northeast corner gouged out and measured 240 rods on the west side and 232 rods on the south side. — (See No. 1 on Map, p. 124.) In 1698 Sergeant Joseph Freeman died and his two sons John and Joseph inherited his part of the land above mentioned. In 1703 Josiah Haynes executor of Sargent Freeman's Will bought for the sons John and Joseph all the land between the Norwich line, which was their west bound and the Quinebaug river, comprising some 150 acres. — (See No. 3 on Map.) In 1709 Josiah Haynes conveyed to John and Joseph his half of the original tract, which he and Sargeant Joseph bought together. Sometime during these years it is presumed but just when and through whom is not known, the Freemans acquired the territory gouged out of their Northeast corner, before mentioned, making the Freeman land a block nearly in the form of a parallelogram and covering a full square mile. — (See No. 2 on Map.) On Feb. 3, 1710/11 John and Joseph divided their farm by an east and west line which ran a part of the way on the path between their two houses (this must have been the lane mentioned later). Joseph was to have the south side and John to have the north side of this line. On the north side of the lane which ran from what is now the main road to the fording place in the river, stood the old Freeman house. It was standing when I was a boy and I remember it well. It was built on the brow of the hill and overlooked goodly portions of three towns. It was a large one story house and when I knew it, was considered the oldest house in the community. It had a large stone chimney in the center and a gambrelled roof, the gables

TOPOGRAPHICAL MAP OF A SECTION OF GRISWOLD, CONN., WITH A PLAN
OF FREEMAN FARM

facing to the east and west. The windows contained many small panes of glass and over the front door which was in the center of the south side was a row of panes of glass, each swelled out in the center with what we called a dimple. This little window furnished light for the entry. Nearly on the east of the house as I remember it was the well, which then and since has played an important part in supplying the farm with water. In front of the house and on the south side of the lane were two ancient and magnificent elms, which are still standing, although somewhat decayed. A few years ago the largest of these trees measured around the trunk 23 feet and cast a shadow at noonday of more than a hundred feet in diameter. Both Sargeant Joseph and his sons owned other tracts of land besids this mentioned in the vicinity."

The above graphic description was kindly communicated to me by Daniel L. Phillips, Historian of the town of Griswold. Sergeant Joseph Freeman soon became a person of note and distinction in the community for he was sent as Representative from Preston in the years of 1695 and 1697. His wife Dorothy died at Preston, 26 Jan. 1697/8, and he died there 2 Feb. 1697/8. In the Inventory of Sergt. Joseph Freeman of Preston, dated 20 Feb. 1706/7 there is mentioned among other items " A new Grant lot in Sudbury called ye Iron Grant." " Ten shillings given by my father Haynes Will." "A bill from Peter Haynes of Sudbury." The total amount being £67 : 08 : 00.

CHILDREN:

> JOHN, b. in Sudbury, 16 Mar. 1680/1, m. Abigail Witter in Preston, 5 Feb. 1706/7; d. between 3 June and 7 Aug. 1725.
> Joseph, b. in Sudbury, 18 Dec. 1684, m. **Hannah Brewster** in Preston, 2 Dec. 1708; d. in Preston 12 May 1733.
> DOROTHY, b. in Sudbury, 4 Aug. 1687.
> ELIZABETH, b. in Sudbury, 25 Oct. 1690, m. Daniel Brewster in Preston, 8 Aug. 1710; d. 2 June 1757.

BREWSTER FAMILY.

BREWSTER William,[1] the famous Elder, claims of liberal Christians everlasting gratitude as the earliest of distinguished Puritan laymen in England. Came in the " Mayflower," 1620, with his wife, two younger sons and the wife of the eldest son and

her oldest son William. He was born 1563 (probably, but earlier
by some computators) at Scrooby in Nottinghamshire at the
Manor Hall of which village belonged to the Archbishop of York,
he afterwards long resided in the same house at which Cardinal
Wolsey had made his last stop, before reaching home in his final
journey, on compulsory retirement from court after banishment
by King Henry VIII, thirty years earlier.   His father, probably
William, was tenant under liberal lease from Archbishop Sandys,
and the son was educated some time at Cambridge University
and his father became, as subtenant of Scrooby Manor, the pos-
sessor of that very residence of the Cardinal, and the son therein
worshiped God, according to the simple forms of the chief
protestants of Protestantism.   After very honorable service with
Davison, Secretary of Queen Elizabeth, he partook in the fall of
that statesman, the consequence·of the Queen's heartless de-
ception and treachery; and abandoned in 1587 political life and
devoting himself for many years to religion, he was the first
prominent layman to reject conformity to the ceremony of
the Church of England. He was in the employment of the
Crown, however, as postmaster before 15 April 1594 at Scrooby
about a dozen years after leaving London; there he married the
wife Mary. With his young friend Bradford (after a dozen
years to be made Governor of New Plymouth) and others; he
passed about 1607 or 8 into Holland for the enjoyment of worship
without the many idle forms on which King James had set his
heart, and was ruling Elder of the church at Leyden of which
John Robinson was teacher, as he had been probably at Scrooby.
The story of the " Mayflower," is too well known to be repeated
here. Suffice to say that he had early removed to Duxbury, and
there under the same roof with his son Love died on 16 April
1643.   His wife died 17 April 1627.

CHILDREN:

Jonathan, b. at Scrooby, 12 Aug. 1593, m. **Lucretia Oldham,** 10 April
1624; d. at Preston, 7 Aug. 1659.

PATIENCE, b. in England, m. Thomas Prence, 5 Aug. 1624; d. 1634.

FEAR, b. in England, m. Isaac Allerton, 1626; d. 1633.

CHILD, b. in England or Holland, d. at Leyden, Holland.

LOVE, b. in England or Holland, m. Sarah Collier, 15 May 1634; d.
soon after 1650.

WRESTLING, b. in England or Holland.   Never married.

JONATHAN BREWSTER MONUMENT
Brewster Plain Cemetery, Preston, Conn.

BREWSTER Jonathan[2] (*William*[1]), oldest son of William and Mary Brewster. Came in the ship "Fortune" in Nov. 1621. He married Lucretia Oldham of Derby, 10 April 1624. She was probably a sister of John Oldham who came to Plymouth on his "perticuler" about 1623 and who was called "brother" by Jonathan Brewster. About 1630 Jonathan removed his family to Duxbury from which place he was deputy to the General Court Plymouth Colony, for the years 1639–41–42–43 and 44. In 1637 he was military commissioner in Pequot War, a member of Duxbury Committee to raise forces in the Narrangansett Alarm of 1642, and a member of Capt. Myles Standish Duxbury Company in the Military enrollment of 1643. Thence he removed to New London, Conn., about 1649. Admitted inhabitant 25 Feb. 1649/50, settled in that part later called Norwich, a Deputy in 1654–55–56–57 and 58. Received a deed of land by Unquas Sachem of Mauhekon 25 Apr. 1650. It comprised the whole neck on which the trading house stood. Mrs. Lucretia Brewster was evidently a woman of note and respectability among her compeers. She has always the prefix of honor (Mrs. or Mistress) and is usually presented to view in some useful capacity, an attendant upon the sick and dying as a nurse, doctress or midwife or as a witness to wills and other transactions. Jonathan Brewster died 7 Aug. 1659 and was buried in Brewster Plain cemetery at Brewster's Neck, Preston (see illustration). His wife died 4 March 1678/9.

CHILDREN:

    WILLIAM, b. at Plymouth, 9 Mar. 1625 (?), m. Mary Pearm or Peirm of London, 15 Oct. 1651; prob. settled in London.

    MARY, b. in Plymouth, 16 Apr. 1627 (?), m. John Turner of Scituate, 10 Nov. 1645.

    JONATHAN, b. at Jones River, 17 July 1629; prob. settled in England.

    RUTH, b. at Duxbury, 3 Oct. 1631, m. (1) 14 Mar. 1651, John Picket, d. 16 Aug. 1667; m. (2) 2 July 1668, Charles Hill; d. at New London, 1 May 1677.

    Benjamin, b. at Duxbury, 17 Nov. 1633, m. **Ann (Addis)** Dart, 28 Feb. 1659/60; d. in Norwich, 14 Sept. 1710.

    ELIZABETH, b. at Duxbury, 1 May 1637, m. (1) 7 Sept. 1653, Peter Bradley of New London, 3 Apr. 1662; m. (2) Christopher Christoper, d. 23 July 1687; d. 1708.

GRACE, b. at Duxbury, 1 Nov. 1639, m. Capt. Daniel Wetherell, 4 Aug.
1659; d. at New London, 22 Apr. 1684.

HANNAH, b. at Duxbury, 3 Nov. 1641, m. Samuel Starr of New London,
23 Dec. 1664.

ADDIS FAMILY.

ADDIS William,[1] Gloucester, was a town officer in 1641.
One of the chief inhabitants, perhaps went home to England for
a short time; but from 1658 to 1662 lived at New London as a
brewer. Who he married is not known by me and his death is
equally obscure, occurring after 1662.

CHILDREN:

MILICENT, b. ———, m. (1) 28 Nov. 1642, William Southmeade; m.
(2) William Ash; m. (3) Thomas Beebe; all of New London, Conn.

Ann, b.———, m. (1) 24 June 1653, Ambrose Dart; m. (2) 28 Feb.
1659/60, **Benjamen Brewster;** d. at Norwich, 9 May 1709.

BREWSTER Benjamin[3] (*Jonathan,*[2] *William*[1]), son of Jonathan and Lucretia (Oldham) Brewster, married Ann Dart, widow
of Ambrose and daughter of William Addis of Gloucester, Mass.,
last day of February 1659/60 according to the "Brewster Book."
He settled upon the "homestead" of his father at Brewster's
Neck, which he acquired from his father and brother-in-law John
Picket. This farm was originally in the town of New London,
but by the alteration of the boundaries and the formation of new
towns, was afterwards successively included in the towns of
Norwich, Preston, Groton and Ledyard. He was a man of
prominence, serving as deputy to the General Court of the Colony
of Connecticut in 1668–89–90–92–93–94–95–96 and 97. Lieutenant of the New London Troops 1673, and Captain of the
Military Company of Norwich 1693. (The "Brewster Book"
undoubtedly had been in his custody from the death of his father
to his own decease and his son Daniel, it is supposed, succeeded
him as custodian of the Book.) His wife died in Norwich, 9 May
1709, and his own death occurred at the same place, 14 Sept.
1710. They both are probably buried in the Brewster Plain
Cemetery at Brewster Neck, Preston.

CHILDREN:

MARY, b. 10 Dec. 1660, m. Samuel Fitch, 28 Nov. 1678.

ANN, b. 29 Sept. 1662, m. Matther Coy of Preston.

JONATHAN, b. 30 Nov. 1664, m. Judith Steven, 18 Dec. 1690; d. 20 Nov. 1704, a. 40 y.

Daniel CAPT., b. 1 March 1666/7, m. (1) 23 Dec. 1686, **Hannah Gager,** d. 25 Sept. 1727; m. (2) 19 Dec. 1727, Dorothy Witter, d. 1757; d. at Preston, 7 May 1735.

WILLIAM, b. 22 March 1669.

RUTH, b. 16 Sept. 1671, m. Thomas Adgate, 15 June 1692.

BENJAMIN, b. 25 Dec. 1673, m. Mary Smith, 17 Dec. 1696.

ELIZABETH, b. 23 June 1676, m. Daniel Meeks, 4 July 1706; d. 9 March 1744.

GAGER FAMILY.

GAGER William,[1] Charlestown, surgeon, from little Waldingfield Co., Suffolk, England. He came in the fleet with Winthrop. Governor Winthrop in a letter of 29 Nov. 1630, says: "I have lost twelve of my family and among them Mr. Gager and his wife and two children." He was original member of the church that formed in Boston. He is numbered " No. 8," on the list being marked "dead, 20 Sept. 1630. Having died from a disease contracted by ill diet at sea," which swept off many of the emigrants. He is characterized by contemporary journalists " a skilful surgeon." His son John is the only child that has been traced.

GAGER John[2] (*William*[1]), was the son of William Gager. He married Elizabeth (maiden name not known) before 1647. Was one of the company that settled at New London, Conn., with John Winthrop the younger. (The elder Gov. Winthrop remembered him in the following item of his last will and testament. "I will that John Gager shall have a cow, one of the best I shall have in recompense of a heifer his father bought of me and two ewe goats and ten bushels of Indian corn.") His name is there found on the earliest extant list of inhabitants. He had a grant from the town of New London of a farm of two hundred acres (sold in 1696 to Ralph Stoddard) east of the river near the straits (now in Ledyard) to which he removed soon after 1650 and there dwelt until he joined in the settlement of Norwich and removed thither, where he had an original home lot and all the privileges of first proprietors, his house lot in the new town bears the date of the oldest surveys, viz., Nov. 1659. He had $11\frac{1}{2}$ acres (1660), part of it a dense swamp and Hammer brook running through it, afterwards in 1697 Bean Hill Cemetery was taken

out of this lot.   He was a constable in 1674 and again in 1688.
The will of John Gager, the proprietor, dated 21 Dec. 1695, has
the descriptive passage "being now aged and full of days," but he
lived eight years longer.   His will provided for wife Elizabeth,
bequeaths all real estate to "only son Samuel," and adds "to
my six sons that married my daughters, viz., John Allyn, *Daniel
Brewster*, Jeremiah Ripley, Simon Huntington, Joshua Abel and
Caleb Forbes, twenty shillings each, having already given their
wives considerable portion in movables and lands."   He died at
Norwich, 10 Dec. 1703.

CHILDREN:

JOHN, b. Sept. 1647, m. Deborah Allyn after 1683; d. 1691.

ELIZABETH, b. March 1649, m. John Allyn, 24 Dec. 1668.   Removed to
Ledyard, Conn.

SARAH, b. Feb. 1651, m. Caleb Forbes, 30 June 1681.

HANNAH 1st, b. March 1653, d. March 1653.

SAMUEL, b. Feb. 1654, m. Rebeckah (Raymond) Lay, Apr. 1695; d.
11 June 1740.

BETHYAH, b. Nov. 1657, m. Joshua Abell, Nov. 1685; d. 31 March
1723.

WILLIAM, b. Aug. 1660, d. Nov. 1662.

LIDIA, b. Aug. 1663, m. Simon Huntington Jr., 8 Oct. 1683.

Hannah 2nd, b. Feb. 1666, m. **Daniel Brewster**, 23 Dec. 1686; d.
25 Sept. 1727.

MARY, b. May 1671, m. Jeremiah Ripley.

BREWSTER Daniel[4] (Capt.) (*Benjamin,[3] Jonathan,[2] William[1]*)
was the son of Benjamin and Ann (Addis) Brewster.   Born
1 March 1666/7, married (1st) 23 Dec. 1686, Hannah, daughter
of John and Elizabeth Gager of Norwich, Conn., born Feb. 1666.
She died at Preston, 25 Sept. 1727.   He married for his second
wife 19 Dec. 1727, Dorothy probably daughter of Joseph and
Dorothy (Parke) Morgan and widow of Ebenezer Witter, all of
Preston.   Daniel Brewster lived at Preston.   He was justice of
the peace for New London County in the years 1717–20–23–25
and 28.   Representative to the General Court of Connecticut
1704–19–21–23–25 and 31.   Was appointed lieutenant of the
militia company of Preston in 1704 and captain in 1716, and was
deacon of the first church of Preston.   He died at Preston
7 May 1735.

PANORAMIC VIEWS, FREEMAN FARM

North-east

South-east

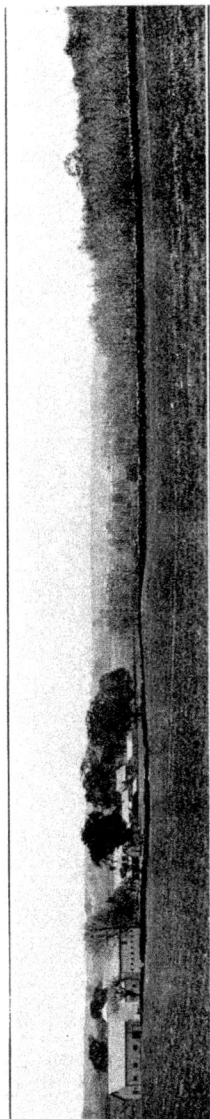

South-west

North-west

GRISWOLD, CONN.

CHILDREN:
DANIEL, b. at Norwich, 11 Oct. 1687, m. Elizabeth Freeman, 8 Aug.
1710; d. at Preston, 14 June 1756, age 69 yrs.
Hannah, b. at Preston, 2 Dec. 1690, m. **Joseph Freeman,** 2 Dec. 1708;
d. at Preston, 6 May 1750.
MARY, b. at Preston, 2 Jan. 1692, m. Christopher Huntington, 4 June
1740; d. 24 Dec. 1749.
JOHN, b. 18 July 1695, m. Dorothy Treat, 20 Sept. 1725.
JERUSHA 1st, b. 18 Nov. 1697, d. 17 Apr. 1704.
RUTH, b. 20 June 1700, m. John Fobes, 14 Jan. 1718/9.
BETHIAH, b. 5 Apr. 1702, m. William Parish of Windham, 23 May 1738,
d. at Windham, Conn., 8 Feb. 1740/1.
JONATHAN, b. 6 June 1705.
JERUSHA 2nd, b. 15 Oct. 1710, d. 7 March 1711.
EBENEZER, b. 19 Sept. 1713, m. Susanna Smith, 28 Aug. 1735; d.
7 Oct. 1739, age 27 years.

FREEMAN Joseph[3] (*Joseph,*[2] *John*[1]), son of Joseph and Dorothy (Haynes) Freeman, was born at Sudbury, 18 Dec. 1684.
He was brought by his father to Preston when a boy. He
married in Preston, Hannah, daughter of Daniel and Hannah
(Gager) Brewster, 2 Dec. 1708. She was born in Preston, 2 Dec.
1690. He settled on the southern part of his father's farm
comprising about 300 acres; his house was situated about one-
quarter of a mile south of his father's house and on the road going
to Norwich. (See illustration.) We find him and wife members
of the First Congregational Church of Preston in 1710, all of his
children having been baptized there. In his will dated 3 Feb.
1732/3 and proved 23 May 1733, he calls himself of Preston and
a yeoman. He mentions wife Hannah, sons *Joseph*, Daniel,
Caleb, Phinas, Benjamin, Nathan, Samuel, and daughters,
Hannah and Jemima; giving husbandry and carpenter tools to
seven sons, Joseph, Caleb, Nathan and Samuel dividing the
home farm. He died 12 May 1733, his wife died 6 May 1750,
and the total inventory of her estate dated 28 Nov. 1750,
amounted to £874 : 18 : 7, while the inventory of his estate
amounted to £3117.6.1.

CHILDREN:
Joseph, b. 4 March 1709/10 at Preston, m. (1) 22 Nov. 1732, **Mehitable
Tyler,** d. 25 July 1743; m. (2) 8 March 1744, Anna Rockwell, d.
12 Jan. 1752; m. (3) 10 May 1757, Mary Story; d. at Preston,
19 March 1780, ae. 71 yrs.

DANIEL, b. 1 Apr. 1712 at Preston, d. at Preston, 28 April 1733.

HANNAH, b. 24 Feb. 1713/14 at Preston, m. William Witter, 7 Nov. 1738.

CALEB, b. 27 Feb. 1715/16 at Preston, m. Ziporah ———, d. at Preston, 10 June 1759, ae. 44 yrs.

PHINEAS, b. 23 Oct. 1718 at Preston, d. at Preston, 9 May 1746.

NATHAN, b. 23 Sept. 1721 at Preston, m. (1) 1748, Lucy Bloggett, d. 2 Nov. 1753; m. (2) 14 Feb. 1753/4, Lucy Barns.

BENJAMIN, b. 27 Nov. 1723 at Preston, m. Abigail Tracy, 2 Jan. 1745.

SAMUEL, b. 25 June 1726 at Preston, m. Elizabeth Brewster, 4 Apr. 1750; d. 28 May 1801.

MARY, b. 12 July 1728 at Preston. Not mentioned in father's will of 1732/3.

RACHEL, bapt. 18 Jan. 1731 at Preston. Not mentioned in father's will of 1732/3.

JEMIMA, b. 13 March 1731/2 at Preston, d. 4 Nov. 1750.

TYLER FAMILY.

TYLER Job,[1] was born about 1619, as in a deposition of 1659 his age is stated as "about 40 years." Called husbandman at Mount Wolleston in 1637. In the Rhode Island Collection, p. 92, is found the following: "Inhabitants admitted at the town of Niew-Port since the 20th of the 3rd 1638 Job Tyler." It is said that the early colonist found him a solitary squatter at Andover about 1639–40. In Roxbury in 1646. Back in Andover again in 1650, for he mortgaged his house 5th of March of that year, and finally sold it 18 April 1662. In 1665 he was at Roxbury and his wife joined the church there 28 May of that year, and next Sunday had John and Samuel baptized there. His wife was Mary ———, she may have been a widow Horton. In 1669 he removed to Mendon, and in 1680 was among those as drawing "for doubling of their houselots"; thence driven by the Indians, he returned to Roxbury, but before 1681 was in Rowley, in that part now called Boxford and again removed to Andover. But in 1688, 1689, 1691 and 1695, he was paying minister's rates in Mendon. After the death of his wife Mary, probably in 1700, he divided his estate amongst his sons, for in a deed to his son Moses he gives land in Mendon and dated 1700 and this is the last heard of Job as no record of his death has been found. At the sixth "Tyler Reunion," at a spot beside the grave of his eldest son Moses in

Andover, a hard-grained boulder, brought from the "Tyler Farm" (now known as the Wood place), four miles distant in West Boxford on which a bronze tablet riveted, is the following legend:

> " In Memoriam,
> JOB TYLER.
> Immigrant, First settler
> Andover, — about MDCXXXIX.
> Born MDCXIX, Died MDCC.
> Dedicated by his whole clan Sept. 4, 1901"

CHILDREN:

MOSES, b. in 1641 or 1642 in Andover or Roxbury, m. (1) 6 July 1666, Prudence Blake, d. 9 Mar. 1689; m. (2) abt. 169?, Sarah (Hasey) Sprague; d. in Andover, 2 Oct. 1727, a. 85 or 6.

MARY, b. abt. 1644 in Andover or Roxbury, m. (1) 18 Nov. 1662, Richard Post of Woburn, d. 14 July 1675; m. (2) 1 Mar. 1677/8, John Bridges.

Hopestill, b. abt. 1646 in Andover or Roxbury, m. **Mary Lovett** at Mendon, 20 Jan. 1668, d. in Preston, 20 Jan. 1733/4, ae. 89 years.

CHILD, d. in infancy, " 1646, month 1, day 28."

HANNAH, b. ———, m. James Lovett at Medfield, 17 Feb. 1668/9.

JOHN 1st, b. abt. 1650 in Andover, d. in Andover, 28 Sept. 1652.

JOHN 2nd, b. 16 April 1653 in Andover, bapt. in Roxbury, 4 June 1665, m. Hannah Parker, 14 Sept. 1682; d. in Mendon, 4 May 1742.

SAMUEL, b. 24 May 1655 in Andover, bapt. in Roxbury, 4 June 1665, m. Hannah ———; d. in Mendon, 17 Dec. 1695.

BLOTT FAMILY.

BLOTT Robert,[1] Charlestown 1634, but had come in 1632 probably to Roxbury, was a Freeman in 1635, and was at Boston 1644. Had wife Susanna who died 20 Jan. 1660. He died 1665 for his will of 27 May 1662 has a codicil dated 27 March 1665 and was probated 2 Feb. 1665/6.

Will of Robert Blott: " I Robert Blott, Being in perfect memory, Doe make this my last Will and testement. I make Edward Ellis, my sonne in Law, Husband to Sarah my Daughter, my Executor, and give unto him my House & lot belonging there unto. Also that he pay my Daughters children named Woodford of Conniticott £3 etc., and to my daughter Tosiors children

£7 & to her eldest sonne John Green, etc. *To daughter Lovetts Children* of Braintree £7 and 3 bushels of wheat and 2 bushells of Indyan, To son-in-Law Daniel Turins Children £8; — To daughter Tosior & my daughter Louet shall have halfe the house hold stuff equally Divided between them & the other half to my daughter Ellis, & 3 bushel of Maulte to be divided Between my three daughters, Also to *Daniel Louett my sonne-in-Law* I give my Best Coat."

CHILDREN:

> MARY, b. ———, m. Thomas Woodford of Roxbury. Removed to Hartford, d. at Hartford, 1656.
>
> SARAH, b. ———, m. Edward Ellis of Boston, 6 Oct. 1652.
>
> **Joanna,** b. abt. 1620, m. **Daniel Lovett** of Braintree before 1648, d. after 1691.
>
> A DAUGHTER, b. ———, m. (1) ——— Green; m. (2) Richard Tozer; d. before 1656.
>
> A DAUGHTER (LYDIA ?), b. ———, m. Daniel Turin before 1646; d. 23 June 1659.

LOVETT FAMILY.

LOVETT Daniel,[1] Salem, was a resident there 1638. He married Joanna, daughter of Robert and Susanna Blott before 1648. She was born about 1620. He removed to Braintree, Mass., where probably all of his children were born. He and his mother had a grant of land in 1639, 12 acres for 3 heads. On 30 (7) 1650, he leased 60 acres of land from the town of Boston. He removed to Mendon with the early settlers, and was Freeman 1673. His wife Joanna deposed on 18 June 1670 giving her age as about 50 years. He made his will on the 26 Dec. 1691 and it was probated 28 April 1692, in which he mentions wife Joanna, son James and daughters *Mary Tyler*, Martha Fairbanks and Hannah Ryder. He died between Dec. 1691 and April 1692.

CHILDREN:

> JAMES, b. 5 Oct. 1648, m. Hannah Teyler at Medfield, 17 Feb. 1668/9.
>
> **Mary,** b. 1 Sept. 1651, m. **Hopestill Tyler** at Mendon, 20 Jan. 1668; d. at Preston, Conn., 3 Mar. 1732.
>
> MARTHA, b. 4 Sept. 1654, m. (Elisezur ?) Fairbanks of Medfield. (A widow, Martha Fairbanks, d. at Sherborn, 22 Jan. 1749.)
>
> HANNAH, b. 30 March 1656, m. William Ryder, 7 or 11 Aug. 1674. (A Hannah, wife of William Rider Sr., d. at Sherborn, 23 Nov. 1715.)

TYLER Hopestill[2] (*Job[1]*), was the son of Job and Mary Tyler of Andover, Mass., where he was born 1646. He married at Mendon, 20 Jan. 1668, Mary, daughter of Daniel and Joanna (Blott) Lovett of Braintree, Mass. She was born 1 Sept. 1651. He was made a freeman at Mendon, Mass., in 1673. Was driven by the Indians to Roxbury and at length returned to Andover. An old record says that he was apprenticed a blacksmith and in 1687 his native town "granted him liberty to set up a shop in ye street near his house." Soon after this the witchcraft persecution began and Mrs. Tyler and two daughters were imprisoned at Salem; they were acquitted however in 1693. Perhaps in part because of this persecution, in 1697, he sold his land and removed to Preston, Conn. The value of the smiths craft to the community in the early days is illustrated by the vote of the town of Preston in 1693, offering fifty acres of land to a smith who should settle there, upon certain conditions, one of which was that " he doe ingage to supply the town with smith work five years." That Mr. Tyler availed himself of this offer when he removed to Preston four years later does not clearly appear. He resided in the forest a mile east of the church.

The following is an extract of his will. "In the name of God Amen. May the fifteenth, 1728. I Hopestill Tyler of Preston being aged and of perfit mind and memory etc. Imprimis: I givi and bequeth to my loving wife Mary, all of my estate as the Law dierets, then to my dafter Mary furnnum I give 50 shillings etc., to my daughter hanna busel, her children teen pounds etc. to dau. Mather 10£ etc. to dau. Abigail 3 score £ etc. To Son Daniel 10£ and *Son James* £5. I give unto my grandson Moses Tiler In Boston 50 Shillings To son Hopestill all lands in Township of Preston, with all my housing & shope tols. executors son James son Hopestill and dau. Abigail." The Inventory of his estate dated 9 Aug. 1734 amounted to £842 : 7 : 3. His wife died at Preston, 3 March 1732 and he died there also the "20 Jan. 1733/4 in ye 89th year of his age," according to a rather rude stone which marks his grave in the old burying ground in Preston.

CHILDREN:

MARY, b. at Mendon, 31 Jan. 1669, m. John Farnum, 30 June 1693.

HANNAH, b. abt. 1672, m. Robert Bushnell, 9 Dec. 1697.

DANIEL, b. ———, m. Ann Geer, 28 May 1700. Mentioned in father's will of 1728.

MATHER, b. at Roxbury, 19 April 1676, m. Robert Geer, 3 April 1700; d. at Groton, Conn., 18 Sept. 1741.

JOHN, b. at Roxbury, 19 Feb. 1677/8, m. Deborah Leatherland, 2 Nov. 1699; d. at Boston, 19 May 1705.

JOHANNAH, b. at Andover, 21 Nov. 1681. Not mentioned in father's will of 1728.

James, b. at Andover, 28 Dec. 1683, m. (1) 8 Oct. 1705, **Hannah Safford,** d. 24 Nov. 1728; m. (2) 2 Sept. 1735, Sarah Juet; d. at Preston, 2 Nov. 1754.

HOPESTILL, b. at Andover, 26 Oct. 1685, m. Anna Gates, 25 Jan. 1709/10; d. at Preston, 7 Oct. 1762.

ABIGAIL, b. at Andover, 4 Jan. 1687/8, m. Daniel Fitch.

MEHITABLE, b. at Andover, 4 Jan. 1687/8. Not mentioned in her father's will of 1728.

SAFFORD FAMILY.

SAFFORD Thomas,[1] husbandman of Ipswich and proprietor in 1641. Bought farm of Henry Kingsbury 8 Feb. 1648. His will dated 20 Feb. 1666 and probated 26 March 1667. In it he gave his farm, etc., to son Joseph, on condition of his care of the father and mother and paying certain amounts to daughters Elizabeth, Mary and Abigail; also mentions daughter " Kilum "; this may be Mary who it is supposed married a Kilham. He died 20 Feb. 1667. A widow Elizabeth Safford died at Ipswich 4 March 1671, probably the wife of Thomas.

SAFFORD Joseph[2] (*Thomas*[1]), son of the preceding, was born in England about 1632. He is called of Ipswich, and took the freeman oath 1678. He married at Ipswich, Mary Baker on the 6th March 1660. He deposed 29 March 1692 giving his age "as about 59 or 60 years. As to what he heard in Ipswich 40 years before." He died at Ipswich on the 29th Aug. 1701 in his 70th year.

CHILDREN:

MARY, b. 20 Feb. 1662.
JOSEPH, b. 11 Aug. 1664.
SARAH, b. 20 March 1667, m. ——— Kimball.
ELIZABETH, b. 3 Aug. 1670, m. ——— Brown.
THOMAS, b. June 1676.

SAMUEL, b. July 1678.

Hannah, b. 11 Jan. 1681, m. at Ipswich, **James Tyler,** 8 Oct. 1705; d. at Preston, 24 Nov. 1728, a. 47 y.

TYLER James[3] (Capt.) (*Hopestill,*[2] *Job*[1]), was born at Andover, Mass., 28 Dec. 1683, the son of Hopestill and Mary (Lovett) Tyler. He married for his first wife, Hannah, daughter of Joseph and Mary (Baker) Safford of Ipswich, Mass., on the 8 Oct. 1705. She was born at Ipswich, 11 Jan. 1681 and was mother of all his children. She died 24 Nov. 1728 in her 47th year. He married for his second wife "Sary Juet" (Sarah Jewett), 2 Sept. 1735. He lived in that part of Preston, Conn., now called Griswold, and died there 2 Nov. 1754. He is called " Captain," on his tombstone and in the town records. In his will dated 3 Oct. 1753 he calls himself of Preston, mentions wife Sarah, sons Moses, Joseph, John and daughters Hannah and Mary. " Grandchildren, *Daniel*, Mary, Mehitable, Amma, Hannah and Elizabeth Freeman, being ye only children of my daughter *Mehitable* Dec." Proved 25 Feb. 1755 in Norwich. " The inventory of Capt. James Tyler of Preston dec." amounted to "£514 : 7 : 10, recorded 2 Jan. 1755."

CHILDREN:

MOSES, b. 19 Feb. 1707, m. (1) 20 Nov. 1729, Mary Belcher, d. 19 April 1742; m. (2) 11 Nov. 1742, Joanna Denison; d. at Preston, 22 Jan. 1787.

JAMES, b. 22 Dec. 1708, m. Esther Bishop, 7 Oct. 1731; d. at Preston, 10 March 1735/6.

HANNAH, b. 11 Oct. 1711, m. William Denison, 30 June 1738; d. in 1797.

MARY, b. 13 Sept. 1714, m. David Perry of Sherbourn, 15 Oct. 1734.

Mehitable, b. 13 Sept. 1714, m. **Joseph Freeman,** 22 Nov. 1732, d. at Preston, 25 July 1743.

JOSEPH, b. 8 Nov. 1717, m. Anna Stephen of Plainfield, 24 Sept. 1741; d. at Preston, 13 Oct. 1807.

SAMUEL, b. 20 Feb. 1719, d. 16 Dec. 1722.

JOHN, GENERAL, b. 29 Dec. 1721, m. Mary (Spaulding) Coit, 14 Dec. 1742; d. at Preston, 29 July 1804. He rendered conspicuous service in the Revolution and became a brigadier-general.

FREEMAN Joseph[4] (Dea.) (*Joseph,*[3] *Joseph,*[2] *John*[1]), son of Joseph and Hannah (Brewster) Freeman, was born at **Preston,**

4 March 1709/10 and married at Preston, Mehitable, daughter of James and Hannah (Safford) Tyler, 22 Nov. 1732. She was born at Preston, 13 Sept. 1714. They were members of the First Congregational Church of Preston in 1740. All but two of their children were baptized there. His wife Mehitable died 25 July 1743, and for his 2nd wife he married 8 March 1743/4 Anna Rockwell, who died 12 Jan. 1751/2. He again married 10 May 1757, Mary Story. He was ensign of a Train Band of the first Company May 1733 and of the fourth Company 1752. Was one of a committee to rectify the dividing line between Norwich and Preston in 1740. The part of his father's farm that fell to him was the central part of the southern half and contained probably a little less than 100 acres. His will is dated 11 March 1778 and proved 10 April 1780, in which he mentions wife Mary, sons Seth, *Daniel* and Ebenezer, also daughters Amy, Elizabeth, wife of John Rude, Mary Leonard, Hannah, wife of Joseph Hatch, "To grandson James Freeman, my son Daniel's son: my shoe-maker's tools," "To son Seth that part of Homestead Farm and Buildings that lie to the west side of Highway that crosses said Farm," "To son Daniel the rest of Home-stead Farm," Daniel being made executor. Inventory of his estate dated 29 June 1780 showed £400 : 1 : 9. He died at Preston, 19 March 1780, and he and wife Mehitable are buried in the Old Cemetery on "Brown Farm." (See † at No. 8 on map, p. 124.)

CHILDREN:

First wife:

Daniel, LIEUT., b. 23 Sept. 1733, m. **Mercy Gates** at Preston, 29 Nov. 1758; d. at Plainfield, N. H., 5 May 1806, a. 72 yrs.

MARY, b. 10 Aug. 1735, m. Samuel Leonard.

MEHITABLE, b. 11 Dec. 1737. May have d. young, is not mentioned in her father's will of 1778.

HANNAH, b. 20 June 1740, m. Joseph Hatch.

AMI, b. 20 June 1740, did not marry, d. at Preston, 29 Jan. 1789, a. 49 yrs.

ELIZABETH, b. 29 Dec. 1742, m. John Rude 20 March 1766.

Second wife:

JOSEPH, b. 16 Dec. 1744, m. Sarah Kimball, 10 April 1766; d. between 17 Jan. 1775 and 27 Mar. 1776.

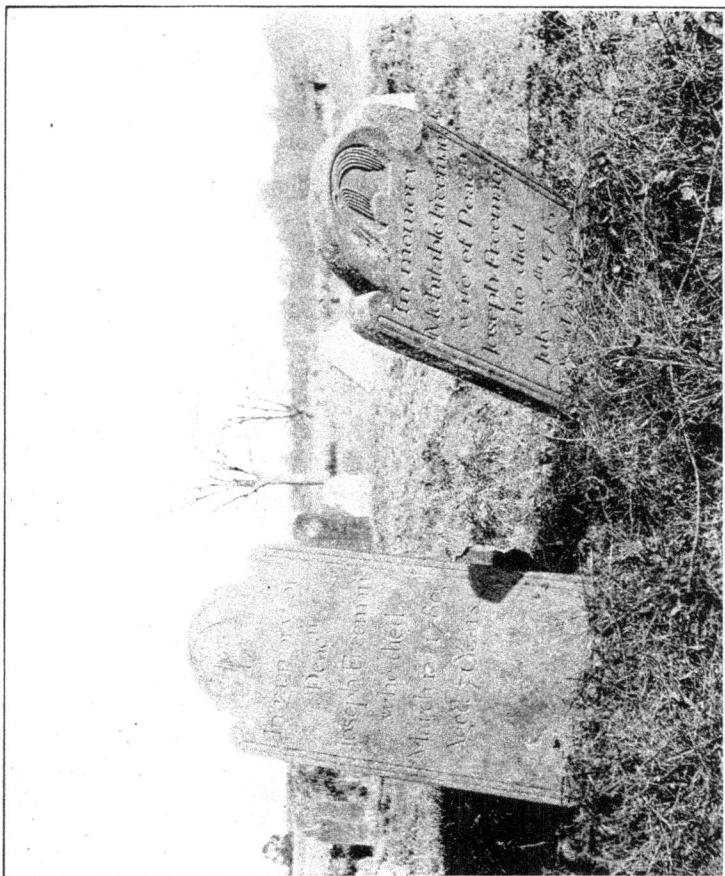

HEADSTONES OF DEACON JOSEPH AND MEHITABLE FREEMAN
Cemetery on "Brown Farm," Griswold, Conn.

PHINEAS, b. 7 Jan. 1747/8, m. Martha Morrison at Fort Ann, N. Y., abt. 1784; d. at Kingston, N. Y., 3 Nov. 1799. Is not mentioned in will of father, of 1778.

EBENEZER, b. 13 May 1749, m. Anna Tyler, 14 Feb. 1771.

Third wife:

SETH, b. 12 March 1758.

CONTENTS

GATES FAMILY.

GATES Stephen,[1] was the second son of Thomas Gates of Norwich, Norfolk County, England. He came from Hingham, England, to Hingham, Massachusetts Bay, America, in the ship "Diligent" of Ipswich, England, in the year 1638. He was accompanied by his wife Ann (The "Chute Genealogy" gives her surname as Hill) and two children. He settled at Hingham, removed thence to Cambridge, Mass., in 1652, and thence the year following to Lancaster, Mass. He signed the town agreement there the 3rd April 1654. Was a freeman 1653, and in 1657 was a constable and had a grant of land near Hog Swamp, also rights in Groton and subsequently returned to Cambridge and died there in 1662. In his will made 9 June 1662 and proved 7 Oct. following he calls himself of Cambridge. *Stephen* the eldest son received the house and lot in Lancaster; his wife Ann and son Simon received his place in Cambridge; his son Thomas was to remain with them at his pleasure. His widow married in 1663, Richard Woodward of Watertown, whom she outlived and died on 5 Feb. 1682/3 at Stow, Mass., where two of her sons resided. In her will she calls herself Anna Gates of Pompasitacutt (now Stow), widow, dated 18 April 1682, proved 9 : 2 : 1683. Mentions daughter Elizabeth, wife of Jno. Lasell, grandchild Mary Maynard daughter of John Maynard, son Simon, Thomas and Elizabeth his wife, Stephen her eldest son to be executor. A footnote added "my last Husbands name was Woodward but I generally went by ye name of Gates, notwithstanding."

CHILDREN:

ELIZABETH, b. in England abt. 1626, m. John Laselle in Hingham, 29 Nov. 1647; d. 3 Aug. 1704.

MARY, b. in England abt. 1636, m. John Maynard of Sudbury, 5 Apr. 1658; d. between 1662 and 1681.

Stephen, b. no doubt in New England abt. 1640, m. **Sarah Woodward** at Cambridge, 1664; d. at Acton, 1706.

THOMAS, b. at Hingham, 1642, m. Elizabeth Freeman, 6 July 1670, of Sudbury. Removed to Norwich and no doubt d. at Preston prob. Oct. 24, 1726 (?).

SIMON, b. at Hingham, 1645, m. Margarit (?) at Cambridge; d. at Brockton, 21 Apr. 1693.

ISAAC, bapt. 3 May 1646, d. 3 Sept. 1651.

REBECCA, bapt. 3 May 1646, d. Jan. 1650.

WOODWARD FAMILY.

WOODWARD Richard,[1] born in England about **1589,** came to New England in the ship "Elizabeth" of Ipswich, embarking there on the 10th April 1634, his age being given as 45 and wife Rose, 50, sons George and John, age 13. He is on the earliest list of proprietors of Watertown. Was admitted freeman 2 Sept. **1635.** He was a miller, and bought a windmill in Boston, 8 Sept. 1648 and sold (or mortgaged) the same on the 26 Dec. 1648. His wife Rose died 6 Oct. 1662, age 80. He married 2nd (settlement dated 18 April 1663) Ann widow of Stephen Gates of Cambridge. He died 16 Feb. 1664–5 and the inventory of his estate filed on 4 April 1665 and was administrated by his sons *George* and John. His widow after his death went by the name of "Gates," name of her first husband, and died 5 Feb. 1682–3 at Stow where she had two sons.

CHILDREN:

George, b. abt. 1619, m. (1) abt. 1640, **Mary,** d. abt. 1658; m. (2) 17 Aug. 1659, Elizabeth Hammond of Newton; d. 31 May 1676.

JOHN, b. abt. 1621, m. (1) Mary, d. 8 July, 1654; m. (2) abt. 16,, Abigail Benjamin (widow Stubbs); d. 17 Feb. 1695/6.

WOODWARD George[2] (*Richard*[1]), was the son of Richard and Rose Woodward. He was born in England about **1619.** He came with his father in the ship "Elizabeth," 1634. He married 1st Mary, about 1640, she died about 1658, he then married 2nd Elizabeth, the daughter of Thomas Hammond of Newton, 17 Aug. 1659. He was admitted freeman 6 May 1646, and lived at Watertown, but nothing further is known of him. He died 31 May 1676 and administration granted the 20th June 1676, to his widow, Elizabeth, and son Amos, and the inventory of his estate is dated 23 June 1676, the amount totaling £143 : 10 : 00.

CHILDREN:

First wife:

MARY, b. 12 Aug. 1641, m. John Waite, 13 Jan. 1663/4; d. 23 Aug. 1718.

Sarah, b. Feb. 1642/3, m. **Stephen Gates,** abt. 1664.

Amos, b. 1646, m. Thankfull Patten; d. 9 Oct. 1679, age 33 yrs.

Rebecca, b. 30 Dec. 1647, m. Thomas Fisher of Dedham, 11 Dec. 1666.

John, b. 28 March 1649, m. (1) abt. 1672, Rebecca Robbins, d. 1696; m. (2) Sarah Goodnow; d. 3 Nov. 1732.

Susanna, b. 30 Sept. 1651, unm., d. 22 Sept. 1676.

Daniel, b. 2 Sept. 1653, m. Elizabeth Dana, 14 Jan. 1679. By Vital Records of Newton it appears that he died at Preston, Conn., 31 July 1713.

Mercy, b. 3 June 1656, m. ———— Eddy.

Second wife:

George, b. 11 Sept. 1660, m. Lydia Brown, 31 Dec. 1686; d. at Brookline, 3 Dec. 1696.

Thomas, b. 15 Sept. 1662, d. 1666.

Elizabeth, b. 8 May 1664, m. Samuel Eddy, 7 Dec. 1693.

Nathaniel, b. 28 May 1668.

GATES Stephen² (*Stephen¹*) was born about 1640 probably in Hingham, son of Stephen and Ann Gates. He married at Cambridge, Sarah, daughter of George and Mary Woodward of Watertown in 1664. She was born 6 Feb. 1642/3. He lived for a time in Cambridge, Boston, Marlborough and finally was among the proprietors of Stow, Mass., 1681. In 1673 he bought a large tract of land of Edward Drinker of Boston and which on the 3rd of June 1684, Benjamin Bowhoe an Indian of Pompacittaquntt (now Stow), quit-claimed to him. " He called himself a yeoman and the amount of land is stated at 300 acres situated in the township of Stow, lying on both sides of a cirtain brook there commonly called by the name of Elsabeth; als. Alsabat Brook." He died possessed of this farm lying on and around Spindle Hill which he left his six sons to be equally divided among them, the division deed being dated 26 March 1710/11 and recorded 1 July 1718. Two sons *Stephen³* and Thomas having previously removed to Preston, Conn., sold their shares to the four remaining brothers, Simon, Isaac, Nathaniel and Daniel. " In Jan. 1886 the Homestead was sold; thus passed out of the family the 'Gates Farm' which had been in its possession for two hundred years It was situated about a mile southwest of the center of the town. at the foot of Spindle Hill. In 1907 the house was still standing, but unoccupied and in need of repair to insure its preservation." But in 1913 it was accidentally burned to the ground. His will is dated at Stow, 5 Sept. 1705 and proved 1707. He died at Acton 1706.

CHILDREN:

Stephen, b. 17 July 1665, m. **Jemima Benjamin** of Plymouth Colony, 8 Nov. 1686; d. 4 Nov. 1732.

SIMON, b. 5 Mar. 1666/7 at Cambridge, m. Hannah Benjamin at Stow, 4 May 1688; d. 1752.

THOMAS, b. 31 Dec. 1669 at Boston, m. Margarit Geer of Preston, Conn., Dec. 1695; d. at Preston, 1740.

ISAAC, b. 1673, m. Elizabeth ———; d. at Stow, 22 Nov. 1748, age 75 yrs.

NATHANIEL, b. 1675, m. Mary Gilson at Concord, 17 Oct. 1700; mentioned in his father's will of 1705.

SARAH, b. 27 April 1679 at Marlborough, never married, d. 27 Jan. 1724.

REBECCA, b. 23 July 1682 at Marlborough, m. Timothy Gilson at Concord, 17 Nov. 1700. Mentioned in his father's will of 1705.

DANIEL, b. 23 April 1685 at Stow, d. 22 March 1759, age 74 yrs.

BENJAMIN FAMILY.

BENJAMIN John[1]. His home is said to have been in Lower Herford, England. He embarked 22 June 1632 on the ship "Lion," and arrived at Boston, 16 Sept., following. His wife was Abigail Eddy, born in England about 1600, daughter of Rev. William Eddy of Cranbrook, Kent Co., England. He was made freeman 6 Nov. 1632 and on 20 May 1633 was appointed constable by the General Court. A proprietor at Cambridge. He purchased 6 acres of land in "New Town" on which he built a house of which Governor Winthrop wrote: "Mr. Benjamin's mansion was unsurpassed in elegance and comfort by any in the vicinity. It was the mansion of intelligence, religion and hospitality, visited by cleargy of all denomination and by the literate at home and abroad." This house was burned on 7 Apr. 1636 with a loss of £100. He removed to Watertown and was a town officer. He was excused from military training on account of his age 7 Nov. 1634; but "was requested to have at all times arms for himself and servants." There is evidence that he was a man of property, education and culture, and the fact that Governor Winthrop designated him as "Mr. Benjamin," indicates that he was a man of some consequence in the colony. There is a tradition that he brought a fine library from England. His will was dated 12 June 1645 and probated 3 July 1645 and mentions " son John to have a double portion; beloved wife: two Cowes and and fourty bushel of Corn out of all my lands to be allowed her towards the bringing up of my smalle Children etc. — All the rest of my lands, goods and chattels shal be equally divided between seven other of my children." He died 14 June 1645 and his wife died 20 May 1687, age 87 years.

CHILDREN:

JOHN, b. in England abt. 1620, m. Lydia Allen; d. 22 Dec. 1706, age 86 years.

ABIGAIL, b. in England abt. 1624, m. (1) abt. 1644, Joshua Stubbs of Watertown, d. abt. 1654; m. (2) abt. 1658, John Woodward of Charlestown.

SAMUEL, b. in England abt. 1628, m. Mary ———— before 1666. Removed to Hartford, Conn., d. 1669.

MARY, b. in England abt. 1629, d. 10 April 1646.

Joseph, b. 16 Sept. 1633, m. (1) 10 June 1661, **Jemima Lumbard;** m. (2) Sarah Clark; d. at New London, 1704.

JOSHUA, b. abt. 1642, m. Thankfull ————, d. 6 May 1684 a. 42 y.

CALEB, b. ————, m. Mary Hale abt. 1670, removed to Weathersfield, Conn.; d. 8 May 1684.

ABEL, b. ————, m. Amity Myrick, 6 Nov. 1671. His will dated 5 July 1710.

LOMBARD FAMILY.

LOMBARD Thomas,[1] of Dorchester, came probably bringing his son Bernard and two other children in the " Mary and John," 1630. Requested to be made freeman 19 Oct. of that year, and was admitted 18th May following, removed in a few years, perhaps to Scituate, but to Barnstable he finally removed, for we find him among the associates of Rev. John Lothrop who settled there on 21 Oct. 1639. In his will, dated 25 March 1662 and probated 7 March 1664, he mentions wife Joyce and children Bernard, Joshua, Joseph, Jedediah, Benjamin, Caleb, *Jemima* and Margaret Coleman, sons-in-law Joseph Benjamin and Edward Colman, grandchild, Abigail Benjamin. Savage says: " He had also younger daughter Jemima which may have made a runaway match with Joseph Benjamin at Boston, 10 June 1661."

CHILDREN:

BERNARD, b. in England about 1608 (deposed in 1668, giving age 60 years.)

JOSHUA, b. in England, m. Abigail Linnell, 27 May 1651.

MARGARET, b. in England, m. Edward Coleman, 27 Oct. 1648.

JOSEPH, b. at Dorchester about 1638, deposed in 1667, giving age as 29 years.

JOBANIAH, bapt. at Dorchester, 23 (4) 1639, prob. d. young.

JEDEDIAH, bapt. at Barnstable, 19 Sept. 1641, m. Hannah Wing, 20 May 1668.

BENJAMIN, bapt. at Barnstable, 27 Aug. 1643, m. (1) 19 Sept. 1672, Jane Warren; d. 27 Feb. 1682, m. (2) 19 Nov. 1683, Sarah Walker; d. 6 Nov. 1693, m. (3) 24 May 1694, Widow Hannah Whetston.

CALEB.

Jemima, m. in Boston 10 June 1661, **Joseph Benjamin.**

BENJAMIN Joseph[2] (*John*[1]) was the son of John and Abigail (Eddy) Benjamin. He was born on this side of the water, 16 Sept. 1633, married at Boston 10 June 1661, Jemima, daughter of Thomas and Joyce Lombard (said to have been a runaway marriage; if so, they had the distinction of being married by Richard Bellingham, Deputy Governor). I do not know when she died, but he married for 2nd wife Sarah Clark. He is called of Barnstable; he sold his estate at Cambridge, 30 Oct. 1686, that came to him, his deed says, "from my father John deceased," and by this means we know of his descent. He lived some years at Yarmouth, where from the imperfect records we find several children, but not all. He removed to New London, Conn. He died 1704, leaving a widow "Sarah, and children, Joseph aged 30, John 22, Abigail, *Jemima*, Sarah, Kezia, Mary and Mercy," according to a probate document.

CHILDREN:

ABIGAIL, b. 1664.

Jemima, b. 1666, m. **Stephen Gates** at Stow, 8 Nov. 1686; d. prob. at Preston, Conn., before 1732.

HANNAH, b. Feb. 1668, m. Simon Gates of Stow, 4 May 1688.

MARY, b. Apr. 1670.

MERCY, b. 12 March 1674.

JOSEPH, b. 1675.

ELIZABETH, b. 14 Jan. 1680.

SARAH.

KEZIA.

JOHN, b. 1682.

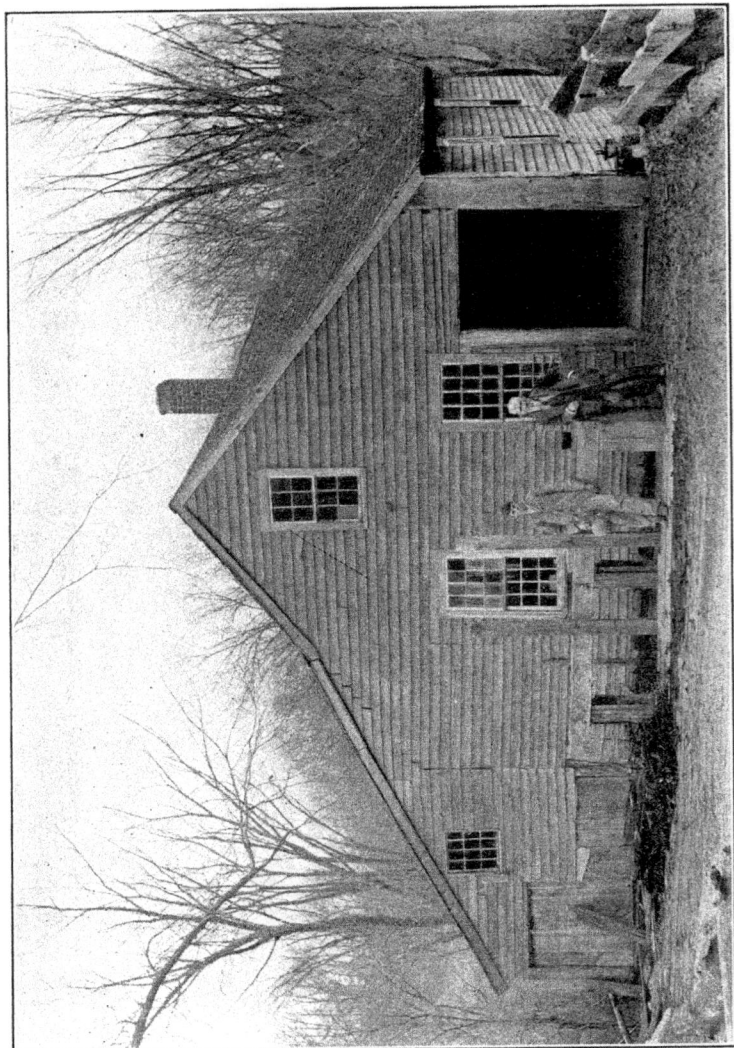

GATES GRIST MILL
Griswold, Conn.

GATES Stephen³ (*Stephen,² Stephen¹*), son of Stephen and Sarah (Woodward) Gates, was born at Watertown or Cambridge (?), 17 July 1665. He married at Stow, Mass., 8 Nov. 1686, Jemima, daughter of Joseph and Jemima (Lombard) Benjamin of Plymouth Colony. She was born 1666. He removed to Preston, Conn., for he is found to have bought land there in Feb. 1696, but after the date of 1707 he is put on the town record as having removed. However, it is certain that he must have returned for after the distribution of his father's farm, 1710/11, he sold his part of the farm at Stow, and I find that the town of Preston in that year granted to Stephen Gates 14 acres of land in consideration that he should build a Grist Mill, and maintain it for the accommodation of the farmers of the town, and for three generations it was run by the Gates family. (For the information concerning the Grist Mill I am indebted to Mr. William Sanders, 83 years old, also for photograph of this mill, in which he appears, being the older man to the right, he having run the mill for several years.) (See illustration.) Stephen Gates lived in that part of Preston now called Hopeville in the town of Griswold. The mill was on the west and south side of Patchaug River. (See No. 5 on map, p. 124.) In his will, proved 6 Sept. 1733, he calls himself of Preston. Does not mention wife and bequeaths his property to sons Stephen and *Isaac* and five daughters, Thankfull Woodward, Mercy Souther, Sarah Clark, Jemimah Clark and Elizabeth Dowing. The amount of his estate totaled £534 : 15 : 5. He died 4 Nov. 1732.

CHILDREN:

THANKFULL, b. 7 Aug. 1687 at Stow, m. ——— Woodward.

STEPHEN, b. abt. 1690, m. (1) Hannah Woodward, 1713; m. (2) Mercy ———; d. at Preston, Conn., 1782.

MERCY, b. ———, m. ——— Souther. Mentioned in her father's will of 1732.

SARAH, b. 10 Nov. 1696 at Preston, m. Benjamin Clark of Preston.

JEMIMA, b. 15 Jan. 1698/9 at Preston, m. Samuel Clark of Preston, 20 June 1723.

Isaac, b. 28 Dec. 1701 at Preston, m. (1) 21 Aug. 1733 **Deborah Partridge**, d. 22 May 1745; m. (2) before 1748, Sarah ———; m. (3) 1765, Charity Lathrop of Norwich; d. at Preston, 16 Aug. 1788, age 87 yrs.

ELIZABETH, b. Feb. 1704/5 at Preston, m. ——— Dowing.

SUZANNA, b. Feb. 1706/7 at Preston. Not mentioned in father's will of 1732.

CONTENTS

TRACY FAMILY.

TRACY Stephen,[1] "Say-maker," young man from England accompanied Anthony Clemens, married at Leyden, Holland, 2 Jan. 1621 Trifosa Le——— maid of England. He came to Plymouth in the "Ann," 1623 with wife Tryphosa and one child, probably Sarah. Counted in the division of lands in the ensuing spring for three heads, and in the division of cattle 1627, another child Rebecca, is counted. From 1633 resided at Duxbury. Town officer 1638-9 and in 1650 or near that time went back to England. In the Colonial Record is recorded a disposition of his property in New England dated at London 20th March 1654/5 and enpowering John Winslow to perform it. He calls himself of St. Yarmouth, England, and says he has five children living in New England, and divides his lands and chattels at Duxbury between his son John, daughter Ruth and the rest of his five children, so we must presume his wife was dead.

CHILDREN:

    Sarah, b. prob. at Leyden, Holland, m. **George Partridge,** Nov. 1638.
    REBECCA, b. at Plymouth between 1624 and 1627. May have d. young.
    RUTH, mentioned in father's will of 1654/5.
    MARY.
    JOHN, ENS., b. 1633, m. (1) Mary Prence; m. (2) Deborah ———; d. abt. 1701.

PARTRIDGE FAMILY.

PARTRIDGE George,[1] of Duxbury. He married Sarah, daughter of Stephen Tracy of Plymouth, in Nov. 1638. He was one of the most respectable yeomanry of the colony and came from the county of Kent, England, about 1636 where he was possessed of an estate which he mentions in his will. In the same year he received a grant at Powder Point, and received permission from the Court to settle there and to build. The next year he was allowed 20 acres at Green Harbor Path, and in the following year 30 acres at Island Creek, and at the same place in 1666 a lot of 40 more and 50 acres at Mile Brook which he sold to Thomas King Jr., of Scituate in 1668. He was made freeman

1646. It is not known what relation he was, if any, to Rev Ralph Partridge. His will is witnessed by Alexander and Josiah Standish and is dated 26 June 1682 and an inventory of his estate showing £86 : 7 : 0, was taken 10 Oct. 1695, so that his death occurred between these dates. The date of his wife Sarah's death has not been obtained.

CHILDREN:

SARAH, b. 1639, m. Dea. Samuel Allen of Bridgewater, abt. 1658.

LYDIA, b. ————, m. Dea. William Brewster, 2 Jan. 1672; d. 3 Feb. 1742/3.

RUTH, b. ————, m. Rudolphus Thacher, 1 Jan. 1669/70.

THRIEPHOSA, b. ————, m. Samuel West, 26 Dec. 1668, d. 5 Nov. 1701.

John, b. 29 Nov. 165[9 ?], m. (1) 24 Dec. 1684, **Hannah Seabury**, d. after 1697; m. (2) 23 May 1700, Mary Brewster. A John d. at Duxbury, 5 Apr. 1731, age 73 yrs.

MERCY.

JAMES, b. ————, m. Mary Stetson of Scituate, 24 Apr. 1712; d. 20 Jan. 1744/5.

SEABURY FAMILY.

SEABURY John,[1] planter, and seaman, is called of Boston, bought house 25 Nov. 1639 and was admitted inhabitant. His wife Grace was admitted to the church 15 May 1642. He removed to Barbadoes and his wife went to her husband there and after his death, but before Feb. 1650, married Anthonie Lane. She approved 14 Oct. 1651 of the sale of a house of her former husband by John Milam.

CHILDREN:

JOHN, b. ————, removed to Barbadoes.

Samuel, b. ————, m. **Patience Kemp,** 9 Nov. 1660; d. 5 Aug. 1681.

AND SOME DAUGHTERS.

KEMP FAMILY.

KEMP William[1] came in the ship " James," 5 Apr. 1635. Settled at Duxbury. Was a juryman and made freeman 5 March 1638-9. Had land granted to him 7 Jan. 1638-9. In 1640 had land at Beaver pond, South river and Namasakeeset. Inventory of his estate was taken 23 Sept. 1641, showing £150 and administration granted to his widow Elizabeth 2 Nov. following.

CHILDREN:

WILLIAM, b. ———, m. Patience Thacher (?).
Patience, b. ———, m. Samuel Seabury, 9 Nov. 1660; d. 29 Oct. 1676.

SEABURY Samuel[2] (*John*[1]) was the son of John and Grace Seabury. Removed to Duxbury, is called physician and also deacon. He married at Weymouth, 9 Nov. 1660, Patience, daughter of William and Elizabeth Kemp of Duxbury. His wife died 29 Oct. 1676 and he married for his second wife, Martha, daughter of William Peabody on 4 Apr. 1677. We find in a Suffolk Deed the following: " Samuel Seaberry sonne of the late John Seaberry, Boston (now living at Duxbury this 10th of Apr 1662), entered his claim to a certain house and parcel of land heretofore belonging to his father, now belonging to his brother John Seaberry of Barbadoes and himself, the said house and land being in possession of one Nathaniel Fryer, who detains it from them under a pretence of a purchase from Alexander Adams and he from John Milom, etc etc, which claim he resolves to prosecute etc." He owned land at Island Creek, North River, the Gurnet, and at the brick-kilns. In his will he gives to his son Samuel his landed property in Duxbury; " To son Joseph those great silver buttons which I usually weare. To son John my birding piece and musket. I will that my negro servant Nimrod (valued at £27) be disposed off either by hire or sale in order to the bringing up of my children especially the three youngest now borne." He died 5 Aug. 1681. The " Seabury house " stood where Wait Wadsworth's now stands (1849), and was a large old-fashioned building very high in front but with the roof nearly reaching to the ground behind. In his wife's will she mentions Elizabeth her daughter (no doubt away from home) and gives her " a negro girl Jane and a cow if she returns."

CHILDREN:

First wife:

ELIZABETH, b. 16 Sept. 1661, may not have married; was living when her mother made her will.
SARAH, b. 18 Aug. 1663.
SAMUEL, b. 20 Apr. 1666, m. Mrs. Abigail Allen, 13 Dec. 1688.

Hannah, b. 7 July 1668, m. **John Partridge,** 24 Dec. 1684; d. after 1697.
JOHN 1st, b. 7 Nov. 1670, d. 18 March 1671/2.
GRACE ⎱ twins, b. 1 March 1672–3, ⎰ d. 16 Mar. 1672–3.
PATIENCE ⎰   ⎱ d. 7 Mar. 1672/3.

Second wife:
JOSEPH, b. 8 June 1678.
MARTHA, b. 23 Sept. 1679.
JOHN 2nd, b. ———, m. Elizabeth Alden, 9 Dec. 1697.
A POSTHUMOUS CHILD.

PARTRIDGE John[2] (*George*[1]) was the son of George and Sarah
(Tracy) Partridge, born at Duxbury, 29 Nov. 165[9?]. He
married for his first wife, Hannah, daughter of Samuel and
Patience (Kemp) Seabury, 24 Dec. 1684 at Duxbury. She was
born 7 July 1668 and died after 1697. He married for his second
wife, Mary Brewster, 23 May 1700, at Duxbury.

He inherited lands in Middleboroug, Mass. I find in the
Duxbury Town records, under date of 24 Feb. 1714, the following:
" Ye said town also gave to their agents formerly chosen by sd
town to pew sd meeting house around &c. Lt. Saml Bradford,
Mr. Thomas Loring, Mr. Saml. Seabury, *Mr. John Partridge* and
Capt. John Alden ye front or free seat in ye upper most or second
gallerie in ye north-west end of ye sd meeting house, etc." In a
deed of land found at Preston, Conn., and dated 14 Nov. 1701,
he and Samuel Seabury buy land of Jonathan Parks of Preston,
Conn.; both are called " of Duxbrough in the county Plimoth
in the province of the Massathusit." It is not known if he ever
removed to Preston (probably not), for we find the death at
Duxbury of John Partridge, who died 5 April 1731 in his 73rd
year.

CHILDREN:
First wife:
SARAH, b. 21 Sept. 1685, d. 18 Nov. 1685.
Samuel, b. 10 Mar. 1687, m. **Deborah Rose,** 15 May 1710; d. 19 Oct.
        1774.
GEORGE, b. 17 Aug. 1690, m. Hannah Foster, widow of Wm. Bradford,
        d. 24 Jan. 1768, age 78 yrs.
MARY, b. 2 May 1693, m. Jona Brewster, 6 Mar. 1710. Removed to
        Windham, Conn., and was alive in 1733.
JOHN, b. 27 Dec. 1697. A John Partridge and Ann Fitch, m. at
        Norwich, 27 Sept. 1722.

Second wife:

BENJAMIN, b. 5 Mar. 1700-1.

ISAAC, b. 2 Mar. 1705/6, m. Grace Sylvester, 10 Mar. 1729/30; d. 26 Jan. 1794, a. 88 yrs.

ALLYN FAMILY.

ALLYN Robert,[1] Salem, 1636. Proprietor at Jeffrey's Creek 1638. His wife Sarah was witness in court in 1642, admitted to the church 15 (3) 1642. Children John and Sarah were bapt. 22 (3) 1642. Mary bapt. 19 (9) 1648. In March 1651 he was one of the principal body of the eastern emigrants from Salem to settle at New London, Conn. He had his lot on the road to Lyme; but in 1656, having obtained a grant of a large farm on the east side of the river, at a place still known as Allyn's Point, now in the town of Ledyard. Here stood the old homestead of the family, on the opposite side of the river from the Mohegan fields, the ancient fort of Uncas was in full view from the house. He was one of the first company of purchasers of Norwich in 1659 and resided for several years in the western part of the " Town plot." In 1661 he styled himself as of " New-Norridge " and held the office of constable in 1669, but in a deed of 1681 used the formula " I Robert Allyn of New London." He had doubtless retired to his farm on the river within the bounds of New London, where he died in 1683, age about 75 years. The heirs to his estate were his son John and four daughters, Sarah, wife of George Geares, Mary, wife of Thomas Parke, *Hannah, wife of Thomas Rose* and Deborah. He left an estate amounting to £530. 16s in money.

CHILDREN:

JOHN, bapt. in Salem, 19 May 1642, m. Elizabeth Gager, 24 Dec. 1668; d. prob. at Ledyard, 1709.

SARAH, bapt. in Salem, 19 May 1642, m. George Geer, 17 Feb. 1659; d. after 1726.

MARY, bapt. in Salem, 19 Nov. 1648, m. Thomas Parke, 4 Jan. 1672.

Hannah, b. prob. in New London after 1651, m. **Thomas Rose** before 1681; d. after 1743.

DEBORAH, b. prob. in New London after 1651, m. John Gager Jr., after 1683.

ROSE FAMILY.

ROSE Thomas.[1] He may have been of Marblehead in 1673. He married Hannah the daughter of Robert Allyn of New London, Conn., and is called son-in-law by him in a deed of land, dated 17 April 1681. He received a grant of land in Preston from the Indians on 2 Sept. 1684, described as being to the north of his house, north of the New London line. So was one of the early settlers in the southern part of Preston and was one of the grantees of Preston in 1686. His name acquired notoriety from the situation of his dwelling house. A large oak tree near the house (separating him from his neighbor Robert Allyn) was a boundary mark between Norwich and New London, standing as a stately warder, precisely at the southeast corner of Norwich. It was directly upon the line running east from the head of Poquetamuck Cove to the bounds of Stonington and is referred to in several surveys, acts and patents. He was a Representative from Preston to the General Court in 1695. Under the shadows of the great boundary tree he and his wife lived to a good old age. He died 1743. His wife survived him, being mentioned in his will dated at Preston, 20 Nov. 1743, also mentioning his daughters Johanna Avery, Dorcas Bellows, *Deborah Partridge*, Mary Pelton, Demaras Gates, Elizabeth Killam, son Joseph and son-in-law *Samuel Partridge*. He left an estate valued at £2498.

CHILDREN:

THOMAS, b. abt. 1681, m. Mary ———; d. at Preston (now Griswold), in May [?], 1733, a. 52 y., buried in "Rose Cemetary," on "Geers Hill."

JOANNA, b. ———, m. Edward Avery, 3 June 1699; d. abt. 1761.

DORCAS, b. ———, m. ——— Bellows.

Deborah, b. ———, m. **Samuel Partridge**, 15 May 1710; d. at Preston, 3 Jan. 1770.

MARY, b. ———, m. ——— Pelton.

DAMARAS, b. ———, m. ——— Gates.

ELIZABETH, b. ———, m. ——— Kellam.

JOSEPH.

PARTRIDGE Samuel[3] (*John,*[2] *George*[1]), son of John and Hannah (Seabury) Partridge, born 10 March 1687 at Duxbury, Mass. He married at Preston, Conn., Deborah, daughter of Thomas and Hannah (Allyn) Rose, 15 May 1710. He settled in that part of

GRAVESTONES OF ISAAC AND DEBORAH GATES
Gates Cemetery (Hopeville), Griswold, Conn.

Preston now called Hopeville in the town of Griswold. His farm extending eastward from the Pachaug River, about one mile, the "Homestead" was located about one-third of a mile east of Hopeville center and to the north of the road, the whole farm containing about 700 acres (see No. 6 on map, p. 124). (For the information concerning this farm I am indebted to Clark C. Palmer, an old inhabitant, age 81 years, whose farm comprised a part, his wife being a descendant of the Partridge family.) Samuel Partridge's wife died at Preston 3rd of Jan. 1770 and he died there also 19 Oct. 1774.

CHILDREN:

HANNAH, b. 10 March 1711/12.

THOMAS, b. 18 May 1714. May have m. Ziporah Freeman, widow of Caleb Freeman, 16 Sept. 1761.

JOHN, b. 28 Jan. 1715/16.

Deborah, b. 28 April 1717, m. **Isaac Gates,** 21 Aug. 1733; d. 22 May 1745, age 29 yrs.

PEREZ, b. 3 May 1720, m. Judith Burton, 5 Feb. 1740/1.

SAMUEL, b. 23 April 1722, m. Ruth Woodward, 5 Nov. 1741.

MARY, b. 3 Aug. 1727, m. Zcphaniah Woodward, 27 Jan. 1747/8.

AMI, b. 11 April 1730, m. Samuel Tracy, 15 May 1755.

GATES Isaac[4] (*Stephen,*[3] *Stephen,*[2] *Stephen*[1]), son of Stephen and Jemima (Benjamin) Gates, was born at Preston, Conn., 28 Dec. 1701. He married at Preston, for his first wife Deborah, daughter of Samuel and Deborah (Rose) Partridge, 21 Aug. 1733. She was born 28 April 1717 and died at Preston, 22 May 1745. He had for second wife Sarah ———— and for his third wife he married Charity Lathrop of Norwich, Conn., in 1765. He lived in that part of Preston (now called Hopeville in the town of Griswold). In his will dated 10 July 1787 he calls himself of Preston, and first mentions his "eight oldest children (viz[t]) Jemima the wife of Benjama Chapman, Deborah, the former wife of Nathan Herrick, *Mercy,* the *wife* of *Daniel Freeman,* Sarah, the wife of Peter Rose my two sons Isaac & Jacob, and my two daughters, Elizabeth the wife of Daniel Gates, and Susanna Whipple." He further mentions "wife Charity" and three daughters, "(viz.) Amy, the wife of Jonathan Church, Anna, the wife of Squire Phillips and Louisa, the wife of William Stanton." The will was proved 26 Sept. 1788. The inventory of his estate, dated 18 Feb. 1789, shows the amount of £91 : 0 : 7. He died 16 Aug. 1788 and buried in "Gates Cemetery," Hopeville (Griswold). (See No. 5 on map, p. 124, also p. 159.)

CHILDREN:

First wife:

JEMIMA, b. 16 April 1735, m. Benjamin Chapman.
DEBORAH, b. 8 Feb. 1737, m. Nathan Herrick.
Mercy, b. 16 May 1739, m. **Daniel Freeman,** 29 Nov. 1758; d. at Plainfield, N. H., 14 Aug. 1806, a. 66 y.
SARAH, b. 4 July 1741, m. Peter Rose.
ISAAC, b. 16 Oct. 1743, m. Priscilla Bundy, 29 June 1764.

Second wife:

ELIZABETH, b. 20 Jan. 1748, m. Daniel Gates, 2nd cousin, 6 Apr. 1769.
SUSANNA, b. 30 April 1749, m. ——— Whipple.
JACOB 1st, b. 30 Jan. 1752, d. Sept. 1754.
AMY, b. 10 April 1754, m. Jonathan Church.
JACOB 2nd, b. 31 May 1757, m. Peggy Stewart, 10 Feb. 1780.
ANNA, b. ———, m. Squeirs Phillips.
Third wife:
LOUISA, b. 1768, m. William Stanton.

FREEMAN Daniel[5] (*Joseph,*[4] *Joseph,*[3] *Joseph,*[2] *John*[1]), son of Joseph and Mehitable (Tyler) Freeman, was born at Preston, Conn., 23 Sept. 1733. He married Mercy, daughter of Isaac and Deborah (Partridge) Gates at Preston, 29 Nov. 1758. She was born at Preston, 16 May 1739. Soon after the settlement of his father's estate in 1780 he with his family removed to Plainfield, N. H. In 1785 we find him and his oldest son James tax payers there. In the year 1788 he is down on a list for the support of the minister. Daniel Freeman had much wealth and surrounded himself with farms and land for his numerous family, much after the old patriarchal style. The home farm was extensive, covering very beautiful sites of hill and dale. A unique feature was the family burial lot, upon a lonely plain under fir trees, containing many monuments and tablets to the Freemans of the earlier settlers and their descendants. (It is of interest to state that upon the death of the last of the direct Daniel Freeman family the old farm at this date, 1915, has just passed into the possession of Winston Churchill, the author, who has made the old house modern and the beautiful spots accessible by roadways and by

HEADSTONES OF LIEUT. DANIEL AND MERCY FREEMAN
"Freeman Cemetery," Plainfield, N. H.

paths.) He died 8 May 1806 and his wife 14 Aug. 1806; both are buried in the " Freeman Burial Lot." (See illustration.)

CHILDREN:

MEHITABLE 1st, b. at Preston, 18 Jan, 1759, d. at Preston, 22 Nov. 1765.

TAMASIN, b. at Preston, 8 Dec. 1760, m. John Lovell Kimball of Cornish, N. H., 19 Mar. 1788, d. at Plainfield, 22 Apr. 1814, a. 53 y.

JAMES, b. at Preston, 23 Jan. 1763. Became a sailor; d. at Demerara, S. A.

DEBORAH, b. at Preston, 2 Nov. 1764, m. Nahum C. Chase of Cornish, 23 Sept. 1784; d. 30 March 1837.

CYRUS, b. at Preston, 25 May 1767, m. (1) Paris Chase of Cornish, d. 22 July 1793; m. (2) Sarah Dow of Plainfield; m. (3) Mary Chase (?); d. at Plainfield, 21 Mar. 1847, a. 80 y.

MEHITABEL 2nd, b. at Preston, 15 July 1769.

Sabra, b. at Preston, 1 July 1773, m. **Oliver Torrey** of Killingly, Conn., 10 June 1792; d. at Canandaigua, N. Y., Aug. 1820.

OLIVE, b. at Preston, 23 Aug. 1775.

DANIEL, b. at Preston, 5 Apr. 1778, d. at Plainfield, 13 Dec. 1855, a. 77 y.

JOSEPH, b. at Preston, 3 May 1780, m. Polly Johnson of Cornish; d. at Plainfield, 13 Feb. 1851, a. 70 y.

BENJAMIN, b. at Plainfield, 6 Aug. 1782, m. Euducia Childs of Cornish, 8 June 1806; d. at Plainfield, 27 June 1828, a. 46 y.

MERCY, b. at Plainfield, 27 July 1785, m. Dr. August Torrey of Killingly, Conn., 11 Oct. 1807. Removed to Canandaigua, N. Y.

TORREY Oliver[6] (**Capt.**) (*Samuel H.,*[5] *Joseph,*[4] *Joseph,*[3] *William,*[2] *William*[1]) was born 18 Dec. 1768 at Killingly, Conn. The fourth son of Dr. Samuel Holden and Anna (Gould) Torrey. He married at Cornish, N. H., 10 June 1792, Sabra, daughter of Daniel and Mercy (Gates) Freeman. His early life and training is not recorded, but from what is known all the sons received a good education, as might be expected from one parent from the home of the Torreys and the mother from the well-known Gould family of Branford, Conn., the family famous for skilled physicians and renowned lawyers. He is known to have had some military training and a knowledge of architecture, but at the death of the father in 1786 evidently the boys were scattered and history tells us that in 1791 he was in Cornish, N. H., as a tax payer, again in 1794, when he paid on a tax of £150 and had two polls. He owned mills and land in Cornish, the family home being on the main street. Here were born the elder members of his family. The homestead was sold and is on record as the "Pike place." In the year 1799 he moved to Chelsea, Vermont, and we have interesting data from the "Town Records," viz.: "March 11th 1800 Voted to receive proposals for building a Court House 40 × 50 feet and to see what the present Court House will sell for toward the cost of building. — The land Tax for building the court amounts to $1320. Amount raised by subscription was $615 making in all the sum of $1935. Oliver Torrey proposed to build the Court House for this sum and what might be raised by subscription; this offer was accepted and Mr. Torrey gave his bond to perform the work." So it is plain he was quite adept in building. He was also "Captain of the Troops," an active citizen and a "good fellow" with his comrades. Just out of the village of Chelsea he bought a farm and I have the record. "Oliver Torrey bought a farm and gave his Horse, Boots and Saddle in payment." His home was also the temporary home of his two younger brothers, Erastus and Augustus, both of them pursuing their studies and later were graduates of "Dartmouth College" at Hanover, N. H. I have in my possession a document in the handwriting of Oliver Torrey, in which he is appointed attorney for his younger brothers which is here inserted. (See illustration.) My mother told me that after her marriage she saw very little of her father and mother, as her home was quite removed, and her parents soon moved to Canandaigua, N. Y., to which place the brother Augustus Torrey had migrated and was there a very successful physician. Dr. Augustus Torrey had married Mercy Freeman, so the tie was very strong to draw the two brothers and two sisters to live their lives in close proximity, also my Aunt Ann Gould Torrey (his first child) had married Galen Holbrook, who owned a large farm at Rushville, N. Y., next town to Canandaigua. Their life here was very brief, both dying of malarial fever in 1820, and they are buried in a small cemetery at Hopewell, N. Y., an adjoining village. The early death of these two worthy people seems very pathetic, and that I know something about the details is owing to my persistent endeavors as a small child to learn the cause of my being without grandparents. By a strange chance I suffered the same loss on the Blake side. Oliver Torrey died at Canandaigua, N. Y., 14 Aug. 1820, and his wife survived him but a few days.

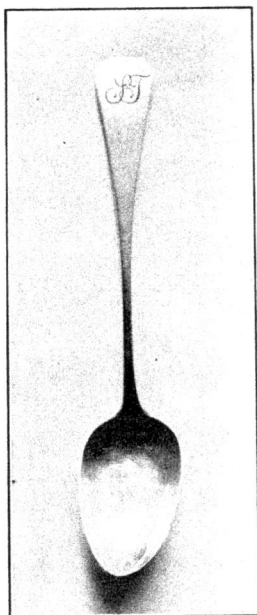

SABRA TORREY SPOON

CHILDREN:

ANNA GOULD, b. at Cornish, N. H., 9 Feb. 1793, m. Galen Holbrook, 26 Oct. 1820; d. at Rushville, N. Y., 3 Jan. 1865.

Susan, b. at Cornish, N. H., 1 July 1795, m. Nathan Blake 3rd, 6 Sept. 1815; d. at Boston, Mass., 18 Sept. 1884, a. 89 y.

OLIVER, b. at Cornish, N. H., 20 Feb. 1797, m. Laura Jenks; lost at sea. S. P.

JAMES FREEMAN, b. at Chelsea, Vt., 1 Dec. 1799, d. young.

CLARISSA, b. at Chelsea, Vt., 15 July 1802, m. Aldridge Watkins, March 1820; removed to Columbus, Ohio.

SABRA, b. at Chelsea, Vt., 24 Apr. 1804, m. John Pratt; d. at Post Mills, Thetford, Vt., Aug. 1867.

SOPHIA, b. at Chelsea, Vt., m. John Tyler; d. at Post Mills, Thetford, Vt. S. P.

ALMIRA, b. at Chelsea, Vt., m. Charles Metcalf; d. at Montgomery, Ala., abt. 1836.

AUGUSTUS, b. at Chelsea, Vt., m. Mary Parks; removed to Birmingham, Mich.

To all People to whom these presents shall come greeting Know ye that I Oliver Torrey of Chelsea in the County of Orange & State of Vermont attorney to my Brother Augustus Torrey of Hanover in the County of Grafton & State of New Hampshire for the Consideration of Two Hundred Dollars ———— Received of William Gould Torrey of Killingly in the County of Windham & State of Connecticut the Receipt whereof I do hereby acknowledge Do by virtue of a Power of attorney from the said Augustus Torrey Constituting and appointing me the said Oliver Torrey his Lawfull Attorney to receive obtain or Recover by Law or otherwise any Legacy or Legacy Left ~~by~~ him the said Augustus Torrey by his Honod Father Samuel Holden Torrey Late of Killingly afored Deceased or any Legacy which is or ought to be left to said Augustus by the Decease of his Brother Joseph Torrey which Power of Attorney is Recorded at Large with Killingly Records for Deeds in Liber & as will fully appears — Do by virtue of said Power Remise Release and forever Quit Claim unto him the said William Torrey his Heirs &c all the Right Title claim or Demand which the said Augustus Torrey hath could or ought to have in and unto any Legacy or Legacies ~~Left to him~~ the said Augustus by his ~~1st Honod Brother Saml Holden Torrey or his Brother Joseph Torrey Both Deceased~~ & I the sd Oliver Torrey Do by virtue of sd Power Engage to warrant & Defend sd acquitted Legacies to him the sd William & his Heirs against the Lawfull Claims or Demand of the said Augustus his Heirs &c In witness whereof I have hereunto set my hand and seal this 22d Day January A D 1796 ———

Signed Sealed & Delivered
in presents of
Sampson Howe
Aaron B. Howe

Oliver Torrey Attorney

AN ORIGINAL INSTRUMENT BY OLIVER TORREY.

SUSAN TORREY BLAKE

NATHAN BLAKE and SUSAN TORREY

LIFE HISTORY
OF MY
FATHER and MOTHER
AT
EAST CORINTH, VERMONT

ALSO BRIEF GENEALOGICAL NOTES AND
REMINISCENCES OF THE FAMILY

BLAKE Nathan[7] (*Nathan,*[6] *Nathan,*[5] *Robert,*[4] *John,*[3] *John,*[2] *William*[1]), was born in Keene, N. H., Oct. 15, 1784, son of Nathan and Bathsheba (Day) Blake. He married Susan, daughter of Oliver and Sabra (Freeman) Torrey, 6 Nov. 1815. She was born in Cornish, N. H., July 1st, 1795. The Torrey family home was on the main road, just under the side of Mt. Ascutney — latterly called the Pike place — as a Mr. Pike erected a new house on the site; at this writing the estate is owned by Dr. Nichols of Boston, who by remodeling has made it an attractive residence, also by relocation of streets in the immediate vicinity, the group of houses, now the summer homes of a city colony, have been given picturesque surroundings, with open ground, ornamented by trees and shrubs.

My mother always referred to this spot as being her ideal of loveliness, recalling that as a child, when lying upon the green grass, watching the white clouds float over the exquisite outline of Mt. Ascutney, she innocently counted that remembrance as the day she was born. Surely her sensitive soul was early attuned to recognize the grand and beautiful. When Susan Torrey was four years of age her family removed to Chelsea, Vermont. The family life there is embodied in the sketch of her father, Oliver Torrey. Of the many sidelights upon New Eng-

land life at that date her " Stories to you children," as she styled
them are interesting. "O yes! I remember my Grandfather
Freeman; what a fine horse he used to ride when he came up from
Plainfield; the Gloves and Top-Boots too were of good style —
he always brought presents to the children. I recollect when he
brought silver-spoons to my mother. My grandfather Freeman
came from Preston, Conn, and took up a large grant of land in
Plainfield — he was prosperous, became wealthy — gave 3 of his
sons Valuable Farms, near his own. He had the ' old country'
idea of giving his daughters, six in number, an ample set-out, as
it was called in those days — In addition to all needful household
Furniture they must have a nice Horse — 2 Cows — 10 Sheep,
and as carriages could not then be used a fine Side Saddle &
Bridle for each. I must acknowledge a certain degree of pride
as I remember riding that horse, knowing it was said there was
not another in Chelsea so elegant."

"My Uncle Erastus and Uncle Augustus Torrey were much in
our home — the latter called me 'Sukey,' brought candy and
sometimes put me upon the saddle with himself for a canter;
you know children, in those days everybody travelled on horse-
back; I well remember the first chaise that came into the town
of Chelsea." Doubtless the educational advantages of this
small and newly settled town were limited; a fact to which she
ever recurred with unfailing regret, and then and there she made
her standard for better and higher education for others. At the
age of twelve years she was sent to Windsor, Vt., to attend a
" select school," at the same time was an inmate in the family of
her Uncle Erastus Torrey, M.D., who had married the daughter
of General Jonathan Chase. This home was one of elegant
appointments for those days; Gen. Chase having fitted out his
daughter Gratia with furniture, wardrobe and jewels of unusual
style and value. "Yes! Aunt Gratia did look very handsome
when dressed for a ' Ball ' and I took great delight in helping
dress her hair — with her handsome combs; an elegant satin
gown and slippers with the pretty buckles gave her an imposing
appearance."

She often referred to the illness and early death of this Aunt
with much feeling.

At Chelsea, Vt., Susan Torrey met and married Nathan
Blake 3rd, the date being Nov. 6, 1815. They first settled at
Waterford, Vt., where Mr. Blake was in mercantile life.

NATHAN BLAKE HOUSE AND STORE
East Corinth. Vermont

In the year 1817, they purchased house, store and property in East Corinth, Vt., from Col. William Barron, and here was spent the remainder of their married life. (See illustration.)

Tradition tells us that the handsome Mrs. Blake soon took a leading place in village activities, in church work, philanthropic and social life and all work for the betterment and progress of the neighborhood. She was a woman who could watch by the bedside of a sick and dying neighbor, visit, console and relieve the suffering and needy; organize and help on in church work; entertain cultivated people from the outer world with a charm and cordiality all her own; step into the mercantile life of her husband's store at times of stress with an understanding and assist with a knowledge not excelled by him.

" Temperance Reform " found in her an ardent helper — her kind words of appeal and persuasion often met with remarkable success.

Here were born to her seven children, six of whom lived to arise and call her blessed.

As a wife and mother the name of Susan Torrey Blake will ever be a star of the first magnitude to her relations and descendants. Her entire life was one of labor and sacrifice for others — being so unselfish that her aid and counsel were sought by those both near and far; if an old woman in an adjoining town had been, or imagined she had been, wronged by her son and family they would all come trooping to her home saying, " Now Mrs. Blake, is not that wrong? Ought I not to complain of it?"

I cannot separate the life story of my father and mother, for it was one of such perfect mutual love and trust, co-working for family happiness and progress, for neighborhood uplift with such constant goodwill and affection that I can truly say it was a home of perfect love and concord.

Many and bitter were the sorrows and losses which came to them through the death of loved children.

The son, William Proctor, aged 3½ years, dying suddenly in, 1833. The eldest daughter Susan Ann died in 1841, aged 20 years, after a long and painful illness of consumption. Soon came declining health to my father, but he kept bravely at his post of duty. In the year 1845 came the death of the second daughter, Sophia Chandler, aged 22, from the same dread malady consumption. Both these daughters had been given unusual advantages at great sacrifice by their parents, were unusually lovely and gifted in person and character. The repeated sorrows and failing health of our father made the home one of constant anxieties, into which my young life was merged. I was retained from school that I might perform the light housework, which I was taught to do in a thorough and expeditious manner. Jan. 26, 1848, Mary Roxanna, the third daughter was married to George Warren Heath and left the home to settle in Boston. In Sept. 1848, I was sent to school at Bradford Academy, but upon returning home for winter vacation our father was very feeble and I remained at home to assist our mother. My father died unexpectedly Jan. 31st, 1849 — he had been in failing health for many months and the end was like the going out of a candle which was spent.

To this period of great sorrow was added the anxieties of the re-adjustment and transference to the son Nathan Day Blake of the long established mercantile business and store—which from mone-tary depressions and other causes had proved less remunerative than in former years — also great solicitude for the son Charles Metcalf, eleven years of age who was in very delicate health. Of this period of gloom I was of an age to receive the most vivid impressions, and no heroine of fiction ever displayed such un-wavering courage, such high loyalty to principle and sacrifice for family interests, mingled with a devout belief and trust in the overruling power of a good God as did our mother. Her faith and prayers were sublime, and to one of her children they have proved a tower of strength, a rock of refuge during a long life. Her character was one of perfect mingling of strength, humility and active doing. The passing years brought changes in the family life. Oct. 1852, the son, N. D. Blake married Matilda C. Thompson of East Topsham, bringing his wife to the home circle — in December of the same year the last and youngest daughter Almira Torrey was married to Isaac Fenno, of Boston, Mass., where her home has always remained. Six months later Mrs. Blake and son Charles followed to join the family life there.

It was truly remarkable that when in her sixtieth year she could thus renounce her lifelong habits, formed in a secluded, rural country and easily adapt herself to city life and formal society — yet more unusual still the fact, that she was at once the center and mingling with young modern life; full of enthusiasm for all that was best and progressive in politics, literature and social life. Her later years were spent in the homes of her two daughters which she illumined by her wealth of wit and humor. She was never old — could always understand and sympathize with those in sorrow — with youth and joy — music and art — could entertain us by long recitations of poems of which no copies are now known, and of funny and witty stories she had no end, saying, "Why! my brain is just like some old attic store room, and when I commence to delve among the records I never know just what I shall bring to light."

I recall her great enjoyment of Shakesperian readings by Fanny Kemble, the Egyptian Lectures of Amelia B. Edwards, the Evening Lectures by Edward Everett, Charles Sumner, H. W. Beecher, Geo. W. Curtis, Wendell Phillips, W. L. Garrison. She attended, when able, the church of Rev. Edward E. Hale. She went at the urgent invitation of her friend John R. Manley to listen to addresses by Theodore Parker — but to the last-named she was rather reluctant to give too much patronage, for she had a good orthodox doubt as to his being a safe leader, with his highly colored liberal doctrines, and what was then considered sacriligious views of sound theology. She was ever alert, appreciating fine scenery, good roads and thrifty towns. Sharing with her a trip to Columbus, Ohio, in the summer of 1865 we found that mother could endure all-night rides, detentions and the unexpected discomforts of travel, with the fortitude of a veteran. She was equal to every emergency — as when we came to a washed-out culvert, where all were obliged to leave the train and walk half a mile around the dislodged rails. As Mr. F——— appeared, much to our surprise with a horse and small express wagon to take our party across in comfort, as she was seated her first thought was for those not so happily placed, and her cheery words rang out "Why! let us carry all their hand-bags and coats." We filled our wagon, and when rejoined by the passengers who reached the other side tired and spent, it was a jolly crowd who claimed their belongings, over which she had assumed charge. This is but a pretty incident, to show her big, generous heart. "The declining years of her life were like a beautiful sunset," said one of her old Vermont contemporaries, who often visited her in the Roxbury home. Her days were spent in reading, knitting and fancy work — of which she completed much of artistic merit — the designs, motives and coloring being original and unique. Her 89th birthday found her completing a handsome silk embroidery she designed for a Fair in aid of the Homeopathic Hospital.

The golden days sped on — the two sons and two daughters vied with each other to lengthen the golden halo and prolong the precious days of their loved mother. A sudden illness, a few weeks of great suffering, through which she never lost her wonderful control of self, or faith and trust in the infinite love and justice of a merciful, and " over-ruling Heavenly Father "; then came the close of this beautiful life — Sept. 18th, 1884. Her funeral was attended by many loved friends — the service conducted by Rev. E. E. Hale, who with wonderful simplicity and eloquence paid a fitting tribute to her life and character. She was carried, as she requested, back to the old home, her body laid by that of our father, in the village cemetery of East Corinth, Vermont.

My father's family played a vital part in the early history of Keene, N. H., of which full accounts have been already given. In the year 1800, Nathan Blake 2d, wife, three sons and three daughters moved to Chelsea, Vermont, where they took up the activities of mill owners and merchants. The elder son, Amplias, acquiring much real estate — the two younger being in mercantile life with him both at Chelsea and Strafford. We have few details of family life; two old documents still preserved are interesting; being commissions from Jonas Galusha, Esquire, Governor, to Nathan Blake Jr. (my father), as cornet of the cavalry in the second Regiment, third Brigade, fourth division State Militia, date June 2d, 1812 — another as Lieutenant of Cavalry in second Regiment, 3d Brigade and fourth division of State Militia, date July 5th, 1813; with the quaint old form of oath, " I, Nathan Blake do solemnly swear that I will support the Constitution of the United States, so help me God.

Nathan Blake Jr." 3d. (See illustration.)

In the life sketch of my mother is recorded her marriage to my father, and the dual life of love and harmony, then commenced, ceased only with his death. As a merchant and owner of mills and landed property he was a man of many activities, who by his strict probity, industry and tolerance soon became one of the leading men of the county — especially in matters pertaining to the church. He was devout, ever led an exemplary Christian

BY HIS EXCELLENCY

JONAS GALUSHA, ESQUIRE,

CAPTAIN-GENERAL, GOVERNOUR, AND COMMANDER IN CHIEF, IN AND OVER THE STATE OF VERMONT.

TO _Nathan Blake_ ———— Esq. Greeting.

You, being elected _Lieutenant_ ———— Division of the Militia of this State,
Lieutenant Regiment of ———— Brigade and ———— Troop, in the name and by the
authority of the Freemen of the State of Vermont, fully authorize and empower you, the said _Nathan Blake_
to take charge of the said _Company_ as their _Lieutenant_ ————

And reposing special trust and confidence in your Patriotism, Valour, and good Conduct—I DO, by virtue of these Presents,

You will, therefore, carefully and diligently discharge the said duty, by doing
and performing every matter and thing thereunto relating. You will observe and follow such orders and directions as you shall from time to time, receive
from the Governor of the State, for the time being, or any other your superior officer according to military discipline and the laws of this State :
And all officers and soldiers under your command, are to take notice hereof, and yield due obedience to your orders, as their _Lieutenant_
in pursuance of the trust in you reposed,

IN TESTIMONY WHEREOF, I HAVE CAUSED THE SEAL OF THIS STATE TO BE HEREUNTO AFFIXED.

GIVEN under my hand in Council Chamber, at Montpelier, this _fifth_ ———— day of _July_ ———— in the
Year of Our Lord, One Thousand Eight Hundred and _13_ ———— and of the Independence of the United
States the Thirty _eighth_ ————

Jonas Galusha

BY HIS EXCELLENCY'S COMMAND,

R. Malloy

SECRETARY.

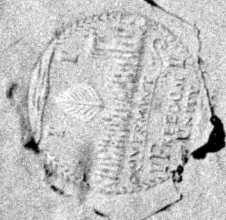

I Nathan Blake Do Solemnly Sware that I will
be true and faithful to the State of Vermont
I will not Directly nor indirectly Do any thing
injurious to the Constitution or Government there
of as is established by convention ———
— So Help Me God —   Nathan Blake

I Nathan Blake Do Solemnly Sware that I will
Support the Constitution of the united
States So Help Me God —   Nathan Blake

Subscribed and Sworn to this fifth Day July
1813 Before Me ——   Daniel Curtis Just

Commission
Lieutenant
Nathan Blake
1813

COMMISSION OF LIEUTENANT NATHAN BLAKE 3rd. 1813.
(Back)

life, was a deacon of the Orthodox Church, active in its support at Corinth Center, and later aiding to establish the branch church at East Corinth. In his early days he sang in the choir at the Center Church — among the first of my childhood memories at four years, I recall the hurry and bustle on Sunday mornings, when we drove, rain or shine, four miles to the church; sat still through a long sermon; ate a luncheon, prepared and carried from home, sat through another long sermon, prayers and hymns; if it was " communion Sunday," my father came down from the choir gallery to assume his official chair with the deacons. His love for, and interest in the education of his children was ardent. I well remember when I was four years of age his methodical methods of instruction, as he seated me in my high-chair and taught me the simple rudiments of music or the lessons from the catechism. One of his great delights was of an evening, when he could early escape from the store and around the household fireside listen to the reading of some important book of history or travel read by one of the elder children. His discipline of the family was lenient to a fault; if very radical measures were needed our mother was often forced to take the helm.

His love of " out-doors " was marked and his garden one of his recreations. Each one of us must be taught how to prepare the earth, make our small garden plot and sow seeds — after one or two failures on our part, because we would dig down to see if our seeds were growing, he impressed upon us the lesson of obedience to the laws of nature and patient observation. My father was quiet and unobtrusive in character, a staunch friend and helpful neighbor — was always active in town meetings, ever zealous in helping in all good works. His interest was great in founding the church in the village — his home was called the " Minister's Tavern," and his labors unceasing to collect the minister's salary. He occupied many positions of trust in town affairs, was Postmaster for four years, also was a Justice of the Peace.

Some details of business methods of his time may prove an interesting landmark and give a glimpse of customs in use one hundred years ago, in 1815. To use a modern phrase, " The merchant must have a plant," but it was radically different from that of today. Home and store must be near each other, also a shed, where customers could "hitch horses" and have them under cover — a small storehouse was necessary to receive the poultry, hogs and produce as taken from the farmers in exchange for " store goods," as it was called. In the purchase of the Barron Estate was included a " Grist Mill," a Potash Factory as well as much woodland and pasture land — in fact, the *big man of a town* must be an owner and factor in all industries desired to promote the growth of the town. The farmers expected long credit, could bring all their produce, butter, cheese, eggs, grain, etc., for which they always exacted the best market price, but rarely paid money for commodities received. " Produce " proved very perishable and before it could reach the distant market had much deteriorated in value, by which a constant loss accrued to the merchant. The flour mill required the service of a " miller " and I distinctly remember " Pa Bergen," who was my good friend and often showed me the big stone wheels go round and the " hopper hop." The grains were stored in separate bins in the chamber of the store, and my childish curiosity was aroused by the slides and chutes by which it was controlled, also I felt an interest in the management as I was often asked the loan of my cats to catch the hordes of mice attracted by the fresh grain. When the dam broke much labor and money were expended to rebuild, for the waterpower must be controlled for the use of the mill, to grind the wheat to make our bread. In very cold weather potatoes, stored in the storehouse froze, in " warm spells " the chickens thawed and were ruined, bringing constant loss and worry to the merchant, but the good old Puritan pluck and courage ever came to the surface, and surmounted difficulties. Twice each year a journey was made to Boston, by a method now obsolete, namely, driving over the road with a horse and chaise. Several times my mother accompanied father; their recitals of those early trips and funny incidents afforded amusement for our youthful imaginations. Boston with its street lights in the evening, big stores, now and then a pig running in the side streets was background for tales equal to fairyland.

It was an event of much expense and importance when the teamster was engaged with his two or four horses, loaded the produce, butter, etc., and left the village, en route for Boston, making the trip in slow stages to meet the endurance of the horses. Often one was left by the way, to rest till the return trip, when the same conveyance brought to the store the big

VILLAGE OF EAST CORINTH, VERMONT

With view of Blake House and Memorial Library

boxes of dry goods, crockery crates, sugar, tea, tobacco and the innumerable small wares of a country store.

Father invariably was in Boston to superintend the arriving cargo and purchase the goods to be returned. The earlier years of the business required the drive over the entire route to Boston; when the railroad was built to Concord, N. H., only a two days drive was needed. One of my earliest recollections was of the marvel and excitement when the steam railroad reached Franklin, N.H., one day's drive and a night then brought the merchant into the city mart on the second day. Yet a few years more and in 1848 the railroad reached Bradford, Vt. The wonder ceased and soon arose, as in this day, the clamor for "rapid transit," and six hours to Boston was slow travel. My father kept his interest and activities in his business to the last and was in Boston to purchase goods only three months before his death. These brief fragments of the life history of my father and mother are written by their loving daughter,

ALMIRA TORREY BLAKE-FENNO-GENDROT.

BLAKE MEMORIAL LIBRARY
East Corinth, Vermont

THE BLAKE MEMORIAL LIBRARY.

In the year 1900 the three children then living of Nathan and Susan Torrey Blake, desiring to make some fitting and enduring memorial to their names, built this Library at East Corinth, Vermont. It is of a fine type of architecture, handsomely and substantially constructed of the best materials; fortunately a most desirable location was obtained upon a large lot of land directly opposite the former Blake Home. The dedication was July 1st and 2nd, 1902 — the people of the town making it a red-letter event, by their hearty enthusiasm and joyful acceptance. Many friends from adjoining towns joined in congratulations, speeches, music and prayers. A bountiful collation was served in the church vestry — in the evening a crowded reception was held in the Library by the rejoicing townspeople, who at once realized the great benefit to be derived from such an institution, erected, furnished and endowed for their benefit.

INDEX

ABBOTT.
Daniel, 102.
ABEL, ABELL.
Bethyah, 130.
Joshua, 130.
ADAMS, ADDAMS.
Alexander, 155.
Edward, 105.
Elizabeth, 105.
George, 106.
Goodman, 107.
Mary, 106.
ADDIS FAMILY, 128.
Ann, 127, 128, 130.
Milicent, 128.
William, 128.
ADGATE.
Ruth, 129.
Thomas, 129.
ALBIN.
Benjamin, 75.
ALCOCK, ALLCOCKE, ALCOTE.
George, 107, 108.
Mr., 107, 108.
Thomas, 107, 108.
ALDEN.
Elizabeth, 156.
John, Capt., 156.
ALLEN.
Abigail, 155.
Lydia, 147.
Martha, 31.
Samuel, 36, 154.
Sarah, 154.
ALLERTON.
Fear, 126.
Isaac, 126.
ALLIS.
Rebecca, 29.
William, 29.
ALLYN FAMILY, 157.
Deborah, 130, 157.
Elizabeth, 130, 157.
Hannah, 157, 158.
John, 130, 157.

ALLYN FAMILY, Cont'd.
Mary, 157.
Robert, 157, 158.
Sarah, 157.
ALMY FAMILY, 91.
Ann, 91.
Anna, 91.
Anne, 90, 94.
Annis, 91.
Audray, 91.
Audrey, 91.
Catharine, 91.
Christopher, 91.
Elizabeth, 91.
Job, 91.
John, 91.
Mary, 91.
William, 91.
ALVORD.
Jeremiah, 30, 31.
Mercy, 30,31.
ANDREWS.
Benjamin, 76.
Richard, 76.
Sarah, 75.
ANDROS, GOV., 92.
ANTHONY.
Elizabeth, 90.
ARNOLD.
Benedict, 92.
Elizabeth, 94.
Freelove, 92.
Stephen, 94.
William, 89, 90.
ASH.
Milicent, 128.
William, 128.
ASPINWALL.
William, 108.
d'AUBIGNE.
Philip, 66.
AVERY.
Edward, 158.
Johanna, 158.
Mary, 22.

BACON.
Keziah, 24.
Mary, 122.
BAIYLYE.
Samuel, 75.
BAKER.
Mary, 136, 137.
BALCH.
Benjamin, 38.
Elizabeth, 38.
BALCOM.
Elizabeth, 123.
Henry, 123.
BALDWIN.
Henry, Hon., 113.
BALL.
Mary, 43.
BAND.
Agnes, 2, 5, 8.
BARDWELL FAMILY, 31.
Abigail, 30, 31.
Ebenezer, 31.
Elijah, 31.
Elizabeth, 31.
Hester, 31.
John, 30, 31.
Martha, 31.
Mary, 30, 31, 32.
Mehitable, 30, 31.
Robert, 30, 31, 32.
Samuel, 31.
Sarah, 31.
Thankfull, 31, 32.
Thomas, 31.
BARKER.
John, 70.
BARNES.
Barbara, 76.
BARNS.
Lucy, 132.
BARRETT.
Jonathan, 31.
Sarah, 31.
BARRON.
William, Col., 167.
BARTON.
Elizabeth, 90.
BATT.
Sarah, 84.
BATTER.
Edward, 72.
BAYLEY.
Samuel, 76.

BAYLIES.
Richard M., 114.
de BEAUVOIR.
Helene, 67.
BEEBE.
Milicent, 128.
Thomas, 128.
BEECHER.
H. W., 169.
Lyman, Rev., 113.
BELCHER.
Mary, 137.
BELDING.
David, 32.
Dorcas, 32.
Hester, 31.
Joseph, 31.
Lucy, 32.
Sarah, 31.
BELL.
Mary, 29.
Samuel, 29.
BELLINGHAM.
Richard, Gov., 148.
BELLOWS.
Dorcas, 158.
BENJAMIN FAMILY, 146.
Abel, 147.
Abigail, 144, 146, 147, 148.
Amity, 147.
Caleb, 147.
Elizabeth, 148.
Hannah, 146, 148.
Jemima, 146, 147, 148, 149, 159.
John, 146, 147, 148.
Joseph, 147, 149.
Joshua, 147.
Kezia, 148.
Lydia, 147.
Mary, 147, 148.
Mercy, 148.
Samuel, 147.
Sarah, 147, 148.
Thankfull, 147.
BENNIT.
Mary, 50.
BERGEN.
Pa, 172.
BETTS.
Martha, 28.
BEVOIR.
Helen, 66.

GILSON.
Mary, 146.
Rebecca, 146.
Timothy, 146.
GLAZIER.
Mary, 46.
GOARD.
Elizabeth, 122.
Roger, 122.
GODDARD.
Leah, 50.
William, 50.
GOLDHAM.
Susanna, 110.
GOLLOPP.
William, 61.
GOODMAN.
Susan, 43.
William, 43.
GOODNOW.
Sarah, 145.
GORTON.
Benjamin, 94.
Mary, 90, 94.
Mr., 92.
Samuel, 89, 90.
GOULD FAMILY, 106.
Abigail, 106, 111, 112, 114.
Ann, 105, 114.
Anna, 112, 113, 114, 161.
Anne, 115, 116.
James, 112, 113.
John, 112.
Mary, 106, 111, 112, 113, 114.
Mehitable, 112.
Richard, 106, 111, 112.
Sally, 113.
Sarah, 103, 106, 112.
Thomas, 106, 112.
Whitehead, 112.
William, 103, 106, 111, 112, 113, 114.
GRAVES FAMILY, 27.
Abigail, 29, 30, 31.
Abner, 32.
Abraham, 30, 31, 32.
Asahel, 32.
Bethiah, 29.
Daniel, 29.
David, 30, 31.
Deliverence, 29.
Dorcas, 32.
Ebenezer, 29.

GRAVES FAMILY, Cont'd.
Elijah, 32.
Elizabeth, 24, 27, 28, 29, 30, 32, 53.
Grace, 30.
Hannah, 29, 30.
Isaac, 27, 29.
John, 27, 28, 29, 32.
Jonathan, 30.
Joshua, 32.
Lucy, 32.
Lydia, 32.
Martha, 28.
Mary, 27, 28, 29, 32.
Mehitable, 30, 31, 32.
Nathaniel, 27, 28, 29.
Noah, 30.
Rachel, 30.
Rebecca, 29, 30.
Samuel, 27, 28, 29, 30, 32.
Sarah, 27, 28, 29, 30, 32, 107.
Submit, 32.
Susanna, 97.
Thankfull, 30, 31, 32.
Thomas, 27, 28, 29, 32.
GRAY.
Edward, 48.
Rachel, 48.
Richard, 112.
GREEN.
John, 134.
GREENE FAMILY, 88.
Alice, 88.
Ann, 93, 94.
Anne, 90, 94.
Annis, 91.
Audray, 93.
Audrey, 94.
Audry, 93.
Catharin, 93, 94.
Deborah, 84, 93, 94, 98.
Deliverance, 90.
Eleanor, 94.
Elizabeth, 90, 94.
James, 90.
Joan, 90.
Joanna, 88, 91.
Job, 93, 94.
John, 88, 89, 90, 91, 92, 94.
Mary, 88, 90, 94.
Peter, 90, 93, 94.
Phebe, 94.
Philip, 88, 94.
Phillip, 89, 90.

HALLE.
  Francis, 107.
HAMMOND.
  Elizabeth, 144.
  Thomas, 144.
HANNAH.
  Mary, 101, 102.
  Robert, 101, 102.
HAPGOOD.
  Shadrach, 119.
HARRIS.
  Dr., 42.
  John, 8.
  Susanna, 8.
  William Torrey, Prof., 64.
  Zipporah, 24.
HART.
  Jemima, 38.
HASEY.
  Sarah, 133.
HATCH.
  Ann, 79.
  Anne, 64.
  Hannah, 138.
  Joseph, 138.
  William, 79.
HAUGH.
  Lemuel, 97.
  Sarah, 97.
de HAVELLAND. HAVELLANDE.
  Cecilia, 67.
  Christofer, 68.
  Christoper, 67.
  Christopher, 68.
  Cysselye, 68.
  Eleanor, 67.
  Elinor, 68.
  Helene, 67.
  James, 67, 68.
  John, 67, 68.
  Julia, 67.
  Julyan, 68.
  Margaret, 68.
  Matthew, 68.
  Nathannell, 68.
  Richard, 67, 68.
  Thomas, 68.
  William, 67, 68.
  Xpofer, 68.
  Xpoffer, 68.
de HAVERLAIN.
  Sieur, 66.

de HAVERLAND.
  Bernard, 66.
  Constance, 76.
  Lord, 65.
  Matthew, 75.
  Peter, 66.
  Robert, 66.
  Thomas, 66.
  William, 66.
HAVILAND FAMILY, 65.
  Anastalia, 73.
  Ann, 73.
  Anne, 72, 73.
  Bartholomew, 71, 72, 73.
  Bernard, 66.
  Burke, 68.
  Cecilia, 67, 68, 70.
  Cecyly, 68.
  Christofer, 68.
  Christoffer, 68.
  Christoper, 67, 70.
  Christopher, 68.
  Constance, 75, 76.
  Cysley, 68.
  Cysselye, 68, 69.
  Eleanor, 67, 69.
  Elianor, 72.
  Elinor, 68.
  Elizabeth, 72, 73, 74, 75, 76, 82.
  Florence, 72, 75, 76.
  Helen, 66.
  Helene, 67.
  James, 66, 67, 68, 69.
  Jane, 64, 72, 75, 76, 77, 82, 94.
  John, 67, 68, 69, 70, 71, 73.
  Joice, 73.
  Joyce, 69, 71, 73.
  Julia, 67.
  Julyan, 68.
  Lord, 65.
  Margaret, 68, 69.
  Maria, 73.
  Mary, 69, 72, 73, 75, 76.
  Mathew, 71, 73.
  Matthew, 68, 69, 70, 71, 72, 73, 74, 75, 76.
  Nathannell, 68, 69.
  Peter, 66.
  Richard, 67, 68, 69.
  Robert, 66, 70, 71, 72, 73, 74, 75, 76, 82.
  Sieur, 66.
  Sister, 74.

HENBURG.
Arthur, 44.
Martha, 44.
HENTLEY.
Ann, 73.
Richard, 73.
HERRICK.
Deborah, 159, 160.
Nathan, 159, 160.
HILEY.
Eleanor, 69.
William, Rev., 69.
HILL.
Ann, 143.
Charles, 127.
John, 49.
Ruth, 49, 127.
HILLS.
Samuel, 32.
Sarah, 32.
HINCKLEY.
Dyer Throop, 55.
Roselinda, 55.
HITCHCOCK, HITCHCOCKE.
Hannah, 28.
Grace, 30.
Mathias, 108.
HOBBS.
Capt., 37.
HOBERT.
Mr., Rev., 87.
HOLBROOK.
Adin, 53.
Ann Gould, 162.
Anna Gould, 163.
Eleazer, 45.
Galen, 162, 163.
Hannah, 53.
John, Capt., 48.
Lydia, 98.
Sarah, 45.
HOLCOMBE.
Henry, 62.
HOLDEN.
Catharin, 93.
Catherin, 94.
Charles, 94.
Randall, 89, 92.
Samuel, 104.
HOLLOWELL.
Ann, 6.
HOLMES.
Obidiah, 80.

HOLMS.
Lois, 116.
HOLWORTH, HOLWORTHY.
Ann, 72.
John, 72.
Mary, 72.
Matthew, 72.
Prudence, 72.
Richard, 72.
Thomas, 72.
HOLWORTHIE.
Anne, 72.
John, 72.
Maria, 73.
Mary, 72, 73.
Mathew, 72.
Richard, 72, 73.
HOOKER.
John, 88.
Mary, 88.
HORTON.
Mary, 132.
HOW.
Josiah, 123.
Mary, 123.
HOWD.
Benjamin, 108, 109, 111.
Elizabeth, 108, 109, 111.
HOWE.
Charles, 32.
John, Hon., 7.
Lydia, 32.
HOWLETT.
Capt., 54.
HUBBARD.
Elizabeth, 109.
George, 110.
Samuel, 80, 81.
William, 83.
HUNT.
Elizabeth, 6.
HUNTING.
Esther, 19.
HUNTINGTON.
Christopher, 124, 131.
Lydia, 130.
Mary, 131.
Simon, 130.
HUNTLEY.
Hannah, 55.
HUTCHINSON.
Ann, 81.
William, 96.

LEATHERLAND.
Deborah, 136.
LEE.
Grace, 41, 42.
LEONARD.
Hannah, 51.
Mary, 138.
Samuel, 138.
LEVITT.
Lydia, 50.
LINNELL.
Abigail, 148.
LOCHARD.
John, 123.
Rachel, 123.
LOMBARD FAMILY, 147.
Abigail, 148.
Benjamin, 147, 148.
Bernard, 147, 148.
Caleb, 147, 148.
Hannah, 148.
Jane, 148.
Jedediah, 147, 148.
Jemima, 147, 148, 149.
Jobaniah, 148.
Joseph, 147, 148.
Joshua, 147, 148.
Joyce, 147, 148.
Margaret, 147, 148.
Sarah, 148.
Thomas, 147, 148.
LORD.
Anne, 18.
LORING.
Thomas, 156.
LORTE.
Ann, 73.
Anne, 72.
Joyce, 72.
Sampson, 72, 73.
LORTT.
Anne, 72.
Joyce, 72.
Sampson, 72.
LOTHROP.
John, Rev., 96, 147.
LOUETT.
Daniel, 134.
LOVETT FAMILY, 134.
Daniel, 134, 135.
Hannah, 133, 134.
James, 133, 134.
Joanna, 134, 135.

LOVETT FAMILY, Cont'd.
Martha, 134.
Mary, 133, 134, 135, 137.
LOWELL.
James Russell, 67.
John, 84.
Naomy, 84.
LUDDINGTON.
Mary, 109.
Mercy, 109, 111.
William, 108, 111.
LUMBARD.
Jemima, 147.
LUSHER.
Eleazer, 19.
LUSON.
Anne, 18.
LYON.
Peter, 51.
Sarah, 51.

MACCANY.
Mary, 51.
MACHERWITH, MACHERWITHY.
Daniel, 47.
James, 47.
Mary, 47.
MALTBIE.
Mary, 112.
MANLEY.
John R., 169.
MANN, MANNE.
Cecilia, 67, 68, 70.
Cecyly, 68.
John, 68.
Phebe, 22.
MARSH.
Mary, 95.
MATHER.
Richard, Rev., 7, 12.
MAY.
Hannah, 50.
MAYNARD.
John, 143.
Mary, 143.
McSPARREN.
Dr., 104.
Mr., 103.
Rev., 103.
MEEKS.
Daniel, 129.
Elizabeth, 129.

SHEPARD FAMILY, Cont'd.
 Rebecca, 43.
 Sarah, 43, 44.
 Susan, 43.
 Violet, 43, 44.
SHEPHARD.
 Benjamin, 24.
 Hephzibah, 24.
SHEPHEARD.
 Edward, 43.
SHEPPARD.
 Hugh, 63.
SHUTTLEWORTH.
 Sarah, 45.
SKINNER.
 Abigail, 46.
 Thomas, 46.
SKINT.
 Robert, 100.
SMEED, 33.
SMITH FAMILY, 25.
 Chileal, 28.
 Christopher, 41.
 Daniel, 30.
 Elizabeth, 28, 30, 31.
 Hannah, 28.
 John, 28.
 Mary, 27, 28, 29, 41, 129.
 Philip, 28.
 Rebecca, 28.
 Samuel, 28, 30.
 Sarah, 30.
 Susanna, 131.
SOUTHER.
 Alice, 8.
 Mary, 6, 8, 11.
 Mercy, 149.
 Nathaniel, 8, 12.
SOUTHMEADE.
 Millicent, 128.
 William, 128.
SPAULDING, 46.
 Mary, 137.
SPENCER.
 Audray, 93.
 Audrey, 94.
 Audry, 93.
 John, 93, 94.
SPRAGUE.
 Sarah, 133.
SPRINT.
 Anne, 75.
 Constance, 76.

SPRINT, Cont'd.
 Rebecka, 76.
 Richard, 75, 76.
 Samuel, 75, 76.
 Zachariah, 76.
STANDISH.
 Alexander, 154.
 Josiah, 154.
 Myles, Capt., 127.
STANETT.
 Edward, Dr., 81.
STANTON.
 Louisa, 159, 160.
 William, 159, 160.
STARR.
 Hannah, 128.
 Samuel, 128.
STEARNES.
 Nathaniell, 21.
STEBBINS.
 Benjamin, 29.
 Edward, 29.
 Mary, 29.
 Rowland, 47.
 Sarah, 29.
STEELE.
 Ann, 110.
 Bethia, 110.
 James, 109, 110.
STEPHEN, STEPHENS.
 Anna, 137.
 Sarah, 10, 14.
STETSON.
 Mary, 154.
STEVEN.
 Judith, 129.
STEWART.
 Peggy, 160.
STODDARD.
 Anthony, 97.
 Mary, 97.
 Ralph, 129.
STONE.
 Rachel, 44, 45.
 Tabitha, 123.
STORY.
 Mary, 131, 138.
STOUGHTON.
 Gov., 21, 87.
 Mr., 21.
STUBBS.
 Abigail, 144, 147.
 Joshua, 147.

TORREY FAMILY, Cont'd.
Jordan, 61.
Joseph, 63, 64, 79, 80, 81, 95, 98,
99, 102, 103, 105, 113, 114,
116, 161.
Josiah, 84, 95.
Judith, 116.
Laura, 163.
Lois, 116.
Lucy, 105.
Margaret, 62.
Marie, 63, 64.
Mary, 62, 64, 79, 84, 87, 95, 98,
99, 105, 163.
Mercy, 116, 161, 162.
Micajah, 84.
Naomy, 84.
Oliver, 105, 115, 116, 161, 162,
163, 165.
Philip, 62, 79.
Phillip, 61, 62, 63, 64, 82, 95.
Rev. Mr., 86.
Richard, 61.
Sabra, 116, 161, 163, 165.
Samuel, 63, 64, 77, 82, 83, 84,
85, 87, 95, 98, 115, 116.
Samuel Holden, 105, 112, 113,
114, 115, 116, 161.
Samuell, 79.
Sarah, 62, 64, 84, 105, 116, 165.
Simon, 61.
Sophia, 163.
Sukey, 115, 116, 166.
Susan, 54, 116, 163, 165, 166.
Tamer, 105.
Thomas, 61.
Tomasyne, 61, 62.
William, 61, 62, 63, 64, 75, 76,
79, 82, 83, 84, 85, 93, 94, 95,
98, 103, 105, 113, 161.
William Gould, 115, 116.
Zacharia, 103.
Zachary, 99.
Zechariah, 99.
Zilpha, 105.
TORRY, TORRIE.
Alice, 62, 63, 64.
Ann, 62.
Dorothy, 62.
Emmett, 62.
James, 63.
Jane, 64, 75, 76.
Joseph, 63.

TORRY, Cont'd.
Margaret, 62.
Marie, 63.
Mary, 62.
Philip, 62, 64.
Phillip, 61, 62, 63.
Samuel, 63, 64.
Sarah, 62.
Thomas, 61.
Tomasyne, 61, 62.
William, 61, 62, 63, 64, 75, 76.
TOZER.
Richard, 134.
TRACY FAMILY, 153.
Abigail, 132.
Ami, 159.
Deborah, 153.
John, 153.
Mary, 153.
Rebecca, 153.
Ruth, 153.
Sally McCurdy, 113.
Samuel, 159.
Sarah, 153, 156.
Stephen, 153.
Trifosa, 153.
Tryphosa, 153.
Uriah, Hon., 113.
TREADAWAY.
Josiah, 121.
Suffrance, 121.
TREAT.
Dorothy, 131.
TURIN.
Daniel, 134.
Lydia, 134.
TURNER.
Capt., 31.
John, 127.
Mary, 127.
DE TURY, TURI, TURRI.
Henry, 61.
Jorden, 61.
Richard, 61.
Simon, 61.
TYLER FAMILY, 132.
Abigail, 135, 136.
Ann, 136.
Anna, 136, 137, 139.
Daniel, 135, 136.
Deborah, 136.
Esther, 137.
James, 135, 136, 137, 138

www.ingramcontent.com/pod-product-compliance
Lightning Source LLC
Chambersburg PA
CBHW071049280326
41928CB00050B/2035